HOW I LEARNED
TO COOK

HOW I LEARNED TO COOK

AND OTHER WRITINGS ON COMPLEX MOTHER-DAUGHTER RELATIONSHIPS

❖ ❖ ❖

EDITED BY

MARGO PERIN

JEREMY P. TARCHER ❖ PENGUIN

a member of Penguin Group (USA) Inc.

New York

Most Tarcher/Penguin books are available at special quantity discounts for bulk purchase for sales promotions, premiums, fund-raising, and educational needs. Special books or book excerpts also can be created to fit specific needs. For details, write Penguin Group (USA) Inc. Special Markets, 375 Hudson Street, New York, NY 10014.

Jeremy P. Tarcher/Penguin
a member of
Penguin Group (USA) Inc.
375 Hudson Street
New York, NY 10014
www.penguin.com

Library of Congress Cataloging-in-Publication Data

How I learned to cook and other writings
on complex mother-daughter relationships / edited by Margo Perin.
p. cm.
ISBN 1-58542-291-6
1. Mothers and daughters.
2. Mothers.
I. Perin, Margo.
HQ755.85.H68   2004   200306194
306.874'3—dc22

Printed in the United States of America
1   3   5   7   9   10   8   6   4   2

Book design by Gretchen Achilles

For Marci,

for teaching me how to love

ACKNOWLEDGMENTS

First and foremost, my deepest thanks to the exceptional writers in this collection, who had the courage and skill to break through the taboo of talking about mothers to tell their stories. To Valerie Mejer, poet, artist, and healer extraordinaire, who taught me to shine a light through the veils of illusion. And most especially to my sisters, who continue to try to make up for the mothering we never had.

Many thanks to Sara Carder and Ashley Shelby at Tarcher/Putnam for understanding and believing in my vision and for their great skill and enthusiasm, and to Janet Rosen and Sheree Bykofsky for representing this book. To Hedgebrook and Norcroft writing colonies, thank you so much for providing the most nurturing space for a writer that can be imagined, allowing me to write my way to the vision that led to this book.

My love and thanks to Dov Mostovoy for his astuteness, artistry, and love; Mardi Louisell for her perception, intelligence, and friendship; Malka Lehmann for her brilliance and insight; Marci Klane for always insisting on my voice; Karen Nani Apana for her intuitive guidance and healing hands; Chinosole, who taught my first writing class and insisted I "don't hold back!" and my dear friends Gordon Smyth, how can I thank you enough; Teresa Camozzi, the most beautiful friend and artist; Rebecca Litwin for her softness, pillows and down; Geoffrey Hayes for friendship and support; and Scott Fisher and Carlos Cancio, chosen brothers—thank you for being family, all of you. To Lisa Kellmann and Dino Lucas at the Scarlet Sage Herb Company in San Francisco, thank you, thank you. To Susan Jacobs and Andrea Ring, with my deepest gratitude, you gave more than you'll ever know, and to Anne Wilson for her exquisite culinary skill and generosity. To Kaila Flexer, who was always there, and to Audrey Daniel and Joey Scudari, my friends and family. To Janet and Joel Klane for your love, thank you. And to all those whom I have forgotten to mention, who I hope will accept my apologies.

CONTENTS

HOW I LEARNED
TO COOK

INTRODUCTION

Mothers everywhere are idealized as the source of eternal love, nurturing, protection, and self-sacrifice. In Western culture, the idealized mother is most clearly represented by the image of the Virgin Mary, whose face radiates the endless compassion, love, and suffering mothers are assumed to feel for their children.

This is the public view, the stuff of myth. But what goes on in the shadows between mothers and their children, and especially their daughters, who, being female, are most closely aligned with their mothers? How to understand the mother in Pam Lewis's "A Little Death," who, on catching her husband in Pam's bed, threatens Pam not to tell anyone? Or Paula Fox's mother in *Borrowed Finery*, who leaves the infant Paula in a foundling home a few days after her birth and, the rare times she shows up throughout Paula's life, continues to reject her? Or Hillary Gamerow's mother, in "How I Learned to Cook," who tells her children she put rat poison in their dinner?

There have been countless stories of the shadow worlds of children and their fathers, stepfathers, and stepmothers that describe complexities within the relationship, ranging from mild intergenerational conflict to extreme sexual and physical abuse. What we haven't seen much of are stories that explore the thoughts and feelings of daughters as they navigate their relationships with their mothers. For along with the myth of mother comes the myth of daughter, who is identified as her mother's companion, helper, defender, and savior. As Meena writes in

1

"Domestic Silence," "Who am I when I am not the dutiful daughter trying to save her mother?"

Even the healthiest relationships between mothers and daughters are not immune from ambiguity. In Kim Chernin's *In My Mother's House*, this is played out on a stage of politics and poetry when Kim tries to assert her identity: "For, whatever else we shouted or declaimed, a single idea was at the heart of our quarrel. I mean of course the fact that we thought different thoughts, and experienced the world differently. That we were no longer the same person." Nawal El Saadawi, growing up in Egypt at a time when her mother was expected to withdraw into the background, even within the family, experienced a lack of mothering in spite of the love she and her mother felt for each other. In *A Daughter of Isis*, El Saadawi writes: "Gradually, my mother was withdrawing from my life. I no longer saw her except in the kitchen. I no longer heard her speak. Most of the time she sat listening to my father's stories. . . . The distance between my mother and me grew bigger and bigger, and the distance between my father and me smaller and smaller. My mother began to sit at the far end of the couch."

The lack of a literary forum for the shadow side of mothering has served to make most women keep their stories secret, ashamed of revealing their feelings and perceptions, afraid of betraying love, frightened of being labeled disloyal, treacherous, or, in our day, antifeminist. (More than one writer I approached in selecting work for this anthology said they couldn't tell their stories until their mothers were dead.) This can be even more true for women who have chosen to have children. Many women are fearful of degrading the role of motherhood, which, ironically in the face of how mothers are mythologized, is uniformly undervalued. This lack of support is not only financial but also physical and emotional, even in countries where mothers are the most revered.

On some level, perhaps we don't speak openly about our mothers because we understand the pressures upon them. These can be socioeconomic pressures or those arising from personal history where our mothers themselves may not have been properly cared for. We know that even among mothers who are not deliberately abusive or neglectful, their skills are not always adequate to fulfill their children's basic needs, needs that are inevitably monumental.

Alice Walker had to work, as her own mother did, leaving her daughter with the same feelings of abandonment that she herself felt about her own working mother. "Because of [my daughter]," she writes in "Sunniness and Shade," "I've reunited with banished bits of my own life; to know again the daughter and the mother I was, and to feel pity and empathy for both; to appreciate the admirable daughter courage that, though self-denying and therefore painful, still springs from a valiant solidarity with the mother who, in this world, always has too much to do and too few to help her. I've also discovered the world is full of mothers who've done their best and still hurt their daughters."

About her mother, who was married at nine years old, Nahid Rachlin writes in "My Two Mothers": "I am not angry at my mother as I used to be. I can see that her life has been limiting, difficult."

Kate Braverman's mother, in *Lithium for Medea,* is having marital problems. "'We have nothing in common,' my father explained. I stood near his shoulder while he picked avocados. . . . 'She's been one hell of a disappointment.'"

After years on the move, Helen Ruggieri's mother, in "Home Is Where Your Stuff Is," attempts to establish permanence through obsessive housekeeping. Ruggieri writes, "We'd never be able to sit on a couch. . . . We'd have to stand in the doorway. Maybe we'd have to detour to get to the stairway so as not to walk on the rug. . . . You had to keep the place clean, like a hospital. . . . My mother liked to brag you could eat off the floor."

Gina Smith's mother, in "Sladjana," is an alcoholic. "I saw why she did it," Smith writes. "Drinking and using drugs makes the happy times happier and the sad times easier to bear. It also helps you to forget all the things you're embarrassed about, and makes it easier to talk to people—the way normal people do."

Jamie Callan's mother suffers from mental illness. In "Just Another Movie Star," Callan writes: "I sat back in the plush red velvet passenger seat next to my mother, as if we were sitting in the audience at one of the opulent theaters of the day and about to see a great movie. . . . I remember looking at my mother and thinking this was the most beautiful, most glamourous woman in the world. She patted my knee and shouted, "Aren't you glad to have such a fun mommy?!" And I screamed back, "Yes! Yes! Yes I am!"

For Elizabeth Payne's mother, the pressures came from sources that remained a mystery to her daughter. Payne writes in "Anybody Could See It": "We were a lot alike that way, grievously good secret keepers. I needed mine, but I also needed hers. Her secrets were evidence of crucial things, a chain of things, that if you followed, shadowing, on her tail, creeping slowly, so she didn't notice you were peeking, you would find a hidden mother, a mother you didn't recognize, but yours nonetheless."

As daughters, we have a primal understanding that all women, especially those of us born before the days of women's liberation, though still true today, have long been defined through our servitude to others, rather than by our own individualized and self-fulfilling journeys through life. Men are thought to realize themselves through work, but for women it has traditionally been motherhood. Because women are seen as being closer to nature, whose primary raison d'être is biological, having children is how women are believed to fulfill their purpose.

In a world that continues to value men over women, daughters are more likely to suffer from the pressures on their mothers, and their mothers' unrealized ambitions and repressed desires, than are their sons. As Rosemary Daniell writes in *Fatal Flowers*: "I perceived my mother, grandmothers, sister, daughters—and all the women whose roots I shared—as . . . trapped in a morass of Spanish moss, Bible Belt guilt, and the pressures of a patriarchy stronger than in any other part of the country." In *At Home in the World*, Joyce Maynard describes her mother's limitless interest in her life as being caused by her mother's lack of fulfillment. Her mother read Maynard's diary, leaving instructive notes between the pages. In *Fierce Attachments*, Vivian Gornick writes: "In refusing to recover from my father's death [my mother] had discovered that her life was endowed with a seriousness her years in the kitchen had denied her. . . . Her pain became my element, the country in which I lived, the rule beneath which I bowed."

Then there are those mothers about whom Ruth Kluger writes: "No one is as dependent as mothers are on the dependency of their children." Her own difficult relationship with her mother continued right through their incarceration in Nazi death camps. "With the increasing isolation of the few Jews left in Vienna," she writes, "my mother became dependent on me for companionship and tortured me with her anxieties. . . . Some years later, in 1944, when she happened to be right, my lack of confidence in her . . . almost cost me my life."

And there are mothers who exhibit darker tendencies and who even seem to take pleasure in harming their daughters. Such is the mother of Jamaica Kincaid in *My Brother*, about whom she writes: "My death now, before her own, would make her feel regal, triumphant that she had outlived all her inferiors: her inferiors are her offspring."

By not fearing the shadows, we can find light, joy, and love. In this collection, every writer has had the skill and courage to also explore her own shadow to become the realized, compassionate, and empowered woman—and writer—that she is. Some have found themselves through discovering a source of love outside their mothers. For others it has been through political or intellectual explorations. Others have developed an inner strength in their search for truth. All exhibit the great sense of self-awareness that comes from writing honestly about one's experiences. That these women became such powerful writers is a testament to the importance of writing the whole story and not perpetuating the myths that deny the complexity of human experience. It is my hope that the stories in this book will encourage others to brave the real story of their own lives.

MARGO PERIN, 2004

BORROWED FINERY

PAULA FOX

❖   ❖   ❖

Car headlights shone on ranks of stunted pine trees and clumps of small weathered gray houses, silent, silvered for an instant as we drove past them. Who was driving, Uncle Elwood, with whom I was living at the time, or my father, I can't recall. We were on our way to Provincetown at the tip of Cape Cod, where my parents were living in a house on Commercial Street. Soon after my stay of a few days, when they were away, it burned to the ground—the fourth fire started by the retarded son of a Portuguese fisherman.

The house, a saltbox, was set back from the street a few hundred feet on the hummocky undernourished ground characteristic of land near salt water. I have a snapshot of myself standing in front of a straggly rosebush growing on a rickety trellis in the yard, its stems like insect feelers. There is another photograph of Uncle Elwood and me by the bay. He kneels to hold me around the waist, although there is no surf; the water is as flat as an ironing board. I suppose my father took the picture with the minister's camera.

A German shepherd my parents owned attacked a cat that was drifting along the narrow cracked sidewalk in front of the house. My heart thudded; my vision narrowed to the two animals, one helpless, the other made monstrous with rage. I grabbed the cat. In its terror, it scratched my hand.

There was no one in the house that day to whom I could report the scratch. I washed my hand at the kitchen sink, standing on a chair to turn on the faucet. The wound bled intermittently for a while. When my parents returned from wherever they had been, I didn't bring it to their attention. I had been left in a Manhattan foundling home a few days after my birth by my reluctant father, and by Elsie, my mother, panic-stricken and ungovernable in her haste to have done with me.

I discovered a steamer trunk in a little room next to the kitchen. It was on end and partly open, like a giant book waiting to be read. Deep drawers lined one side. Suits and dresses hung in the other. They looked as though they'd been pitched across the room, arrested in their flight by small hangers attached to a metal bar, to which they clung, half on, half off.

I had never seen so many women's clothes before. I touched them, felt them, pressed against them, breathing in their close bodily smell until I grew dizzy. I pulled open a drawer and discovered a pile of cosmetics.

I hardly knew what they were for, but memories stirred of Uncle Elwood's mother, asking that her face be powdered when she was about to be taken for an outing in the car and a large powder puff in his hand as he bent toward her face, or the lips of some of his parishioners, too red to be true.

My mother was suddenly in the room, as though deposited there by a violent wind. I gasped with embarrassment and fear. She began to speak; I saw her lips move. I bent toward her, feeling the fiery skin of my face.

"What are you doing?" She was asking me over and over again. I heard her repeat "doing . . . doing" in the same measured voice, as she stared at my forehead covered with her powder, at my mouth, enlarged and thickened with lip rouge I had discovered in a tiny circular box.

I began to cry silently. Her face loomed in front of mine like a dark moon. She began to whisper with a kind of ferocity, "Don't cry! Don't you dare! Don't! Don't cry!"

I covered my face with my hands. She pushed in the trunk drawers and straightened the clothes. I sensed that if she could have hidden the act, she would have killed me.

I stood there, waiting for permission to stay or leave. She left the room as though I weren't there.

There was a party that evening. The noise of it came up the narrow stairs to the alcove where I lay on a cot, listening. It was like the sound of the ocean roaring in a seashell.

A year passed between the long drive to Provincetown and several visits I made to apartments where my parents stayed in New York City, one visit to a rented cabin in the Adirondack Mountains, and a few hours in a restaurant on the Coney Island boardwalk, midday in the spring.

A scene occurred there that displayed the pleasure my mother, Elsie, took in her own mockery. I was sitting at a table with her and my father and several of their acquaintances. A small band was playing popular songs of the day. She turned to me suddenly. Would I go over to the bandstand and request a song called "Blasé"?

I felt excitement at the thought of carrying out her wish,

but I was abashed by her smile of amusement and the secret it implied.

I made my way among the tables to the bandleader, who was in the middle of a number. I stood beside the bandstand where the musicians sat in scissorlike wooden chairs, blowing and fiddling on their instruments. At last I caught the eye of the bandleader. My voice to him must have been nearly inaudible. What I said was, "'Blasé' for *her*," and pointed to the table where my mother was sitting. His sour expression gave way to a startled smile. He waved in her direction and bowed slightly. Everyone was laughing: my parents and their friends, people at tables close enough to the platform to have heard my request, and now the conductor himself. My face blazed. I knew, without understanding what it was, that their laughter was about something ridiculous I had done.

My parents were staying temporarily—their arrangements, as far as I could work out, were permanently temporary—in a small borrowed apartment in New York City. The minister arranged with my father to leave me there for a few hours and then return to take me home.

A large dog lay on the floor, its eyes watchful. I recognized it as the same animal that had attacked the cat in Provincetown a year or so earlier. It got up to sniff my shoes. My father filled in the silence with his voice. I wasn't listening to him. Where was my mother?

Suddenly she appeared in the doorway that led to a second room. I saw an unmade bed behind her. She pressed one hand against the doorframe. The other was holding a drink. My father's tone changed; his voice was barely above a whisper. "Puppy . . . puppy . . . puppy," he called her softly, as though he feared but hoped to wake her. She stared at me, her eyes like embers.

All at once she flung the glass and its contents in my direction. Water and pieces of ice slid down my arms and over my dress. The dog crouched at my feet. My father was in the doorway, holding my mother tight in his arms. Then he took me away from the apartment.

At some hour he must have returned with me. Perhaps we waited for the minister outside the front door.

For years I assumed responsibility for all that happened in my life, even for events over which I had not the slightest control. It was not out of generosity of mind or spirit that I did so. It was a hopeless wish that I would discover why my birth and my existence were so calamitous for my mother.

A few months later Uncle Elwood took me to the city again to visit my parents. This time they were staying in a hotel owned by a family they were acquainted with, whose wealth included vast land tracts on the west side of the Hudson River, just north of the Palisades, as my father explained to me. I was to stay overnight, and for that purpose the rich family provided a room for me across the corridor from Paul and Elsie.

The idea of spending so much time with them filled me with alarm. But the visit began cheerfully, though a malaise gripped me as soon as I saw them together in the hotel room. I mistook the feeling for excitement.

Humorously, my parents played with the idea that I should marry the son of the hotel owners, a boy only a year or so older than I was, I guessed. They would arrange the marriage first thing in the morning, they promised, both smiling broadly. I strained to match their mood. It would be like the marriages of children in India. I had seen such children in an issue of the *National Geographic*. They looked so little. They wore bands of jewels across their brows and large brilliantly colored flowers behind their ears.

Evening approached. The dark, like ink, filled up the airshaft of their room on the fourteenth floor. My father asked me what I would like for supper; he would order it from room service. My experience was only with the minister's cooking. "Lamb chop and peas," I said, partially aware that this was a special occasion: hotel rooms, Paul and Elsie, so tall, so slender, both, a marriage planned for the future so I would be able to live in this room for years, the excitement of great things about to happen. We hardly ever had lamb chops at Uncle Elwood's house, though we often had little canned peas. When the tray was delivered by a waiter, I looked at it and saw I had forgotten something.

"There's no milk," I observed.

At once, my father carried the tray to the window, opened it, and dropped the tray into the airshaft.

Moments later, as I stood there stunned by what my father had done—nothing Elsie did ever surprised me—I heard the tray crash. Through tight lips, my father said mildly, "Okay, pal. Since it wasn't to your pleasure. . . ." My mother, behind the half-closed door of the bathroom, where she had gone at the very moment he walked to the window, exclaimed, "Paul!" in a muffled voice, as though she spoke through a towel.

Again, as in the episode of the trunk in Provincetown, I was profoundly embarrassed, as though I were implicated in my father's act. But nearly as painful was the gnawing hunger I suddenly felt for that lamb chop lying fourteen stories below.

As the two of them were leaving for the evening, for whatever entertainment they anticipated, there was a loud knocking at the door. My father opened it to a laughing young man, possessed by what was to me an inexplicable merriment. "Foxes!" he cried, clapping his hands, fluttering and capering, calling out praises to my mother. "Your costume, darling!" My father murmured, "Dick is to keep an eye on you," and at that the young man spotted me and held out his hand, which I took. "Come along, Paula," he called, even though I was standing next to him.

I followed him across the corridor to another room. He threw himself down on one of the twin beds, still smiling. "Well, dear little one. What shall we play?" he said, and promptly closed his eyes and fell asleep. Even if it had not been his purpose, he had rescued me from two incomprehensible people. I looked over at his pretty sleeping face in the other bed, and I was overcome with an emotion I had no word for—a kind of love for that stranger.

I put myself to sleep with pictures of everything I could envisage in the Balmville house, the way I felt its walls around me, and Uncle Elwood, coming and going, the animated spirit of it all.

It seems unlikely that I would have been allowed to go unaccompanied on a train to New York City, yet in the winter of 1928, you could place a child safely in the care of a conductor or a porter. In any event, several months after the Visit of the Dropped Tray, as I named it in my thoughts, I went to the city on the train and was met at Grand Central Station, not by my father but by a married couple, actors, who took me to their tiny apartment, which they shared with two enormous dogs—Great Danes, they told me. A large window in the living room looked out on Central Park.

They both had roles in the play *Animal Crackers*, and except on matinee days they were always at home during the day. They expected my father to "turn up" at any moment, as they smilingly told me. I spent two nights with the actors, going to sleep in their bedroom, carried into the living room and deposited on a sofa when they were ready to retire.

During the day the dogs kept watch over the two rooms, pacing restlessly the length of the living room or sleeping sluggishly in great canine heaps.

My father came to get me on a matinee day as the actors were on their way out the door. "Thanks, dear pals," he said to them. He told me he had lifted a few too many glasses two evenings earlier and had not been able to meet me at the station. "I was— ahem, ahem—indisposed," he said, with comical exaggeration, and I, without comprehending what he meant, smiled up at him. Now we were going to take a bus to Schroon Lake, New York, in the Adirondack Mountains, where he and my "sainted mother" had rented a cabin. I puzzled over his words about Elsie for a while, then gave it up as another mystery.

He looked tired, as though the glasses he had lifted had weighed too much for him. His water-color eyes were bloodshot; his voice, usually so deep, so melodic, as though he were always on the point of breaking into song, had a cranky, querulous note; and his words, usually so finely cut, were blurred.

He slept on the bus, falling against me as it lurched. I had not seen him since he had dropped the supper tray out the window, and I felt wary and nervous. As he slept, I investigated his face, his hands, one of which held an unlit cigarette, his trembling eyelids.

After hours of traveling, we arrived in the hamlet of Schroon Lake. My mother and a friend, a slender, spidery, dark-haired man, were waiting in front of a general store, a dusty, cheese-smelling, dark space in front of which stood a single gas pump. Nearby was a beat-up little car that apparently belonged to my parents. As I stepped from the bus, the spidery man's eyes widened with amusement. "Oh, she's a one!" he exclaimed to Elsie.

We drove several miles and turned off the paved road to a rutted lane. Soon a small cabin appeared. Behind it was Schroon Lake. A pale strip of shoreline was still visible, but it vanished as night spread over the water. The cabin was meagerly furnished; the smell of old fires emanated from a stove that stood at one end of the living room.

Recalling the evening in the hotel, I said nothing about meals, although I was hungry. My father fixed me supper with particular effort, noticeable effort, as if he too remembered that evening and was determined to erase it from both our memories. He laughed and talked ceaselessly. Now that I think of it, his movements and gestures might have been a dance of contrition.

The next evening we drove to the hamlet of Schroon Lake, parking the car on a country road across the street from a wooden building that served various community purposes that included movie showings. In the one that we saw Warner Baxter played the lead. When the film was over, I walked beside Elsie into the small anteroom that served as a lobby.

I startled myself by asking her how babies were made. The spidery man on her other side burst into laughter. After a moment, she replied, in an impersonal voice, "Sexual intercourse."

At that moment, we reached the car. She drove, with my father in the passenger seat and the spidery man and me in the rear. She spoke animatedly about other matters. No one mentioned the movie or my question and her answer.

Sober or drunk, my father spoke dismissively about the places he had lived in over the years. After downing a few drinks, he would fall in love with his own voice, theatrically honeyed, filled with significant whispers and pauses. He was in thrall to his voice; his thoughts stumbled behind.

From fragments of sentences that fell from his lips, I understood him to be claiming that he'd been on his way to his true and noble destination when he was sidetracked by women. He himself, he asserted, would have been contented with an unadorned life, a roof over his head to shelter him from weather, a cot to sleep on, a stove to keep him warm when cold winds blew, and upon which he could prepare spartan meals.

All men aspire toward the mountain peaks, but women drive them down into the valleys of domesticity where they are ambushed by family life and other degrading and petty tyrannies.

As we drew near to his rented house in the car he had met us with at the Los Angeles railroad station, he gestured toward it, saying disdainfully that it was furnished with "yard upon yard of Spanish junk." The road we were on ended a half a mile farther among bare hills. At their summit rose a gigantic sign: HOLLY-WOODLAND.

When I recall the few days I spent at the house, I'm always outdoors and it is nighttime. The dark is thinned by stepping stones of amber light cast on the sidewalk by streetlamps. The house is large, its windows partially hidden by elaborate ironwork grilles. An outside staircase reaches the top floor. Big shadowed houses stand back from the street, separated by extensive gardens and trees unfamiliar to me.

Aunt Jessie, her task to deliver me to California completed, departed after a week or so for the East and her mother, whom she'd left in a housekeeper's care. On the evening of the day she boarded a train bound for New York, Daddy and my mother went out to a party, leaving me on my own.

In the long dusk, I wandered through doorless, cavelike rooms with beamed ceilings and rough white plaster walls, turning on the lights where I could reach a switch. A chill rose from the red tiles of the floor. Tables and chairs were made of some dark wood. A plump pink sofa squatted in the center of one of the larger rooms. The sudden barking of a dog startled me, each bark like a gunshot.

I came to the front door, opened it, and stepped outside. It swung shut behind me. I tried the metal handle. Even as I moved it back and forth, I knew I was locked out.

The dark tightened around me, and for a moment I couldn't draw breath. It was as if the night were a black sack into which I'd been dropped. I listened. A faint breeze rustled the leaves of the trees; a car suddenly speeded up with a grinding of gears on an unseen street. There was the steady splash of a waterfall at the back of the house. I tiptoed toward it across the grass.

It fell into a shallow pool like a serpent sliding from a tree branch, the water shimmering in the lights from the house. In the pool swam a few torpid goldfish. I had spent hours beside that pool, and one morning I had fallen into it.

A man appeared suddenly a few feet away. His head was

cocked at an angle as though he too were listening. When he saw me, he said—and his voice surprised me in a world only seconds ago empty of human life—"I've made the same mistake before. I think I've left on my lawn sprinkler. Then I find out it's the sound of your little waterfall." He waved toward it.

"I'm locked out," I told him

He nodded in agreement. He seemed to know that no one was home. He said, "We'll go to my house. Are you hungry?" I said yes, though I wasn't. He held out his hand and I took it. We walked a short distance to his house.

In the kitchen, his wife sliced a banana into a bowl. I ate it at the kitchen table, observed by their grave, friendly faces. When I had finished the banana, I was so sleepy I could hardly hold my head up. The wife led me up a staircase to a spare bedroom, un-used since their son had grown up and moved to another state to live and work. I crawled beneath the sheet in my underwear, and she drew up a quilt over me. I was nearly asleep when she whispered she had made the quilt herself.

It was warm, bright with color. My last thought was of Joseph's coat, which I'd heard about in Sunday school in Uncle Elwood's church.

Early the next morning, I walked back to my parents' house and climbed up the outside steps to a door. It was unlocked. I opened it, at the same time calling, "Daddy!"

From one of two beds, a blanket rose into the air like a large animal getting to its four feet. Suddenly my father was holding me like a rag doll and running down the back stairs. His pajama top was unbuttoned. I glimpsed patches of pale skin as we entered the kitchen, where a black maid was ironing. He seemed unaware of her presence as he whirled about looking for a chair. What he'd wanted was to get me out of the bedroom.

I knew it wasn't my mother in the other bed. I'd seen yellow hair on the pillow.

He lighted on a chair, put me across his knees, and began to spank me.

"Mr. Fox! That isn't right! It isn't fair!" the black maid protested.

My father looked up at her as if surprised by her presence. I was astonished that she had defended me and lifted my head from his knee to stare at her. Years later, when I thought about her—and I thought about her often—about how much she had had to overcome in the way of an enforced and habitual discretion, how a sense of justice in her had outweighed the risk—I realized how brave she had been.

A decade after the incident, my father told me, in what he deemed to be a comical voice, that that night he had pretended to be a childless bachelor and had "brought home a girl from the party." Then I had burst into the bedroom at a heathen hour of the morning, shouting "Daddy!"

I never discovered where my mother had spent the night. Nor did my father ask me where I had been before I opened the door to the bedroom.

A few days later, my father drove me to Redlands, a small town thirty-five or forty miles from Hollywood. He left me there in the care of an old woman, Mrs. Cummings. She kept house for Sophie, her enormous daughter, who ran a summer camp for girls in the Big Bear Mountains.

Years later, I told my father that I had returned to the camp when I was sixteen. He said, "Ah, well . . . people who've been parceled out and knocked around are always returning to the past, retracing their steps." He spoke distantly, in a detached voice.

It was during that same exchange that he told me what my mother had said—after I'd spent a week or so in Hollywood in the house with the waterfall—which had resulted in his leaving me in old Mrs. Cummings's care.

"She gave me an ultimatum," he began. "She said, 'Either *she* goes or I go.'" He shook his head ruefully. "I had no choice," he said, in a faintly self-pitying tone of voice.

"I had only a few days to find someone to take care of you." Then he repeated his words: "I had no choice."

I learned that if I were to see my parents, I had to live away from them. The four or five times I visited them during that year I spent in Redlands, Mrs. Cummings would put me on a train to Los Angeles, placing me in the charge of a porter. Once, a friend of my father's, Vin Lawrence, met the train. He drove directly from the station to an all-night miniature golf course. It was brightly lit up, like a small-town circus. Vin loved golf, which he called "the green mistress."

He talked to me as if I were grown up, in a voice that sounded like soft barking. Now and then he whistled or made popping sounds with his mouth and clapped his small hands together— especially when his stroke had been good—resting the golf club he was using against one leg. He explained that my father had been unable to meet me because he had "lifted a few too many glasses," an explanation I had heard before that wasn't one.

He played the little course with utmost seriousness as I walked or waited beside him. He kept up a running commentary. A story about my mother held my attention. He called her "Spain."

He and my father had searched for and found an elegant black gown for her to wear at a movie opening at Grauman's Chinese. They didn't know she had spent the day stuffing herself with olive oil and garlic on dark bread, food for which she had been suddenly possessed by intense longing. She arrived at the theater in time, wearing the velvet gown but stinking to high heaven. It was the first story I'd heard about her. Until then I had had only my own stories.

Another time, no one met the train. It was early evening. I sat for a while on a station bench, a small suitcase next to me. I worked out the words on a sign over a booth a few yards away. TRAVELER'S AID, it read.

I was a traveler and I needed aid. I went over. I don't recall any conversation, but I do remember the outcome. The woman behind the booth gave me taxi fare, and she smiled as she put the bills in both my hands.

My parents moved to Malibu Beach, where they rented a house built to look like the midsection of a small ship. A deck jutted out over the sand. At the top there was a large square room, like a captain's bridge, my father said, from which I could see the vast ocean.

I spent several weekends at the Malibu house. At a fated hour all the mornings I was there, my father gripped my resistant hands and lifted me over the foaming waves of the surf toward the dreadful green waters of the Pacific, into which he dropped me.

I sank at once, then rose, running in the water, keeping afloat in a way that every second left me in doubt about whether I would live to the next. I heard myself gasping and sputtering; it frightened me further. I knew there were miles of water-filled space below me. The only thing keeping me above it was the frenzied movement of my feet. "I'm drowning!" I'd cry. "No you aren't!" my father called out in a hard, jocular voice from a few yards away. And I wasn't.

Malibu was a beach movie palace. Actors and actresses, oiled with various preparations to keep themselves from getting sunburned, lay gleaming on the sand, or walked along the edge of the surf, as I once saw Richard Barthelmess do. On a morning, the next-door neighbors appeared, Lilyan Tashman in a startling white bathing suit, her face a polar snowfield of cold cream, and her husband, Edmund Lowe, with his black thread of mustache.

One Sunday morning, John Gilbert took me for a long walk holding my hand and talking to me in his high, thin voice. Most weekends I was there, one of my father's actor friends, Charles Bickford, would drop by from somewhere to sit on the beach and talk to Daddy in his deep voice.

After he had gone, Daddy said, "Actors are so dumb. You wouldn't believe how dumb they are!"

Mary Barthelmess, a few years older than I, gave me a pair of rose-colored beach pajamas she had outgrown. When I tried them on, I was stung on my rear end by a bee trapped inside the cotton folds. I had learned it was dangerous to complain within my mother's hearing. My hand flew to cover my mouth and hold in my startled cry.

Several weeks earlier, I had murmured to Daddy that I had a toothache. My mother just then entered the room. In a neutral voice she said, "I'll fix that for you." She turned, smiling, to my father. "Would you put her in the rumble seat?" It may have seemed to him that she had nothing in mind but a short drive in the open air, but I heard sounds of distant thunder.

She drove on the steep, curving hills that rose across from Malibu. Through the back window, I saw how rigidly she held her back, how stiff her neck was, as she drove like the wind and I was shaken like a rattle.

The drive lasted twenty minutes or so—the drive lasted forever. When we returned to the beach house, she emerged from the car and stood like a statue for a moment, staring at me in the rumble seat with her great dark eyes, her face stony. "Do you still have a toothache?" she inquired politely. Driving me on the mountain roads had not lessened her rage but intensified it.

My parents returned from Europe after a sojourn of three or four years, when I was eleven. They slid into my sight standing on the deck of a small passenger ship out of Marseille that docked in New York City on the Hudson River alongside a cavernous shed. They were returning home after their adventures, the most recent being their flight a few weeks earlier from the Balearic island of Ibiza during the early days of the Spanish Civil War.

My mother had draped a polo coat over her shoulders—I

suppose because it was a cool spring day—and she smiled down at my grandmother and me as we waited in the shadowed darkness of the shed. Sunlight fell in daggers through holes in the roof high above us.

It had been years since I'd seen them. They were as handsome as movie stars. Smoke trailed like a festive streamer from the cigarette my mother held between two fingers of her right hand. When she realized we'd spotted her, she waved once and her head was momentarily wreathed in smoke. The gangplank was lowered thunderously across the abyss between the deck and the pier. Passengers began to trickle across it. Suddenly my parents were standing before us, a steamer trunk like a third presence between them. I knew that trunk; I'd seen it in Provincetown years earlier.

"Hello . . . hello . . . hello," they called to us, as if we were far away. They pointed out their luggage for porters, speaking to my grandmother and me in voices that were deep, melodious—not everyday voices like those I heard in Kew Gardens, but of an unbroken suavity, as though they'd memorized whole pages written for them on this occasion of their homecoming.

They spoke of shipboard life; about a cave in Ibiza outside of which my father had crouched for hours—embarrassed by a fit of claustrophobia that had paralyzed him not two feet from the entrance, while my mother hid inside along with other refugees—before escaping the next day to the ship that carried them to Marseille; about the fact, ruefully acknowledged by both of them with charming smiles, that no troops from either side especially wanted to capture them; about the demeanor and somewhat hostile behavior of the French in the port; with serio-comic emphasis, they warned us both about the pitfalls of British filmmaking—as though either of us might be about to launch ourselves into it—and such a myriad of subjects that although I stood there motionless and listening ravenously, I felt I was tumbling down a mountainside, an avalanche a few yards behind me.

Unlike her brother Fermin, my mother had not a trace of a foreign accent, although as I learned over the next few months, she spoke English with a foreigner's extreme caution, as though entering an unexplored forest full of dangers. She wanted, I guessed, to speak impeccably, and she would often pause in the middle of a sentence to make a kind of grammar drama. "Is it sort or kind?" "Is it were or was?" "Is it me or I?" she would ask, pondering the perilous choices and looking up at the ceiling as though it might contain the answer.

Now, in mid-sentence, she switched to Spanish and bent suddenly to embrace my grandmother with nearly human warmth as if she'd all at once recalled that the elderly woman standing so submissively behind her, a stunned smile on her face, was her own mother, who, with her poor grasp of English, would not have understood even a part of what had been said.

My mother's eyes stared at me over my grandmother's shoulder. Her mouth formed a cold radiant smile. My soul shivered.

My father leaned toward me at that moment, reaching out a hand to push a clump of hair behind my ear. The tips of his fingers were damp. He laughed. He murmured, "Well, pal. Well, well. . . . Here we all are."

I saw my mother twice during the autumn I was a Juilliard student. I can't imagine that she requested my company; I must have gone to see her on my own the first time.

"Come in, Paula," I hear her say, a half century later. It sounded to me then as if she'd said, "Go away, Paula."

Was it she who always imposed a painful formality between us? Or by then was it a collaboration of the two of us? As some people are inclined to do in such tense circumstances, she simulated frankness and told me personal stories about herself, more detailed perhaps than she intended, or else a certain brutal self-revelation was her specialty. Perhaps she didn't know any better.

She smoked constantly, lighting one cigarette from the end of another.

The second time I saw her was when I was taken by taxi to her apartment accompanied by my El Paso friend, Paul, and another acquaintance from International House. My face was red with fever. She was expecting me. Friends had telephoned her to tell her that I was ill. They half carried me up the stairs.

When she opened the door, I saw she was dressed in a coat. An open sack of oranges sat on a table. She waited until my friends had gone and then said to me politely, "Take care of yourself," and left. I spent the night there.

Perhaps to atone for what even I could judge as utter neglect, she invited me a few weeks later to a concert conducted by Arturo Toscanini. I had a date with a Columbia University medical student. I told her I had an engagement that night. "Engagement?" she asked lightly, with sardonic disbelief.

My life was incoherent to me. I felt it quivering, spitting out broken teeth. When I thought of the purposes I had tried to find for myself the last year, to show my father that I "wanted" something—piano, voice lessons, sculpture, none of the least use to me—when I thought of the madness of my parents where I was concerned, I felt the bleakest misery.

I would have been one of those children found in a wilderness, written about in case histories, if it had not been for Uncle Elwood; I had learned civility and kindness from him. I knew how to behave in parlous circumstances, to temporize and compromise—a lesson taught me by my father. From my mother I had gained the knowledge of how to contend with the madness of people. And from black servants, I had learned what justice was.

When Elsie was ninety-two, dying of old age and emphysema, two of my three children urged me to visit her on the island of Nantucket, where, as far as I knew, she had been living for more than three decades. I had not seen her for thirty-eight years.

I wanted to please them. I had no desire to see her. With my permission, my daughter had given her my telephone number. She called me. I heard the old seductive voice, deep and familiar as my own. I felt the same harrowing tension for a moment; then it went, and it was as if I were speaking politely to an utter stranger.

I went to the airport the next day, but Nantucket was fogged in and the flight was canceled. I hardly had the nerve for a second try. But I made it without the nerve. I landed on Nantucket around noon. I took a taxi to her address; the driver was a voluble old bohemian who had lived on the island since the late sixties.

Her house was one of several like it in a new community extending out from the port town. As I got out of the car, I thought of my grandmother, dead and buried without my having been told. "She wouldn't have been interested," Elsie had said of me, one of my uncles reported. Perhaps I had deserved it. But not from the woman who was my mother. I looked at the house and shuddered. The door was unlocked.

I walked into a conventionally furnished living room. From a small room on the left came a sound that I told myself, grimly, was a minotaur breathing, but it was only an oxygen-supplying machine. I looked inside. My mother was asleep on a big bed. I averted my eyes from the figure beneath the bedclothes.

I must have sat in the living room for twenty-five or so minutes, looking at a magazine I had found on a table, when I was aware that someone was looking at me.

I put the magazine down. My mother was standing a few feet away, swaying slightly. She reminded me of an old conquistador, thin, tall, white hair like a helmet. I would have recognized her anywhere.

"Paula?" she asked, beginning to smile.

"Yes," I answered, as I stood up. She was wearing a thin white cotton nightgown. Her chest bones protruded slightly. Her skin was transparent and tinged with a bluish cast.

We shook hands. I followed her into her bedroom just as the front door opened and a young couple entered. They were her caretakers, a South American Indian from Peru and his plump young American wife, pale, with frizzy dyed-blonde hair. They lived in a spare room upstairs.

He addressed my mother as Señora. They had been out on an errand. He was a trained nurse. While I sat in a chair next to her bed, he brought her a drink that looked like malted milk. With a winsome smile, she commanded him never to leave her. Then, still smiling, she asked me if he didn't have a "perfect Indian head." I thought of Francisco Pizarro cutting off such heads.

I detected panic behind her effort to keep him charmed, an infant's fear of the dark.

She asked me to go to a room across from hers and bring her a photograph. I went, found a closed door, opened it, and saw the floor was covered with boxes filled with paper. On the top of one box was a sepia-colored photograph of a man standing in front of a horse and carriage in parkland. I brought it to her.

"Who do you think this is?" she asked archly.

I shrugged. She answered her own question dramatically. "Your grandfather! And the horse? It was his own, sent him from Cuba to New York City. Her name was Beauty. He said American horses were too slow for him."

She laughed and then had to use the oxygen machine. I put her drink down on a table. She had barely touched it.

"I want you to have this photograph," she gasped. She stopped speaking, and the nurse came into the room.

I went out, and when I came back she had played her trick; she had hidden the picture under the bedclothes knowing, somehow, that I wouldn't want to search there for it. I didn't ask her where it was, although I couldn't help casting glances at the bed.

I needed to urinate. I excused myself and went outside and walked until I found a field and a tree. I couldn't use a toilet Elsie might have used. My revulsion was so deep, I took the chance that someone might spot me crouching next to the tree trunk.

I went to the airport an hour earlier than I needed to, hitching a ride with the nurse who, as we drove off, told me he had a part-time job: standing on the small Nantucket airfield holding two lighted rods to guide incoming airplanes.

He parked in front of a small airport restaurant I had been too tense to notice when I landed that day. It was dark now, and patches of light from the windows glowed on the ground.

I walked inside. There were tables, a counter with a plastic cake stand, a coffee machine, a waitress wearing a short black shirt beneath her apron, and an open window to the kitchen. The customers were few: a family with two children, a young middle-aged couple, two men holding hands, a man in a business suit reading a newspaper, two young women speaking earnestly to each other. I sat down at a table, its surface gritty with grains of sugar.

I was surrounded by the saints of ordinary life, and for an instant I felt that God was in the restaurant. After Elsie.

A few months later, the nurse's wife telephoned me at home to say Elsie had died that morning. I murmured something comforting and realized I had spoken as if Elsie's death was the wife's loss.

When I hung up, I felt hollow, listless. I had lost out on a daughter's last privilege: I couldn't mourn my mother.

JUST ANOTHER
MOVIE STAR

JAMIE CALLAN

❖ ❖ ❖

In 1962, I was eight years old. My family lived in a big blue
Dutch Colonial house in North Stamford, Connecticut.

John F. Kennedy was the president. Chubby Checker and
Elvis Presley were at the top of the pop chart. Only a few years
earlier, Marilyn Monroe had appeared nude in the premiere issue
of *Playboy*. She had just starred in *Gentlemen Prefer Blondes* and
Some Like It Hot and was voted America's top film star. Her magic
only grew after her death.

But it was my mother who truly taught me about the power of
magic and illusion. She introduced me to the movies.

This love affair with the movies began with Shirley Temple.
My mother would come into my bedroom at three in the morning, wearing a pink chiffon negligee, and pull me out of bed, whispering, "Wake up. Come downstairs." I came into the living room,
sleepy-eyed, barely awake, and tried to focus on the small black-
and-white television set. Shirley Temple, the little girl in the
impossibly short white ruffled dress, bounced up and down, her
lacy-pantied bottom showing, her eyes wide, her winning dimples

and that sudden flashing smile pulling us into her make-believe world.

I watched in my nightgown, curled up on the couch next to my mother as if still in a dream, my mother's arms around me, her breast pressed against my cheek, the aroma of the day-old Chanel No. 5 enveloping me.

Four-year-old Shirley sang "On the Good Ship Lollipop," and she danced a little soft-shoe with a grown-up man in a top hat, a delicious love affair that could only take place in the safety of the movie screen.

In the afternoon on television, there was *The Million Dollar Movie*. At night, *The Late Late Show*. While my father and older brother slept, my mother and I sat together on the couch, and I learned how to hitchhike from Claudette Colbert, what a lady keeps in the fridge—only perfume and champagne—what to eat when you're having breakfast at Tiffany's—croissants—how to keep cool during August—keep your panties in the icebox.

Next came the Marilyn Monroe festival on Channel Eleven for an entire week at the end of August, and I began to study Marilyn. Her little-girl voice, the tilt of her head, the way her curves swam and pressed against a silk dress, flashes of flesh emerging unexpectantly. Mother put her arm around me, and we settled into the couch, the shades drawn, shutting out the afternoon sun. "She is so *feminine*," my mother whispered as Marilyn ran to catch a train, struggling with her luggage, her curvy hips swaying to a jazzy up-tempo beat. We watched her through Jack Lemmon's eyes, male voyeurs, sneaking a peek at the Female. I was learning how to be a *female*. And even though I didn't know it at the time, I was beginning to understand something about the power and the dangers of female sexuality.

But sitting there, I was aware that I was a girl watching a grown-up man as he watched a woman—as she played a woman who was not aware of the fact that she was being watched. And neither one of them knew that they were being watched by us, the ordinary people in the shadows of their living rooms. I was learning to see life through the eyes of a man and a woman. Later, I realized the movies introduced me to the delicious joys of voyeurism. But at the time, I was little girl, watching my mother as she watched Jack Lemmon watching Marilyn Monroe, and all I truly understood was the exquisite pleasure of watching.

During the commercials, I went to the bathroom and sat on the counter by the sink and posed in front of the mirror, pouting like Marilyn. I stuffed tissue paper into my cotton shirt and put on my mother's red lipstick. I cooed at myself with my eyes half closed, trying out that sleepy-eyed, open-mouthed Marilyn Monroe look. But truth be told, I felt more like Jack Lemmon, a voyeur with breasts made of paper.

That year *Long Day's Journey Into Night* with Katharine Hepburn came out. My mother, my father, my twelve-year-old brother, Johnny, and I all went to see the film on a muggy night in July. I don't think my parents knew anything about the movie or Eugene O'Neill or the original play. All they knew was that Katharine Hepburn played the lead. When it became clear that the movie was about a wife and mother addicted to morphine, my father made us all leave in the middle of a scene where Katharine Hepburn descends down the stairs in the middle of the night to launch into a drug-induced monologue about her lost girlhood.

This was the summer my mother invented The Thrill Ride. The kids in our neighborhood had been to Playland and kept bragging about going on the roller-coaster ride. My mother said we didn't need to drive all the way to New York for a roller-coaster ride, that we could have one right there on our very own street. She renamed her car The Blue Devil and started charging the kids in the neighborhood for a thrill ride.

My mother stood in front of the bathroom mirror, putting on bright red lipstick from a gold tube. Her hair was slicked back with Dippity-do. Before she put the scarf on she looked a lot like Jean Seberg.

She applied rouge, and I quickly looked out her bedroom window. "Where are my customers?" she asked me.

"They're sitting on the front lawn," I told her.

"Give me a pill. *S'il vous plait.*"

"What color?"

I asked this because her pills came in all sorts of colors, shapes, sizes. She had drawers full of them. Doctors prescribed them for nerves, to keep her peppy, busy, and to make her a happy suburban housewife. Nobody seemed to think there was anything wrong with this. It would be another two years before *Valley of the Dolls* was published. My mother believed in the power of pharmaceuticals. She gave me orange-flavored St. Joseph's baby aspirin to "calm me down."

Outside, there must have been eight kids waiting for their thrill ride. My brother, Johnny, had already taken off for the beach, but the Frickers were there, and my best friend, Camille Vassano, and the Wilcox twins—Barbie and Suzie—and Donna Fuscaldo, who was almost twelve and hardly ever played with the little kids anymore, all waited in line. The Good Humor man had just come and gone, so everyone was licking the remainder of the ice cream bars as the melted chocolate ran down their sticky fingers.

My mother came out of the house. She took her time walking down the front path. She wore her Audrey Hepburn sunglasses, and she stopped in front of the Ford parked in the driveway and caressed it lightly before giving the bumper a little slap. The car was huge and blue. It had silver trim and "Ford" written in script across the back by the trunk. My mother balanced herself with one hand on the rear of the car and then leaned down and adjusted the strap on her white high-heeled sandal. She stood up and smoothed out her yellow cotton sundress with the scooped-out neckline and jangled the bangles around her wrists. One of the older boys whistled at her.

"Okay, who's got a nickel?" she asked.

"Mrs. Callan!" shouted David Westhouser. "Can I owe you till tomorrow?"

"No, you cannot," she said, and jangled her bracelets in the air.

"Please?"

My mother put her arms out and stopped the kids from rushing into the car. "No one under four feet allowed!" They settled down and waited in line as she took out her purse. "Okay, give me your money, then you can get on." She turned to David. "If there's room, you can give me an IOU. Just sit there and wait." Mother turned to me.

"You can get in for free." She smiled at me and I got in line with the others, and my mother began collecting money.

"Hey, this isn't a nickel, Billy. This is a pebble."

Billy Taylor looked up at her, his extended hand, grubby and covered in chocolate ice cream.

"Billy, this is a pebble, not a nickel. Are you retarded?"

"No," he whispered.

"Do you have a nickel?"

"No, Mrs. Callan."

"Then you can't ride with us."

Billy held back tears and sat on the front lawn, his head buried in his lap. "All right, get in. Hurry up."

Mother collected the rest of the nickels, and we scrambled into the car.

David pulled on my mother's dress. "Mrs. Callan, I have the money at home."

"It's not about the money, David. It's about your mother."

"My mother?"

"Yes, your mother. Why does she wear her mink to the PTA meetings?"

"I don't know."

"Well, everyone is wondering about it, David. I mean, the PTA *meeting*." Mother smiled. "Doesn't your father satisfy that woman?"

"What do you mean?"

My mother lowered her sunglasses and smiled at David. "Satisfy, David. You know." She lowered her voice. "In the *bedroom*. I hear your daddy has a small weenie."

"Mrs. Callan, I have the nickel at home."

"Never mind, David." She rumpled his hair. "This one's on me." He ran to the car, and she followed quickly, then stepped inside and adjusted her sunglasses to check her makeup in the rearview mirror, the kids laughing and poking one another all the while.

"This is not for the squeamish," she announced, arranging herself behind the enormous ivory-colored steering wheel and fluffing up her hair. She started up the engine, making it roar, black smoke exploded out of the exhaust pipe, and then she turned the radio up full blast. The Isley Brothers belted out "Twist and Shout!"

I sat back in the plush red-velvet passenger seat next to my mother, as if we were sitting in the audience at one of the opulent theaters of the day and about to see a great movie. She grabbed my hand and pressed down on the gas pedal hard, and suddenly we were climbing up to the top of Ledge Lane, then down the hill at what seemed like a million miles an hour, then swerving up over to Belltown Road with the breaks squealing and the kids in back laughing and screaming as if we really were on a roller-coaster ride at Playland with the cool air rushing around us and the smell of cotton candy on our fingers.

I remember looking at my mother and thinking this was the most beautiful, most glamorous woman in the world. She patted my knee and shouted, "Aren't you glad you have such a fun mommy!?"

And I screamed back, "Yes! Yes! Yes I am!"

Later that summer, Mother and I spent an entire Saturday shopping at Saks Fifth Avenue on High Ridge Road. My father and mother had spent the night fighting, and now she had his credit card and wanted to get back at him for being cold and Irish and not understanding her because she was hot and French.

We walked into the air-conditioned store and headed right for the beauty counter, where an Helena Rubinstein representative gave us free makeovers. I was painted and rouged, just like my mother. We tried on hats and boots, wigs and silk scarves.

Mother circled her arm around mine every time she pulled out the Saks Fifth Avenue credit card. "You need these, Jamie," she whispered, holding out the three-layer lace white ankle socks she had chosen for me. She turned to the clerk and handed her my father's plastic card. "Charge it," she said. "Charge away!" She laughed. "That's my battle cry!"

We left the store with shopping bags full of cotton shifts in mod Mondrian patterns, pink sandals, and a puffy one-piece sunsuit with blue butterflies floating all over it. Mother bought a black fringed twist dress, cat-eyed sunglasses with rhinestones, a red lace bustier, and a bottle of Evening in Paris.

A few days later, I stood in front of my mother's mirror when she was downstairs in the kitchen and I was supposed to be making her bed. I tried on her silver lamé evening gown and all her jewelry—gold pins in the shape of flowers, cats with tiny rubies for eyes, a lizard made of rhinestones and garnets. I put on the Hawaiian shell necklace that the boy who died in Pearl Harbor had given to her.

I took the lace curtains out of the linen closet and draped them around my shoulders and pretended I was Marilyn Monroe. I opened the dresser drawers, looking for more of my mother's loot: her silk lingerie, the delicate pearls, her stockings and garters.

Mother came into the room. "What are you doing?" she asked.

"Playing dress-up."

"With my things? This is dangerous stuff," she said, and she closed the door and then took the pearls out of my hands. She put them back in her jewelry box, then turned to me and grabbed my arm. "I want to give you something," she said, and pulled me into her closet.

She opened her closet door and took out a green silk dress. It had a cinched waist with panels of chiffon floating around the skirt. "I can't fit into this anymore. Why don't you take it?"

"Are you sure?"

"Yes," she said, and slipped it over my head, zipped it up, her fingers gliding up the small of my back. I looked at myself in the mirror. It fit except that the bosoms were empty shells, filled with air.

"You need tissue paper," she said, and opened her night table drawer.

I leaned over her and looked inside the drawer and caught sight of her pills. Vials and vials of them. Speckled ones. Pastels. Orange. Green. Yellow. Blue. They looked like candy. She uncapped a vial and popped a little green pill. Marilyn Monroe took pills. Judy Garland took pills. Ann Margret probably took pills. Why shouldn't my mother take pills? But, I confess. Even then, I began to wonder about the pills and what they were doing to my mother. She was funny and crazy, but she slept until noon every day and she had a lock put on the kitchen drawer where she kept her wallet. She worried a lot about my brother and me going into her "money drawer." And she began to scratch her left wrist until it was raw. I would tell her to stop, and she would tell me to shut up.

They were mostly diet pills. Dexamils. Phenobarbitol. The same doctors who said they would help her, suddenly wouldn't prescribe them anymore.

I was in the fourth grade when my mother returned from the doctor one afternoon, got into bed, and refused to get out the next day or the day after that. She stayed in bed and cried for three days.

And then on the third day, I was awakened by the sound of her singing "We're Havin' a Party" in the middle of the night. I looked out my bedroom window to see her dancing and running around the backyard in her bare feet. Then I heard my father and my brother go downstairs, and I followed. It was raining out, and I stood at the door watching my mother in her purple negligee as she picked up a stick out of the mud and waved it in the air as if it were a magic wand.

My father yelled for her to come inside, but she laughed at him, and so he tied his bathrobe around his waist and went out there. My father was a lieutenant commander in the naval reserve, and he had a military gait. He quickly marched up to my mother and grabbed her by the waist and began pulling her. She twisted away from him and ran to the other side of the yard and stood there in the wet grass, waiting and watching.

Then my father leapt at her and wrestled her to the ground, tackling her with his body. She tried to hit him with her fists and she got mud on his face, but he pinned her down by the wrists, until she went still. I held my breath. I thought about Elizabeth Taylor. I thought about *Suddenly, Last Summer*. I watched as he picked her up off the ground and lifted her easily up into his arms.

She was perfectly still, and then suddenly she kicked up her muddy feet and grabbed a hold of his neck. I could see her nails digging into his flesh, but I couldn't tell if she was crying or laughing. She whispered something into his ear and slid her hand down the nape of his neck to where his crew cut ended. He nodded his head as if agreeing with her. Even then, I knew there was something sexual about this moment. Something secret and adult. Something I would store away in my brain for later reference—when I got older, when I could understand more completely.

My father lifted her higher and whisked her through the muddy grass and up to the house. I remember noticing that his bathrobe was open, and I could see his white boxer shorts. His hair was wet, dripping water down his cheeks, and he was kissing the top of my mother's head, brushing the strawberry blonde bangs out of her eyes.

Her nightgown was soaked, and I could see her breasts, the dark outline of her nipples through the thin purple fabric. My father pressed his lips against hers as he kicked the back door wide open with a crash of his foot and rushed her through the kitchen.

My brother and I stood there on the linoleum floor, anchored between the stove and the washing machine. My father turned to us for a second. "Go to bed, you two," he said before carrying our mother up the stairs and slamming the bedroom door shut.

The next day my mother put vodka in our lunch-box Thermoses.

In the following weeks, she fed Jell-O to the cats.

She put thumbtacks in my father's shoes.

She bought a used pink Cadillac because the Ford was in

the shop. She drove it to the shopping center and then left it
there.

She served shoelaces for dinner and said it was spaghetti.
When Johnny and I told her it was not spaghetti, it was shoelaces,
she said leather is a protein.

She gave my brother's cat, Nemo, away to a girl who lived
down the street.

She got in the car and ran down all the neighbors' mailboxes.

She threw eggs at Mrs. Westhouser's front porch because she
said she didn't understand why she wore her mink to the PTA
meetings.

She wrote letters to the Coca-Cola Company claiming their
product made her daughter break out in red spots in the shape of
Rhode Island.

She showed up at the PTA meeting wearing nothing but a
pair of black lace panties and matching bra, underneath her blue
raincoat.

She bit my father in the arm and left two crescent-moon
marks.

She took me to the Ford Modeling Agency and demanded
they put me on the cover of *Glamour* magazine immediately.

She crashed the Ford into a police car.

My father put my mother into Fairfield Hills Mental Hospital.

Your mother is nervous," Aunt Dolores said as she scrubbed out
our kitchen sink with Comet cleanser. "She needs a rest."

Aunt Dolores was my father's little sister, a tough-minded gal
from Brooklyn who never married and basically raised her five

brothers and sisters after their parents died. She had taken a train from New York City to baby-sit me and my brother, Johnny. She pulled off the pair of pink rubber cleaning gloves and turned to me. "What's this frou-frou?" she asked, picking up my mother's ostrich-feather duster.

"It's for dusting furniture," I told her, but the truth was my mother used it for waking up the fireflies in our back yard during summer nights when we danced in our nightgowns and played at being fairies.

"Where's the Pledge?" Aunt Dolores asked.

"In there," I said, pointing to the cupboard under the sink. I left her and went outside. My mother was sitting in the front of my grandparents' shiny black Chrysler about to leave for the hospital.

She was wedged in between her mother and father, wearing a pink cotton shift dress, clutching a white straw purse in her lap. She wore a kerchief over her hair and dark glasses. Her head was bowed as if she were saying a prayer. My grandmother was wearing a navy blue dress, her church hat, and white cotton gloves.

My grandfather started up the car's engine. He was wearing his best gray suit, a white shirt, a black tie, and his good hat.

Exhaust fumes billowed out the back end of the car, filling our front yard with blue puffs of smoke. The maple tree stood there, oblivious. It was just happening, without smell or taste, like a movie rushing in front of my eyes, until suddenly she screamed my name. "Jamie!" And then the silence was ripped open, and I tasted the gasoline on my lips, felt the heat of the day on my eyelids, and smelled the sweet odor of earth and pollen, bushes and bees.

Suddenly my mother reached across her mother, my grandmother. She took off her sunglasses and stretched her arms out the window for me, and I ran to her. I begged my grandparents not to take her away, and when they wouldn't listen to me, I stuck my head inside the half-opened window and I grabbed my mother's arms and she turned and grabbed my face, my head, trying to pull me inside with her, but I couldn't fit and my grandmother pushed me out.

My mother's hands were wet—maybe from crying. I'm not sure. She smelled like lemons and salt water. The Atlantic Ocean. "Jamie, I love you!" she cried, and I held on to her. I wouldn't let her go. I wouldn't let them take her from me. I told her I loved her and she told me she loved me again and again, and I tried to pull her out of the car, but my grandmother grabbed her away and finally managed to unhook our arms, separating us, as she pulled my mother in and pushed me back out of the window.

My mother stared at me, sobbing now, as my grandmother closed the window shut. "Don't forget about me. Promise. Girl Scouts' honor."

"Girl Scouts' honor," I repeated, and I crossed my heart to show her, because I don't think she could hear me. And then my grandfather put the car in first gear. I stood there on the front lawn and watched as the black Chrysler jerked forward, slowly at first, then faster and faster, up Ledge Lane and over the hill, then suddenly gone.

I stood there for a long time, and waved and watched. I watched her as if she were in a movie playing someone else and I was safe in the living room. I pretended she was Marilyn Monroe playing my mother and that she was going to a glamorous institution where she would play tennis and attend dance therapy classes, and a handsome psychiatrist—possibly Claude Rains—would sit in his office with her lying on a leather couch and as he puffed on his pipe, he would finally figure out what made her tick. That was the thing in those days: finding out "what made you tick." It was as if we were all clocks with numbers and hands, and if we could just figure out what made the hands go, what made us "tick," then all would be well.

But in 1962 at Fairfield Hills Mental Hospital, they were still routinely performing lobotomies. There was no Betty Ford Center, and women addicted to prescription drugs were locked away in Georgian brick institutions with bars on the windows painted white to look like they were on ordinary windows. And right next door was the men's prison. There were underground tunnels where patients were transported from one building to another. I recently visited the now empty mental hospital, and a nurse who had worked there during the sixties told me how there were liaisons between patients in these tunnels—sometimes consensual, sometimes not. Women addicted to prescription drugs were taught how to clean house properly and allowed to go to the mental institution beauty parlor to get their hair done, when they were good. They were also given electroshock treatments. My mother was given several, and when she came out of Fairfield Hills Mental Hospital three months later, she had gained twenty pounds and her hair was cut in a ragged Dutch boy with crooked bangs. She was wearing a green flowered cotton dress that she had made herself in the hospital sewing class. She made one exactly like it for me. It was called a mother-daughter dress. I wore it once and then "lost" it, just as I had lost my mother.

I decided I would not grow up to be my mother. I would certainly not grow up to be Marilyn Monroe. Or Ann-Margret. Or Elizabeth Taylor. I would remain fluid and unreachable.

This is what my mother taught me.

DOMESTIC SILENCE

MEENA

❖ ❖ ❖

My mother has always been an elusive and demanding figure in my life. Sarasvathy Ramalingam. When I try to think of what she means to me, my brain staggers and lurches for a concept. I have a black-and-white photograph of her on her wedding day in Sri Lanka, 1963. She is smiling, wearing a beautiful silk sari. She looks so young, pure, and innocent—doelike in her slenderness and elegance. My father is standing beside her, tall, handsome, wearing a white tunic and pants, a turban. Flower garlands are draped around both their necks. They didn't have an arranged marriage. They fell in love. Here they are in black and white, in their late twenties, with their whole lives ahead of them.

Every time I look at this picture a part of me screams, "No! Don't do it! Run away!" But it's too late. Thirty-eight years later they are still married. My mother has been married to a loving, caring man for thirty-eight years. She has also been married to a tortured soul who has controlled, abused, and terrorized her. And one way or another I have been trying to protect and look after her since I was a little girl. She wasn't able to protect me from the trauma of growing up with domestic violence. She chose to stay with my father for various complicated reasons that have changed over the years. I've stopped waiting for my mother to *be* a mother to me. We reversed roles long ago.

My father arrived in Toronto in 1972 and sponsored his wife and daughters two years later, once he had settled into a factory job and a two-bedroom apartment at Eglinton and Kennedy. My mother brought my sister and me to Toronto in 1974. I have flashes of memory of the journey we three took from Sri Lanka to Canada. My mother was thirty-seven years old, terrified, and on her own for the first time in her life with two young children. Bombay was our first stopover. It must have been such a shock for my mother to be out in the Western world, with very little knowledge of the English language, on an airplane for the first time, and on her way to a cold climate, to her husband and a new life.

My mother still wore a sari almost everywhere she went then, before she became comfortable in Western clothes. Her hair was long, and she wore it in a single braid down her back. I forget that my mother was once young. Only when I look at old pictures of her from the late seventies, wearing jeans and a T-shirt with a Kate Jackson/Charlie's Angels haircut, do I think of her life as having colour and shape. Now, having lived in Canada for twenty-seven years, she has become Westernized to such a degree that she probably couldn't function in a traditional Sri Lankan lifestyle. One of her first jobs was to work the intimidating night-shift at Canada Post with a hardened, motley crew of men and women that included derelicts, drug dealers, and racists. It terrified her, and she didn't do it for long. She later worked in banks, as a teller, for years and became accustomed to commuting to King and Bay from the suburbs and shopping at the First Canadian Place on her lunch breaks. But she has been traditional enough to the point where she has allowed her life to be shaped by her husband's choices and pretensions. She was so intimidated by life in Canada for several years that she always deferred to my father's judgment. The truth is, he was and is so controlling that he expected no less from his wife.

I think of my mother as someone who has been shaped by circumstances beyond her control and who eventually gave up trying to exert any control over the direction of her life. She never had the experience of having a mother. Her mother died of pneumonia at the age of twenty-seven, when my mother was a baby. My mother and her brother and three sisters were all raised by aunts and uncles and only peripherally by an alcoholic father. My mother tells me that my grandfather was not a violent or unpleasant drunk. She tells me she had a relatively happy childhood without any real traumas. I believe her. I can also see that she was probably raised without the kind of stimulating guidance that allows you to explore your own potential, only encouraged to learn how to cook and sew, much like all women of her generation and culture.

When my father first came to Canada, the weight of backbreaking work, outside, all night long, on the coldest winter nights, and the financial pressure of trying to build a life that could support his family was more than he had ever had to deal with. He once told me he used to cry waiting for the bus, in the dead of winter, on his way to work. He told me he used to walk around shopping malls in awe of the cornucopia of products and services available. He especially liked walking into the Canadian Tire store to admire all the tools he would buy in the future. A typical immigrant experience. At one point he sent a stuffed panda bear to Sri Lanka for me. It must have cost him a fortune. I remember the bear, which was bigger than I was. I also remember not knowing where it had come from.

Two years after my father, my mother, sister, and I arrived in Canada. There was more to worry about. My father has never known how to ask for help. He always keeps his fears and worries to himself until he can't take it anymore, and then he explodes in violence. The worst of it happened one day in 1976. My father had been working long hours and was burnt out. He was so emotionally unbalanced that he just couldn't cope with the stress and financial demands of a new house, trying to take care of his family, and working. My mother was not working at the time.

I am in my bedroom, sitting on my bed, flipping through my colouring book. I am five years old. I hear something, but it's more like I sense a tension, a vibration of something amiss. My body stiffens in fear. Please God, no. Don't let it be my dad hurting my mom. Please don't let it be anything. I get off the bed and try not to make any noise as I tiptoe down the hall to the kitchen. Mom is sitting in a chair beside the kitchen table, limp, tired, passive, and sad. She is not making a sound. Dad slaps Mom across the face with the back of his hand. Again. And again. "Is there anything I haven't done for you?" he shouts at her. "Is there anything I haven't given you?" He waits a second for her to respond, and then he hits her again. I freeze. I can't believe what I'm seeing. Dad turns and sees me. He tells me to go back to my room. As if I could just go back to my room. My sister, Arulmori, is sitting across from my mother at the table, crying, begging my dad to stop, to let her speak. "Give her a chance!" she cries. Arulmori is twelve years old. I take a step back into the hallway, out of sight, but I can still hear everything. I take a step forward again and watch. "Is there anything I haven't given you?" he asks her again. My mother whispers, "A sewing machine." He hits her again.

I can't remember how we get to the next point. I'm sitting on the floor next to Arulmori in the spare room. Mom is sitting on the bed. Dad is sitting on the big, brown desk, talking, talking, and talking to us. I am straining my mind, body, and soul to understand what he is asking me. Arulmori cries and says, "She can't understand you, Dad; she's only five!" Dad is threatening to slit his wrist with a razor he's holding in his hand. And then, after more talking, he decides he won't kill himself. He tells me to remind him to give me a good beating when I turn fourteen. (Years later, before I turned fourteen, I asked if he was still going to beat me. He smiled and shook his head.) He tells Arulmori and me to leave the room and promises he won't hurt Mom. Arulmori and I walk into the next bedroom and wait. Silence. I tiptoe out and look back into the other room. Mom is half on the bed and half off. Dad is choking her with both hands. I run back to Arulmori and say, "Hold me! Hold me!" As if she could squeeze me tight and crush the pain. Arulmori looks at me with horror and walks out to see for herself. She runs back and we hold each other, screaming and crying.

Again, I don't remember how we get to the next part. Dad has pulled the phone jack out of the wall. Mom is sleeping. He asks us what are we going to do now. We both quickly give him a response. Arulmori says she'll watch TV. She turns on the TV and sits stone-faced on the big, green sofa chair. I say I'm going to colour in my colouring book. Dad is standing in front of the dining room window, looking outside. He turns to me and says, "Your mother called me a monster. She thinks I'm a monster." I say, "You're not a monster, Dad." I say this slowly, with hesitation, because he doesn't fit the cartoon character of a monster I have in my head.

❖ ❖ ❖

What can you say to a child who has seen so much evil? You can't replace the innocence that's gone. It's like something broke inside, and I continue to carry that sense of being broken. I would like to glue that piece back together again, but I can't. For years I blamed myself for not intervening, for not stopping my father. I am thirty-one, and it has really been only in the last few years that I can say, "There is nothing I could have done to stop it. It was not my responsibility. It was not my fault."

A friend of mine suggested to me that trauma affects a person's ability to learn. I'm not sure what that means exactly. But I do know that the trauma of domestic violence has shaped my sister, my mother, and me irrevocably. Perhaps it is more a matter of what is learned and not learned. Growing up with the fear of violence prevented us from focusing on other aspects of our lives and our personalities. My father has such a warped view of the world around him, and it was this warped view that was the lens through which we looked at life for a long time.

I don't know how my mother put herself back together again in 1976. I doubt that she even considered leaving as an option. She had no money of her own, she had only been in Canada for a little over two years, and she had two young children to look after. Where would she have gone? The city of Toronto didn't have the kinds of social services it has today for abused women. And even if it had, my mother wouldn't have known about them. She wouldn't have known how to work her way through the web of social workers who might or might not have understood her English. And besides, she loved her husband and would never leave him. She had not been raised to be independent and assertive. She was raised to be a dutiful Hindu wife. She was raised to revolve her life around her husband and her children, to depend on her husband for every kind of guidance in a society that supported male dominance.

There were other violent episodes throughout the seventies and eighties, not as bad as '76 but traumatic enough. The explosions never happened in a void. My father would display all kinds of warning signals for months leading up to his loss of control. He lost his temper easily; he was controlling and miserable to be around. And, of course, there were always the honeymoon periods when I thought, "The violence is behind us now, I don't have to worry anymore. Look at them, they look so happy now. . . ." There were still moments of tension and fights caused by my father's moods, but no explosions. Out of guilt and remorse for what he had done that day in 1976, my father went out three days later and bought my mother a sewing machine.

My mother may have thought she was protecting us by staying in the marriage. In her own way she was being as brave as she could be. She didn't check out of herself. She didn't suffer from clinical depression. She didn't start drinking. She kept cooking our food and washing our clothes. She stayed and looked after her husband and children because it was the only kind of life she knew in a Sri Lankan community where wife abuse was never talked about and if it was, people turned their backs on it. As long as my sister and I were unharmed, clothed, fed, and healthy, all our needs were being met. She was probably too stressed and traumatized to even begin to think that we had other needs. And besides, no one had considered her own creative, emotional needs as a child, so why should she consider ours? I still don't know how my mother absorbed the violence. Maybe she went into denial; too terrified to leave, she stayed and made the best of her life. She must have a strange reserve of strength.

I have a blur of memories of my father's drinking, his loud, menacing, threatening voice saying, "Sarasvathy! Open the door or I'll break it down! If you don't . . . I'll break everything in this house!" One time, we had come back from a party, and my mother lay down on the living room couch. I was standing in front of the radio in the dining room. I must have been fourteen or fifteen years old. My father walked over to my mother and stood over her saying something in Tamil I couldn't quite hear. But I could hear the rage building up in his voice and see the violence emanating from his stance, arms akimbo. I knew what was coming and I wanted to stop it, but instead I froze. The trauma of knowing what was ahead and the confusion of not knowing how to deal with it paralyzed me. He slapped her face with the back of his hand. I was by her side in an instant. My sister appeared in that same instant. "I'm going to break every bone in your body!" he shouted as he lunged for her. My sister and I threw ourselves onto him, and it took all our strength to hold him back.

My mother taught me how to live with the fear of violence. To be afraid and to accept it as a way of life. My parents taught my sister and me how to keep things hidden in silence. No one ever talked about the violence, why it happened, and why it continued to happen. My mother showed us that it was something we had to learn to survive, over and over again. My parents wouldn't talk to each other for days, weeks. Eventually, life would ease back into its normal routine, back into the warm comfort of denial. During the stable periods my parents got along, my sister and I got involved with school, with our friends, with life in general. But it's the silence that kills you; it muffles, suffocates, and distorts your confusion and pain. To this day, my mother doesn't realize how terrifying it was for my sister and me to witness so much violence and how damaging it was for us to take on the role of bodyguards.

There were nights that I thought would never end. Long, long nights of listening to my father's drunken monologues, which went on for hours. He would pick a fight with my mother and give her a litany of all the things he had done for her and all the ways she had betrayed him. My sister and I would stand by to protect her. One time he was sitting across from her on their bed. He said, "Sarasvathy, you're a fat cow. You're a lard-ass fat-cow bitch!" He reached out and punched her in the stomach. She didn't even flinch. She just asked him in a soft voice, "Why did you do that?" For days after an episode my mother would be so raw and tender that she would be kinder to my sister and me. She would yell less, nag less. My father always referred to having to curb my mother's behaviour as if she were a problem child. He wanted to squelch her yelling and nagging. She does nag. Men who are abusive often say, "She nagged me." And I bought into that at times. I once thought, "At least she won't be yelling at me for a while." As if that was the desired outcome of my father's abuse. I felt like I was betraying my mother, seeing her through the eyes of the abuser and silencing her.

My sister and I were too undeveloped and insecure and just too young to have much perspective on what was happening to us. There was a time when I thought everybody's dad got drunk and hit his wife. I thought everyone had deep, dark, violent family secrets. It completely warped my sense of what was healthy and acceptable. I used to look at other children my age and observe their fathers. I would think to myself, "Hmm, he looks like a stable dad, why can't I have a stable dad?" The irony was that my father was completely different in public. He was very socially affable, and many of my relatives thought my father was the ideal father figure because he always gave my sister and I so much attention and spoiled us with all kinds of material things. On a surface level, my sister and I came across as happy, confident children.

My mother taught me how to appease my father. She wanted all of us to be passive and to pacify him because that protected her. And lord knows, what I wanted most of all was to protect her.

My mother hit me a few times when I was very young. I may have been about seven or eight years old. She was angry and frustrated with me over something, who knows what. She threatened to get the stick, pulled open the kitchen drawer, and made all kinds of rattling noises as she looked for the wooden spoon. As soon as I heard the drawer open I tensed up. Once she hit me so hard she broke the spoon into two pieces, giving me red welts on my thigh. I was deeply confused at what she was doing to me. How could she hit me when she knew how awful it was to be hit? She felt terrible afterward and gently applied baby oil to the welts on my leg. It would all be over in a few minutes. I was never *afraid* of my mother. She wasn't a violent person, and she never did it again. Compared to a lot of things in life, such as starving to death in Uganda or the violence she had been through, it was a small event. I thought that I could never tell my father what she had done because he would be furious at her for hurting me. He would have hurt her to protect me. The irony would have escaped him, I'm sure.

My mother feared many things and held us back with her fears. I thought I would never leave home because, without me, my mother would never be safe. But I had it backward. I didn't realize there could have been a choice. Instead of my mother leaving the unsafe place and taking us with her, my sister and I stayed, adapted ourselves to living with violence, and protected her. She may have saved us from poverty and, in doing so, gave us opportunities we would not have had otherwise. But we paid a price for our comfort. We always had nice clothes, and my sister and I had our own cars when we were in our teens and into our twenties, but we did not have peace of mind. We lived in a kind of intermittent fear, always waiting for the next blowup. I grew up having nightmares of my father beating up my mother. The nightmares would be fewer and far between during the stable periods. I still have them, maybe once a year, sometimes more often. I once had a dream where I came home and my mother was so beat up she was as flat as a paper doll. In the dream, I picked her up gingerly, hoping to get her to the hospital, where the doctors could put her back together again. I was trapped. I never would have run away from home. Who would protect her? And how could I leave my sister to face my parents alone? But my sister and I did grow up and move out. In 1989 I went away to university in another town. I was nineteen. My sister, who was twenty-five at the time, moved in with her boyfriend. My mother resented us for leaving, for escaping and getting on with our lives. She continues to feel we owe it to her to go back home, to continue to rescue and protect her. *I* am the child. She is supposed to protect *me*.

Life in Sri Lanka before we came to Canada was life without a father (in fact, I didn't know who he was when I first came to Canada), and it was a precious capsule, free of violence. I often stood on the porch of my aunt's house eating mango slices, which the crows would steal out of my hands. My mother would scoop me up when I screamed as the swarming red ants bit into my chubby legs and carry me off to the bathroom to wash them off. I remember the well in the backyard and my mother and her sisters lining up all the babies for a wash. I remember how the pond across the street from the house would completely dry up during the dry season and my cousins, my sister, and I would climb down into this big empty bowl to fly our handmade kites. I remember the simplicity of our lives and my own profound sense of safety.

My mother can't win. She is the victim of abuse. She is the failure as a mother and as a strong role model. She is the martyr mom that no one reveres. What is she when she isn't destroying herself or betraying her children? What is left? Even as I write this I struggle to keep her as the focus. She slips through my fingers as my father's violence dominates the writing just as he has dominated our lives.

My mother is sixty-four years old. She is five feet tall, rotund, and has been dying her short hair Clairol black for so long now that I have no idea how much grey hair she actually has. She is a very cute woman. Sometimes I like to reach out and pinch both her cheeks. She usually yelps in protest, but I keep doing it anyway. It always makes my father laugh. She is a fantastic cook, and shopping is her favourite hobby. She's not a very literary person. She never reads books and limits herself to the newspaper and crosswords in magazines. She's been on holiday to visit relatives in Paris and London, but you'd never know it from anything she says. She is not interested in politics or world events. She's very feisty and is always on the phone talking to a hundred relatives. You could say she has her finger on the pulse of her extended family. (In some cases, the only reason people speak to my father is because they like and respect my mother.) My mother generates a lot of noise. She talks loud; she's always banging pots and pans in the kitchen. She goes on vacation for a few weeks every year, alone. She likes to visit friends and relatives in Vancouver, California, or Florida. When she is away, the house is as silent as a tomb. My father can't function without her. He *misses* her. He misses her laughter, her movement within the house, her presence.

My parents have not slept in the same room since 1987. Summer 1987 my dad had one of his explosions. My sister and I were out, he got drunk, and my mother had a few drinks and called him an asshole. He went over the edge, pulled her by her hair, hit her several times. By the time I got home he was so drunk he could barely stand up. I put him to bed and stayed with him until he had fallen asleep. My mother had called the police, and by the time they arrived my father was fast asleep. My mother and I went outside to talk to the police. In 1987 the police couldn't press charges. Only my mother could do that, and she was too scared to charge my father with assault. My hands were tied.

He has not hit her since 1987. He has pushed and shoved her; he has broken many many dishes and thrown things around. Ten years later, in 1997, he got drunk, yelled and cried, broke several dishes, and finally went to bed and passed out, all because he didn't like the way my mother said something to him. He didn't like her tone of voice. He felt left out of something she was doing. He had called me in the middle of this night of terror to cry and complain to me; he often does this to me. I was living downtown at my own apartment. It would have taken me close to two hours to reach my parents' house in the suburbs, late at night. I spoke to my mother and asked her if she was all right, and she told me it was OK and that I didn't need to come home. I asked her several times if she wanted me to come home. He hadn't broken any dishes at that point. I couldn't sleep after the phone call. My mother later called the police and again, by the time they arrived, my father had passed out and she sent the police away. It is supposed to be unusual for men to become more violent as their testosterone levels go down, as they get older.

t's July 2001; my father is sixty-five years old.

The phone rings, and I leap out of bed to answer it. It is one o'clock in the morning, and my father's voice comes on the line.

"Meena," he cries in a drunken, weeping voice. "Your mother called the police!" I am not awake. This is a nightmare, and my heart shreds into a million pieces.

"Dad, it's OK. You're going to be fine. Can I talk to the police?" I say this as soothingly as I can.

"What's going on officer?" I ask.

"We don't know yet," he says. He promises to call me back as soon as he knows. My whole body is shaking. I call my best friend. By some minor miracle her cell phone is on and she is awake.

"Van, where are you?" I fire out the words as fast as I can.

"Hiii maa love!" she chirrups.

"Van, where are you?" I ask again. I'm frantic, and I don't know what to tell her because I don't know what has happened. But I know it's bad. Real bad. Van is in Hamilton—an hour's drive away from Toronto.

"My mom called the police. My dad is drunk. I don't know what's happened!" My voice is shaking as I say this. I am completely ripped up inside and out. I can barely speak. Van calls her roommate in Toronto and asks her to pick me up and drive me to my parents' house. Van tells me to drink some water. My father calls me again.

"Dad, can I speak to Mom?" I can hear him slurring his words as he says, "Officer, would you permit my daughter to speak to her mother?" My mother's tiny voice comes on the line. She tells me she is OK and that the police are taking her to my aunt's house. I talk to my mother over the phone once she reaches my aunt's house. My mother gives me a summary of what happened. It takes me days to get the story straight. I arrive at my parents' house at two in the morning and listen to my father rant and rave and cry for half an hour before he agrees to go to bed. I sweep up the broken dishes in the kitchen. My uncle, who I didn't know was there, is visiting from Rochester. He is very shaken and finally goes to bed as well. It is close to four in the morning by the time I go to bed. Nobody sleeps. I am as far from sleep as I can be, and I jolt at the slightest sound.

My mother was so traumatized that I am certain she only gave an incomplete account of what had happened to the female police officer who sat her down and spoke to her. When she was asked if my father assaulted her, she said, "No." In her mind he had grabbed her and broken her chain. For her that didn't count as assault.

My mother stayed at my aunt's house for the weekend. I stayed with my father. I was in such shock that I couldn't cope with discussing what had happened. I wanted to run away, to disappear. My mother called me from my aunt's house. She was a wreck. "Meena, I don't have any clothes! I don't have my toothbrush!" I went back and forth between my father and mother, taking clothes to my mother, making sure my father was stable. He couldn't remember exactly what had happened. "Mom is too terrified to come home," I told him. He rolled his eyes. I am still astounded that he could be so out of touch with the pain he creates. Men who are abusive never remember what they've done and tend to minimize what they do remember. I had to sit down and tell him what he had done, and only then did he begin to feel the impact.

My mother came to stay with me for a week. We did not tell my father where she was staying. I moved back home for ten days after that because my mom was too scared to be in the house with my father. I was too scared for her to be there with him. It was complicated and painful. She needed to be at home so that she could drive to work. She works part-time at Canada Post as a sorting clerk. My mother is too scared to drive on the highway, and I live downtown, where she would have to take the highway to get to work in the suburbs. She didn't want to go to a women's shelter, and who could blame her. The ones closest to work were full. The other ones were located in the farthest reaches of the city. So I commuted for over two hours every day to get to work and back. My father drove me to the subway station in the morning and picked me up in the evening. He put on a bold front and acted as if nothing had happened. He kept busy with his exercise routine and errands. Here I was, once again, the trained dog who goes running to rescue and protect my mother and cope with my father's terrifyingly irrational state of mind.

My mother was the most emotionally unstable I have ever seen her. It had been years since my father had freaked out. The shock of his rage and the terror of his behaviour completely unhinged both of us. There is always residual trauma. It is never just one night of terror. The detritus of years of abuse comes back to constrict your heart anew each time; it feels like 1976 all over again. The day after the incident she was completely drained, exhausted, and incoherent. She was barely able to take a shower or eat anything. For the next week I had to repeat myself constantly to get anything across to her fragile mind. Severely depressed, for the next two months she struggled to function enough to drive, to work, buy groceries, do errands.

One day, during the week that she stayed with me, she decided to meet me at the bookstore near my workplace, after I finished working. But there was a miscommunication. I thought she was going to meet me at my apartment, so I went home after work and waited for her on my front steps. She waited for me at the bookstore. I finally realized what had happened and went back to look for her. I was tired, irritated, and stressed from the trauma of the week's events. "Mom! Where were you? You have my keys! How could I get inside the apartment without you!" She said, "Oh Meena! I'm sorry. Sorry, sorry, sorry." I felt so sad. She was so broken, and she looked like a lost child whom I had to retrieve and bring back home. It broke my heart.

I started to breathe fire down her neck about moving out. She told me she wanted to move out, but I didn't really believe her. I was frantic, full of anxiety, and I felt defeated every day. "Mom! You have to move out! You can't stay. This is going to happen again. Do you want me to spend the rest of my life doing this?" Feeling desperate and hopeless, I ran around the city getting information on affordable housing for seniors in abusive situations, on support groups for battered women, on free counseling for battered women to present to my mother. She was lifeless and withdrawn, working against herself and against my own efforts. I was fighting an uphill battle on her behalf, feeling like it was all a waste of time. Out of my frustration I would lecture her, "Come on, Mom! You have to help me! I can't do this all by myself!" I was overbearing and on the cusp of being verbally abusive.

❖ ❖ ❖

couldn't focus on anything. I couldn't read a book or watch a film. The landscape and details of what would have been my life just faded. I should have been writing and devouring the piles of books in my apartment. The books stared back at me, collecting dust. I should have been plotting my next travel or work adventure into Asia. Instead, I suffered from inertia. It took all my energy to manoeuvre myself through my day-to-day functions. I lost my appetite for food for several weeks. I was exhausted. Having to go to work was the only distraction that saved me. Having a job and being able to provide for myself became the most important thing to me so that I would never have to fall back on my parents in any way.

I clung to anything positive: my best friend's voice, laughter, a cup of Ceylon tea, the echoes of a Buddhist nun I once met in Vietnam, a hot bath. All these things came together like a fine silk thread acting as my lifeline. Every day I fought the overwhelming desire to slip into denial and run away. I thought about suicide, but then I decided it was too much work. I felt like I was lost at sea in a tropical storm. If the phone rang after 10 P.M., I was afraid to answer it. Everything I did was a massive effort. I felt as if someone had given me a hundred-pound sack and told me to carry it up Mount Everest. The sack was my mother's life. I couldn't stand to see her psyche so battered and bruised. It just put more pressure on me to look after her. Out of panic and stress I would bombard her with questions about how much money she had and the apartments we could look into. I told her I would give her money for the first and last month's rent. I repeatedly asked her how she felt, as if she would feel better if I just kept asking her.

I drove her crazy. "Meena! Stop asking me! I know. I know. What do you think I am doing? I can't think. My mind is gone."

My apartment became my refuge and safe house, far from the psychotic mind of my father and wilting soul of my mother. I was pathetically grateful for being able to cook dinner in my kitchen, sit on the couch, and watch TV while I ate. I cried often. I cried for an hour one Saturday morning. I cried in the shower. I cried in the washroom stall at work. I cried on the phone to my friends. I cried my heart out talking to my therapist. I met my mother at Chester subway station one day to take her to her first therapy session. My mother was beyond exhausted. She was completely disoriented and deluded about her life. "I'll retire and go live somewhere else," she said.

"Where?" I asked.

"The States. California."

"The States!" I gasped. "Mom! You can't afford to go live in the States! Your $900 per month retirement income will be worth nothing in the U.S.!"

"No, no, no. . . . Not the States. India," she said.

India! That was it. I lost it. "Are you crazy?" I shouted at her. "You'll die there! WHAT ARE YOU TALKING ABOUT?!!" I was beyond myself. This kind of delusion was too much. My mother knows no one in India. After close to twenty-eight years of good roads, strong infrastructure, and health care, she would go live in India at the age of sixty-four, where millions barely eat and have no clean water, where corruption controls your electricity and your phone lines. I felt like the sky was falling down, just on top of me. I was almost hysterical, and I wanted to hurl myself in front of a speeding car. I felt utterly alone.

My mother desperately wanted to run away to a safe space.

But more than that she wanted her life back—her life with my father before the explosion. Normally, they have a pretty good life together. My father finds it soothing to hear my mother puttering around in the kitchen. My mother likes to have him around to talk to. They take great comfort in each other's company. A week before my father lost it, the two of them had come over to my place for a visit. They were laughing and teasing me.

My mother's mind was in so much pain that she didn't want to deal with the present reality. Years of control and trauma have shaped who and what she has become. I don't know if there is a person underneath the layers of abuse. Maybe she is too scattered to ever be whole. Abuse can do that to a person.

And abuse has made me who I am. I've been railing against it my whole life. In a way it has informed almost every decision I have ever made. Abuse has taught me to blame my mother for everything, just like my father does. Abuse has taught me to treat her like someone who isn't capable of much without my help, just like my father does. It is a matter of accountability. I can't blame my father enough because he will never be able to function as a healthy person. Someone has to take the responsibility for all that went wrong. The journey from understanding to forgiveness is too much for me right now. I am tired, and I am not yet ready to cover that distance.

I can't control everything and everyone. Abuse is trying to teach me how to let go. It has also scattered, terrorized, and stomped me into the ground. My happiness is tied into the behaviour of the abuser. I have spent the last ten years trying to disentangle myself from its influence, and I feel like I'm just getting started.

People in abusive relationships sometimes bond through the

pain. My mother thinks she is the only one who understands my father and his pain. Her loyalty to him makes her vulnerable. The thought of breaking this bond with him is excruciatingly painful. Dealing with all his emotional issues, his controlling behaviour, his potential violence, cooking for him, worrying about him when he's sick—all this takes up a large space in her life. If she leaves him, what will she fill this void with? Who will she watch TV with on a cold winter's night? Who will accompany her to the movies, weddings, and funerals? Who will get on her nerves? After a lifetime together, who will she laugh with and at about all sorts of things? And what if he goes crazy and does something to himself, or to her, if she tries to leave him?

And me? If my mother no longer needed me how would I fill the void of her needs? Maybe I would go to Ecuador and teach English or travel through India again for a few months, worry free. The nightmares would stop. I could go to sleep at night without being afraid of getting an urgent phone call at 2 A.M.

Who am I when I am not the dutiful daughter trying to save her mother? And why am I getting up every day and trying to fight the fight when no one else is? Why do I feel compelled to be the parent?

I've been holding on so tight for so many years that I'm afraid I'm going to have to amputate my hand in order to let go. But now I realize I have to give back responsibility to my mother. I have to let go of trying to figure out how to protect her, how to look after her. Maybe there will be more violence in the future, maybe not. If my mother won't leave him, I can't make her leave him. The hell state they live in is stronger than I am. The forces and emotions that keep her tied to him are more powerful than I am.

If something like Rwanda can happen, then why not have

violence and terror unfold in my life? If nothing intervened to save 800,000 Rwandans from genocide, then why should I be able to single-handedly stop evil from taking over the lives of people I love?

My mother has gone back to cooking chicken curry and asking my father to pick up string hoppers from the local Sri Lankan restaurant for dinner. My father has stopped drinking, for now. Life has slipped back into the comfort and tenuous stability of routine. My mother tells me not to worry too much. Maybe I *will* go to Taiwan next year to teach English. Maybe I will turn my back and feel safe with an ocean between me and my parents—no matter what happens while I'm gone. Maybe, one day, I will just get on with my life.

STILL ALIVE

RUTH KLUGER

❖ ❖ ❖

My mother's life spanned the twentieth century. She was born into the old Austro-Hungarian Empire in the days when a lady didn't show more of her leg than her ankles. Her father was a respected and well-to-do chemist who sent her to a girls' finishing school in Prague and then selected a husband for her whom he judged to be a good provider. My mother had met a medical student whom she preferred, but she obeyed her father, married, had a son, then decided she couldn't stand to live with a man who, according to family lore, was boring and stingy.

My mother divorced her husband, a rather unusual step in those days. Her father forgave her and helped her out financially in her second marriage. She got custody of my half brother, Schorschi, as he was called in the Austrian vernacular. (He was Georg in German and Jiří in his native Czech.) He came to Vienna with our mother, who finally and for a few years had what she wished for: the dashing medical student from a poor family of ten siblings with a widowed mother. My father, the seventh child, now a full-fledged doctor, got a handsome wife with a dowry, and after a year they had a child. Just a girl, to be sure, but any child makes for happiness. They were well-off and presumably contented.

The dawn of memory: my brother, six years older than I, owned a flashlight, which he would turn on under the blanket so that you could clearly see everything, even though the big light in the room was turned off. (This was not exactly an approved game, because in Sigmund Freud's town, brother and sister weren't supposed to play together in bed.) My brother read Jules Verne on the toilet when he was supposed to be on his way to school and got scolded. He played Indian games with his friends, which I could join only on rare occasions, given the limited number and subordinate nature of Indian girl roles (Pocahontas wasn't part of the Austrian Indian mythology). And in Grandfather's garden he turned into a patriotic Czech, fighting the good fight for President Masaryk, despite the assertion of Austrian friends and cousins that Chancellor Schuschnigg was "better." My brother had a bicycle and could ride it, while I didn't and couldn't. He also had a library of Czech children's books, which he actually was able to read. After he was gone, I sometimes leafed through them and marveled at the curly diacritical marks, in awe of Schorschi's secret knowledge. And I frequently annoyed him, and sometimes he would play with me.

That's all I know about my brother; all else is hearsay. He was my first role model, and I loved him with that peculiar craving of a small child to be more and bigger and someone else. One day I'd be like him, as far as a girl could be. One day he was gone.

My mother cried and berated her ex-husband, who hadn't let the boy come back after a summer vacation in Prague. The court there had reversed an earlier decision and granted custody to the father on the ground that no Czech child (even a little Jew) should be subjected to a "German" education in Vienna. As my mother said, resentfully and not incorrectly: "After 1918 the Jews

became more Czech than Old King Wenceslas himself." National-
ism struck the small boy and the small country like one of the
Egyptian plagues. In retrospect, I am pleased that Schorschi was
on the right side in Grandfather's garden, when he defended Tomáš
Masaryk, the first president of the Czech Republic, a democrat
and a liberal, against the Austro-Fascist Chancellor Schuschnigg,
but I also know that his choice was accidental. The boys took
sides solely on the basis of "my country, right or wrong," because
they thought they had a country.

Schorschi was my first great loss, and every subsequent loss
has seemed a replay of that first. I had not only lost a beloved family member but also a role: little sister. "He'll return," my parents
comforted me. "You have to learn to wait."

Not so. If you wait long enough, death comes for you. Don't
learn to wait, learn to run away. Once, in a meadow of dandelions
in bloom, you said to me: "Look, little sister, they're lions, ready to
bite us." (The pun is more obvious in German, which calls the
flower Löwenzahn, lion's tooth.) So we started running until we
were out of breath, yelling in pretended fear, and then we rolled in
the grass, laughing our heads off. My dear, dead brother, we should
never have stopped running. Running from danger, a heady game.

My mother, later: "If it hadn't been for you, I would have
saved him. I couldn't leave you alone in Vienna while I went to
fetch him." So was it my fault? Or did she have a bad conscience
because of her divorce, which had led to her separation from her
older child? To be reunited with him became an obsession with
her, but she did nothing to bring it about. Once I asked her the
foolish question "Whom do you like better, him or me?" And she
actually said, "Schorschi, because I have known him longer." I
thought that was a fair enough reason and comforted myself that

there was surely enough love left for me. Sixty years later, however, I still hear her say it.

It should be obvious by now that these pages hardly deal with the Nazis. I didn't know any Nazis, but I knew the difficult, neurotic people whom they oppressed, families who hadn't had ideal lives anymore than their Christian neighbors had. When I tell people that my mother worried about my father's possible love affairs while he was a refugee in France, and that my parents had not been a harmonious couple in their last year together, or that my mother and her sister literally tore each other's hair in my presence, so that their aunt, my great-aunt Irene, threw herself between her nieces to separate them, or that I feel no compunction about citing examples of my mother's petty cruelties towards me, my hearers act surprised, assume a stance of virtuous indignation, and tell me that, given the hardships we had to endure during the Hitler period, the victims should have come closer together and formed strong bonds. Particularly young people should have done so, say the elderly. But this is sentimental rubbish and depends on a false concept of suffering as a source of moral education. In our heart of hearts, we all know the reality: the more we have to put up with, the less tolerant we get, and the texture of family relations becomes progressively more threadbare. During an earthquake, more china gets broken than at other times.

I often wonder at the spontaneous intimacy I see in the families of my younger friends and envy them a bit. I didn't become an overtly affectionate mother, probably because I was revolted by my own mother's intrusive possessiveness, which would alternate with unforeseeable punishments and reprimands. It wasn't she whom I learned to trust, but my nanny, whom I called Anya, and loved dearly. She was young and funny and never laid a guilt trip on you. I can still see her putting on a pair of silk stockings in preparation for going out with her boyfriend, Egon, and I watch her and hope that I, too, will grow up to have long, smooth legs like my Anya. Unlike my mother, she was never suspicious that I meant something other than what I said. I remember walking with her in the country and her devout expression as she crossed herself before a crucifix. I watch her, curious, trying to understand this unusual behavior. Among my few olfactory memories is an association of Anya with cyclamen, the mountain violet.

Again, this is all. She couldn't stay with us because of the Nuremberg laws, but she visited us once, months later. I jumped with joy like a puppy, wanting to be held and cuddled: my very own Anya. My mother was embarrassed, or perhaps jealous of this display, which the young woman took for granted. I don't know what became of her. Probably she was sucked into the Nazi "Movement." I can't look for her because I don't know her real name, and I wouldn't know whom to ask, since for my mother she was simply an employee of long ago.

For in the beginning I didn't see much of my mother. I had to be careful not to bother her when she was taking a nap, and she made me wear uncomfortable clothes: woolen underwear, which felt like hair shirts; cute little dresses, which mustn't get dirty or wrinkled; and, worst of all, heavy boots with laces, which absolutely never fit and made your feet sweat. I noticed that *she* didn't wear such underwear or shoes, but nice things in which she moved gracefully, and I looked forward to the day when I could do likewise. If my face was dirty, she spat on a handkerchief and rubbed my cheek with it. That was revolting: it made me want to puke and I would loudly protest, but to no avail. Once I cut up a handbag of hers out of sheer spite, because I was so mad at her. I wasn't even six then, and wasn't supposed to touch the scissors I used in this act of revolt.

And then there were my mother's birthdays: she expected presents, but any giver of gifts acquires in the act a certain authority, or at least there is a claim of equality when inferiors or dependents give gifts. If you reject a gift, it means that you won't make any concessions. My mother demanded that we solemnly acknowledge her birthdays, but then she reacted with exaggeration to her presents, often without having looked at them. She made it clear that she didn't so much enjoy the carefully chosen gift, as she wanted us to know that her ostentatious thanks were a gift on her part. Even my birthday poems for her were insufficiently admired, I felt, for she didn't feed my authorial pride by commenting on them.

This pattern never changed. Whenever I bought her something to wear, it was the wrong color or size, which she wouldn't tell me soon enough to exchange it; instead of flowers, she would want candy on Mother's Day, or the other way around, no telling in advance which. But she had to get *some* presents, or she would be hurt. I have to add in fairness that I am no better: her gifts were impossible, and I used to pass them on to the Salvation Army, especially those she made herself. Formal occasions for giving, like those ill-fated birthdays, can be a source of conflict, which one can only escape by rejecting both gift and occasion. In our case, the symptoms of this flourishing mother-daughter neurosis were textbook-perfect, and it's amazing that not only the neurosis itself, but the symptoms go back so far. Yet this awareness was of little help. Freud was an optimist.

❖ ❖ ❖

With the increasing isolation of the few Jews left in Vienna, my mother became dependent on me for companionship and tortured me with her anxieties. She alluded to the suicide attempts of unnamed women; she talked about fatal illnesses and the imagined destination of the ever more frequent transports of deportees. I didn't know what to believe, let alone how to cope with these veiled threats to my existence. Out there was a deadly secret, but I could only suspect, not fathom, what it was.

I was like a young dog without exercise, and she tried to keep me from the few games which were left. We were allowed to use the library and recreation room of the Jewish Community Center, and the Jewish cemetery was our park and playground. When I came home to our cramped quarters from a rare outing with other Jewish kids, happy and exhausted from running around in the open air, she'd paint the specter of deadly pneumonia, which I was very likely to have caught, she said. She persuaded me that I had flat feet (I don't) and massaged my soles to prevent a future limp. My mother would have been an admirable nurse for an invalid child. She confessed that she sometimes dreamt of sitting beside a bedridden daughter. Apparently it is not a disturbing dream. Psychiatric jargon speaks of castration when the hapless subjects are sons. The term is one-sided and therefore harmful, for it excludes the possibility that daughters can be just as much incapacitated and stunted by their mothers' maneuvers.

When I embraced my mother too vigorously at the end of a lonely day, she would assure me that I had just then almost strangled her, and that the hand of a child who has hurt her mother, even though inadvertently, grows out of the grave for all to see.

She told me so much nonsense that I ceased to believe anything she told me. By insisting what a brave child she had been, she tried to make me timid and fearful. For a while she succeeded, but I became more and more alienated from her. She claimed to have gotten the better of six boys in a fist fight as a girl, and I was much relieved when a friend of hers discounted the credibility of that story with a smile, because my only impulse when Aryan boys taunted me on the street was to run away.

There was nothing that she hadn't done better than I, and my only recourse was to doubt her word. As a little girl she had written both stories and poems, but when I asked to see some, none had survived. She had composed her poems very quickly, she said. She must have worked much faster than I did, I had to admit, for she needed only half an hour per poem, while a single stanza sometimes took me whole days. And my lack of knowledge, compared to all the things she knew when she was my age! I stopped asking her for help to avoid these put-downs. She would often slap me or kiss me from sheer nervousness, simply because I was there.

My first two homes were bright and sunny, but after we had to leave my grandparents' house, we lived in two dark apartments which we shared with a couple of other Jewish families. My mother and I had a small room, which got its only light from an inner courtyard. I picture sadistic architects designing these holes deliberately to exclude the daylight in spite of existent windows. There were bedbugs. You turn out the light and imagine the bugs crawling out of the mattresses. Then you get bitten and turn on the light and complain bitterly that the repulsive vermin are indeed sharing your bed.

My scalp was itching. My mother dismissed my complaints, but when she finally listened, she realized that I had lice. What to do with lice had not been part of the curriculum at her girls' finishing school in Prague. One of our co-tenants advised a kerosene cure. I didn't like the idea because the stuff stank. I begged, "Can't we wait until tomorrow?" but the two women had already found what they needed, made me bend my head with its long, unruly hair over a washbasin, poured on a generous amount of the liquid, tied my head in a towel, and sent me to bed.

I couldn't sleep. My head seemed on fire. Since I shared the room with my mother, I didn't give her much rest either. In spite of all my whining, I couldn't get her to take the towel off my head or allow me to take it off. Would I please stop sniveling? She needed her sleep; she had to go to work in the morning. Next day, when my tormented head finally got some air, the lice were gone, but so was much of my scalp. I was shaved clean and got ointment for the sore skin, but it was weeks before the burns were fully healed. What really haunted me, though, was why she hadn't paid attention to me when I was so obviously in pain. And while she admitted her fault, even afterwards she didn't seem all that sympathetic. I began to doubt that adult cruelties were wholly fortuitous or for the good of the children, as they always maintained. It's essentially the question we ask when we observe civilizations, alien to our own, that practice exorcism by inflicting harm on the bodies of the women and children who are said to host devils and demons.

My mother turned superstitious and regularly frequented a fortune-teller, much as she had employed a seamstress to make her dresses in the good old days. She talked about a miracle-working rabbi who had been an ancestor of hers and whose spirit protected the family in times of need. She implored me never to marry a goy, because all goyim beat their wives. "All of them?" I asked. "You think even Goethe beat his wife?" Goethe not only is Germany's greatest poet but also is traditionally invoked as a role model for all kinds of conduct. For a moment my mother is nonplussed. Then she says yes, of course he must have beaten his wife. After all, he was a goy.

The catastrophe seemed to have come out of the blue sky, even though, with hindsight, everyone recited the forewarnings with relish. Politics was not meant to be a feminine domain, and in my mother's Czech finishing school they didn't teach the girls how to read a newspaper critically any more than they instructed them on how to delouse the heads of children. Neither did her social experience prepare her for the harsh realities we faced, since by definition anti-Semites didn't move in Jewish circles. And didn't we live in an enlightened country, unlike Russia or Poland, the traditional lands of pogroms? Before the German invasion there were enough worries that were closer to home than politics, such as family disagreements, inheritance feuds, and in the aftermath of her divorce, the Czech-Austrian custody case. In addition she had started what we would now call a small fitness program, where housewives who were beginning to put on weight could take some of it off by means of light workouts. But after the German invasion nothing mattered more than politics.

Once when she and I were at the Jewish Community Center, a young man asked us whether she would consider sending me by myself with a children's transport to Palestine (or was it England? I am not sure). It was a last chance he said, just in the nick of time. Very advisable. My heart pounded, for I would dearly have loved to leave Vienna, even if meant betraying my mother. But she didn't ask me and didn't even look at me as she answered in an even voice: "No. A child and its mother belong together." On the way home I fought down my disappointment without mentioning it, since there was no point in hurting her. But I never forgot that brief glimpse of another life which would have made me a different person. What kind of a person? Who knows? Should she have asked my opinion? Not have treated me exclusively as her property? In her last years, when she was a broken old woman who had seen most of the century, with her faculties failing, I still now and then got a glimpse of this powerful claim to ownership, disguised as love and expressed as criticism. ("Why can't you visit me tomorrow?" "Do you *have* to travel?" "Where is your coat? It's too cold to go without." "You are wearing the wrong shoes.")

But in those years she had so little and was deprived of all that had made her life worthwhile. When my children left me, they went to college, not into a Nazi concentration camp, and I had a profession and friends, a sprawling country, and a free life. She was so nervous that she developed a tic, an automatic twitch of her leg. I found this tic appealing, because it was part of my mother. She fantasized about what else she could lose, and typically for the women of her generation, she didn't worry that her husband might be murdered, but that he might be unfaithful. There is a story that he had a girlfriend in France. Maybe. Who cares? After the war she got some letters from people who knew him in Drancy, the French camp from which he was deported, and they said that he was helpful and full of jokes to the end.

She made me her confidante in this matter of marital infidelity, though I was hardly the right person for it and had no idea how to respond. She had some mail from him (I never did, much to my chagrin), and later she would say: "Your papa wrote me such a loving letter from Drancy. I still had it in Auschwitz and lost it there." She said "lost," as if it disappeared inadvertently, as if she could have taken anything along from that hellhole. And she acted as if she had forgotten her Viennese jealousy, as she probably had.

I was a nuisance and often in the way, useless and lazy, yet all that was left. In the course of three or four years she had been uprooted, her life had shrunk, and she was engulfed in the isolation of the persecuted. Her husband was on the run, her son in an occupied country, her sister's family underground in Hungary. Her circle of friends had emigrated to America, England, and Palestine, or had been deported to Theresienstadt or "to Poland," a vague phrase, but much in use. And here she was with her *Reichsfluchtsteuer*, the tax she couldn't pay. Then came the news my half brother and his father had been deported to Theresienstadt. My mother received a few postcards from there. The prospect of seeing him again made her own impending deportation acceptable.

And still I ask: Why didn't we get out in time? When others ask, I get irritated and answer that it's a stupid question: don't look at the emigrés who were lucky or rich or both; think of the hundreds of thousands of German and Austrian Jews (the Polish ones didn't have a chance in the first place) who perished. We happened to be among those who were pulled into that vortex. But I did ask *her*, many times, when she was still of sound mind: "Why? You had connections, you are pretty savvy, what happened to you?" She came back to that tax. (And I think, Could it have been your neuroses, your cumulative madness, aggravated by the mad new social order, that prevented you from finding a way to save us?) "And I couldn't leave Schorschi alone in Prague." "So

why didn't you go and get him?" "That would have been dangerous, and I would have had to leave you behind." The snake biting
its own tail. A vicious circle.

There came a point where nothing could be done. She tried
to remain in Vienna as long as possible. She had a job as a nurse
and physical therapist at the Jewish hospital. She left early. I slept
late, read in bed, walked over to the hospital, where I got a meal
and could take a shower. Then I spent the rest of the day alone
with a book in the hospital yard. We were pretty much among the
last Jews to be deported from Vienna to Theresienstadt, on the so-
called hospital transport of September 1942.

In 1940, when I was eight or nine, the local movie theater
showed Walt Disney's *Snow White*. I loved movies. I had been
weaned on Mickey Mouse shorts and traded pictures of Shirley
Temple with classmates. I badly wanted to see this film, but since
I was Jewish, I naturally wasn't permitted to. I groused and bitched
about this unfairness, until finally my mother proposed that I
should leave her alone and just go and forget about what was permitted and what wasn't.

I hesitated a bit at this unexpected go-ahead, for it was a Sunday, we were known in the neighborhood, and to go to a movie
right there in broad daylight was a kind of dare. My mother
couldn't accept the absurdity of blatant discrimination. She assured me that no one would care who sat in an audience of children. I shouldn't think I was that important, and I should stop
being a coward, because she was never a coward, not even when
she was my age. So of course I went, not only for the movie, but
to prove myself. I bought the most expensive type of ticket, think-

ing that sitting in a loge would make me less noticeable, and thus I ended up next to the nineteen-year-old baker's daughter from next door with her little siblings, enthusiastic Nazis one and all.

I sweated it out for the next ninety minutes and have never before or afterwards understood so little of what happened on the screen. All I could think of was whether the baker's daughter was really glaring at me, or if I was only imagining it. The wicked queen of the film merged with my neighbor, her fairy-tale malice a poor imitation of the real thing, and it was I, and no innocent princess, who was out on a limb, being offered poisoned apples, in fear of glass coffins.

Why didn't I get up and walk out? Perhaps in order not to face my mother, or because any move might attract attention. Perhaps merely because one doesn't leave a theater before the film is over, or most likely, because this solution didn't occur to me, frightened as I was. Consider that I still wonder why my people didn't leave Vienna in time—and perhaps there is a family resemblance between that question and why I stayed glued to my seat.

When the lights came on, I wanted to wait until the house had emptied out, but my enemy stood her ground and waited, too. She told her little brother to hush and fixed me sternly. There I was, trapped, as I had surmised. The baker's daughter put on her gloves and coat and finally addressed me.

She spoke firmly and with conviction, in the manner of a member of the Bund Deutscher Mädchen, the female branch of the Hitler Youth, to which she surely belonged. Hadn't I seen the sign at the box office? (I nodded, what else could I do? It was a rhetorical question.) Didn't I know what it meant? I could read, couldn't I? It said "No Jews." I had broken a law. She was using her best High German—none of Vienna's easy-going dialect for this patriotic occasion. If it happened again she would call the police. I was lucky that she was letting me off this once.

The story of Snow White can be reduced to one question: who is entitled to live in the king's palace and who is the outsider. The baker's daughter and I followed this formula. She, in her own house, the magic mirror of her racial purity before her eyes, and I, also at home here, a native, but without permission and at this moment expelled and exposed. Even though I despised the law that excluded me, I still felt ashamed to have been found out. For shame doesn't arise from the shameful action, but from discovery and exposure. If I had got away with my transgression, I would have been proud of my daring. But I had been unmasked. . . .

It was over pretty soon. The girl had asserted the superiority of her Germanic forefathers as opposed to the vermin race I belonged to, and there was nothing more to say. I was in a state of shock. This was new and terrible. Tears welled up, but I held them back. The usher, an older woman, helped me into my coat and handed me my purse, which I was about to leave on the seat. She was sorry for me and said a few soothing words. I nodded, incapable of answering because I was choking on my tears of humiliation, but grateful for this bit of kindness, these alms for the poor.

It was still light outside, so I walked at random through the streets of my neighborhood in a daze. I had found out, for myself and by myself, how things stood between us and the Nazis and had paid for knowledge with the coin of pain. To be sure, I was overreacting to a minor incident, but that didn't change the fact that now I knew. I had had the feeling of deadly danger, and this feeling didn't leave me, but escalated until it was justified. Without having to think it through, from now on I was ahead of the grown-ups.

I came home crying and furious, blaming my mother for what seemed a near catastrophe. She shrugged her shoulders. Who would think of bothering a child watching a fairy tale? To my exasperation, she acted as if what had happened hadn't happened, because it oughtn't to have happened. And even if it did, she implied, don't get upset. There are worse things. But that was exactly the problem. Wasn't this bad enough? Hadn't I almost been arrested? What were the worse things? How was I to learn the priorities of danger? It was easy for my mother, who presumably knew where you drown and where you can still barely tread water. But I didn't know and wanted explanations, instructions, directives. What was the worst, and could it be something other than death? Later I realized that the grown-ups around me didn't know much themselves, that they were entirely flummoxed by the turn of events, and that, in fact, I was learning faster than they. I got the impression that I shouldn't trust my mother, that she had only bad advice for me. This impression was wrong. Like other people's advice, my mother's varied between good, bad, and indifferent. Sometimes its source was paranoia, sometimes reason and evidence. Goodwill or malice might be part of it. Mostly, however, it came from an undifferentiated instinct, a mixture of unexamined experiences, a bubbling stew of indistinguishable thoughts and emotions. Some years later, in 1944, when she happened to be right, my lack of confidence in her, dating from that afternoon at the movies, almost cost me my life.

The "ghetto" Theresienstadt was a transit camp for Jews, most of whom were sent on to their extinction further East. My mother and I were sent on to Auschwitz after about twenty months. Birkenau was the extermination camp of Auschwitz and consisted of many smaller camps and subdivisions. Each had a main street, lined on both sides with wooden barracks. The barracks were backed by barbed wire, which divided them from a similar subdivision on the other side. B2B was an exception, inasmuch as it warehoused men, women, and children—babies, too. Hence its heartwarming name, Theresienstadt Family Camp.

Each building had two rows of three-tiered bunk beds along the walls. Between them stretched a brick structure called the chimney (not to be confused with the crematoria), which divided the room in two. Our first evening in the camp, the block eldest, herself a prisoner, stood on this structure, while we cowered in our bunks, and screamed, cursed, and gave orders which I don't remember, words whose purpose was intimidation and nothing else. We know this trick in talking to animals: what is said doesn't have to make sense, since it's the tone that carries the meaning, and I listened that way, like a puppy. But one sentence struck me: "You are no longer in Theresienstadt." She made it sound as if we had just been expelled from paradise. It occurred to me that this woman treated us as inferiors because she had been in Auschwitz longer than we. I felt confused: wasn't she an inmate like us? I learned the hierarchy of the numbers: those with the lower numbers were socially above those with the higher ones, because they had had to live for more days, weeks, and months in a place where no one wanted to live. A topsy-turvy world.

The same evening, when we finally lay down to rest in the middle row of the bunk, five to a row, my mother explained to me that the electric barbed wire outside was lethal and proposed that she and I should get up and walk into that wire. I thought I hadn't heard correctly. If to love life and to cling to it is the same, then life has never been dearer to me than in the summer of 1944, in camp B2B in Birkenau. I was twelve years old, and the thought of dying, now, without delay, in contortions, by running into electrically charged metal on the advice of my very own mother, whom God had created to protect me, was simply beyond my comprehension. The idea of it! I couldn't grasp it. I fled into the comfort of believing that she couldn't have meant it. Persuaded myself that she was only out to frighten me. Resented that she was up to bad tricks. Hadn't she often scared me before for nothing? My mother accepted my refusal nonchalantly, as if she had merely offered me a walk in the country in peacetime. "Okay, whatever you say." And she never returned to her suggestion.

I knew my mother no better than most children know their parents, which isn't very well. Perhaps a certain wild, destructive pleasure was at the root of her proposal. But more probably she was quite serious and quite desperate. As I think back, I ask myself if I have ever forgiven her that worst evening of my life. Of course I have: but who can count the sparks in the ashes? We never talked about this exchange again, not in all the years that passed before her death at ninety-seven. Yes, there were moments when I had the urge to say: "That first evening in Birkenau, did you mean it or not?" But then I pulled in my feelers like a snail that has learned a bit more than it needs to about the outside world and is happy enough in its shell. I figured she was not going to give me an honest answer, but would say whatever happened to suit her at the given moment. Besides, I detested any intimacy with my mother, and what could be more intimate than such a question?

Only when I had children of my own did I realize that one might well decide to kill them in Auschwitz rather than wait. I now believe that I would have had the same thought and perhaps carried it out more efficiently. For to kill oneself is a relatively familiar idea, especially if you come from a country like Austria, where the suicide rate is high, "doing oneself in" is a common topic of small talk, and a remarkable number of people have tried to do just that, one or more times. But then, committing suicide is a homespun, almost cozy, idea for many cultures, and certainly more acceptable than the prearranged death at Birkenau.

Selection, there was to be a selection. At a certain barracks at a certain time, women between the ages of fifteen and forty-five were to be chosen for a transport to a labor camp. Some argued that up to now every move had been for the worse, that one should therefore avoid the selection, stay away, try to remain here. My mother believed—and the world has since agreed with her—that Birkenau was the pits, and to get out was better than to stay. But the word *Selektion* was not a good word in Auschwitz, because it usually meant the gas chambers. One couldn't be sure that there really was a labor camp at the end of the process, though it seemed a reasonable assumption, given the parameters of age group they were taking. But then, Auschwitz was not run on reasonable principles.

My mother had reacted correctly to the extermination camp from the outset, that is, with the sure instinct of the paranoid. Her suicide proposal of the first night is evidence of her understanding. And when I wouldn't go along with her then, she managed to take the first and the only way out. Time has proved that she was right all along, and yet I still think it was not her reasonableness, but an old and deep-seated sense of being persecuted, which enabled her to save our lives. Psychologists like Bruno Bettelheim have tried to persuade us that a sane person who hasn't been spoiled by a disabling bourgeois education should be able to adjust to new conditions, even if they are as outlandish as those of a concentration camp. The saner, the better the chance of survival is the bottom line of this type of argument. I think the opposite is true. I think that people suffering from compulsive disorders, such as paranoia, had a better chance to pick their way out of mass destruction, because in Auschwitz they were finally in a place where the social order (or social chaos) had caught up with their delusions. If you think that your mind is the most precious thing you own, you are right, because what have we got that defines us other than reason and love? But in Auschwitz love couldn't save you, and neither could reason. Madness, perhaps. There are no absolute means of salvation, and there are times when even paranoia may work. It wasn't the last time that my mother thought she was pursued, and maybe it wasn't the first time. But it took the Shoah to prove her right for once.

But isn't the price she paid too high: this madness that she carried inside her, like a sleeping tomcat? The cat would occasionally stretch, yawn, arch his back, softly case the joint, suddenly chatter with his teeth, reach with sharp claws for a bird, and go to sleep again—leaving the bloody feathers for me to clean up. I don't want to carry such a predator inside of me, even if he could save my life in the next extermination camp.

Two SS men conducted the selection, both with their backs to the rear wall. They stood on opposite sides of the so-called chimney, which divided the room. In front of each was a line of naked, or almost naked, women, waiting to be judged. The selec-

tor in whose line I stood had a round, wicked mask of a face and
was so tall that I had to crane my neck to look up at him. I told
him my age, and he turned me down with a shake of his head,
simply, like that. Next to him, the woman clerk, a prisoner, too,
was not to write down my number. He condemned me as if I had
stolen my life and had no right to keep it, as if my life were a book
that an adult was taking from me, just as my uncle had taken the
Bible from me because I was too young to read it. Later I saw the
selector's image in Kafka's door keeper, who won't grant a man entrance to his own space and light.

My mother had been chosen. No wonder: she was the right
age, a grown-up woman. Her number had been written down, and
she would leave the camp shortly. We stood on the street between
the two rows of barracks and argued. She tried to persuade me
that I should try a second time, with the other SS man in the
other line.

The month of June 1944 was very hot in Poland, and therefore both the front and the rear doors of the barracks stood open.
The back entrance was guarded, but the detail consisted of inmates, and my mother felt I could sneak by and take another turn.
And this time, please don't be a fool and tell them your real age of
twelve. I got angry and was half desperate. "I don't look older," I
remonstrated. I felt she half wanted me to step in a pile of shit,
like the time a few years earlier when she had urged me to go to
the movies despite the legal prohibition. (I repeat: my mother and
I were very unfair to each other.) The difference between twelve
and fifteen is enormous for a twelve-year-old. I was to add a quarter of my entire life. In Theresienstadt, in L414, they had put the
different age groups into different rooms. A mere difference of

one year had meant another room, another community. The lie which my mother proposed was so transparent: three years! Where was I to find them?

I was anguished and frightened, but this was not the profound fear that overwhelmed me when I looked at the chimneys, the crematoria, spitting flames at night and smoke by day. When that fear gripped me, it was like the psychological equivalent of epileptic fits. The fear I felt now was more like the bearable fear of malicious grown-ups, a fear with which I could cope. For what would become of me if I had to stay in Birkenau without my mother? Well, that was out of the question, she assured me. If I wouldn't try the selection a second time, she would stay, too. She'd like to see who could separate her from her child. Only it wasn't a good idea, and would I please listen to what she was telling me, she said, without paying attention to my conclusive counterarguments. "You are a coward," she said half desperately, half contemptuously, and added, "I wasn't ever a coward." So what could I do but go in a second time, but with the proviso that I would try thirteen, never fifteen. Fifteen was preposterous. And if I get into trouble, it's your fault.

The space between the barracks I was to invade in order to reach the back door was guarded by a cordon of men. My mother and I watched them carefully for a minute or so. "Now!" we realized, and I sneaked by as the two men in charge happened to call out to each other. I bent over a little to appear smaller, or to make use of the shadow of the wall, turned the corner, and entered through the door, unobserved.

The room was still full of women. A kind of orderly chaos reigned which I associate with Auschwitz. The much-touted Prussian perfection of camp administration is a German myth. Behind every good organization is the presumption that there is something worth keeping and organizing. Here the organization was superficial, because there was nothing valuable to organize or retain. We were worthless by definition. We had been brought here to be disposed of, and hence the waste of *Menschenmaterial*, human substance, as the inhuman German term has it, was immaterial, to use another inhuman term. Basically the Nazis didn't care what went on in the Jew camps, as long as they were no bother. The selecting SS officers and their helpers stood with their backs to me. I went unobtrusively to the front door, took off my clothes once more, and quietly went to the end of the line. I breathed a sigh of relief to have managed so far so well, and was happy to have been smarter than the rules. I had proved to my mother that I wasn't chicken. But I was the smallest, and obviously the youngest, female around, undeveloped, undernourished, and nowhere near puberty.

I have read a lot about the selections since that time, and all reports insist that the first decision was always the final one, that no prisoner who had been sent to one side, and thus condemned to death, ever made it to the other side. All right, I am the proverbial exception.

What happened next is loosely suspended from memory, as the world before Copernicus dangled on a thin chain from Heaven. It was an act of the kind that is always unique, no matter how often it occurs: an incomprehensible act of grace, or put more modestly, a good deed. Yet the first term, an act of grace, is perhaps closer to the truth, although the agent was human and the term is religious. For it came out of the blue sky and was as undeserved as if its originator had been up in the clouds. I was saved by a young woman who was in as helpless a situation as the rest of us, and who nonetheless wanted nothing other than to help me. The more I think about the following scene, the more astonished I am about its essence, about someone making a free decision to save another person, in a place which promoted the instinct of self-preservation to the point of crime and beyond. It was both unrivaled and exemplary. Neither psychology nor biology explains it. Only free will does. Simone Weil was suspicious of practically all literature, because literature tends to make good actions boring and evil ones interesting, thus reversing the truth, she argued. Perhaps women know more about what is good than men do, since men tend to trivialize it. In any case, Weil was right, as I learned that day in Birkenau: the good is incomparable and inexplicable, as well, because it doesn't have a proper cause outside itself, and because it doesn't reach for anything beyond itself.

I can't keep SS men apart—to me they are all the same uniformed wire puppet with polished boots. Even when Eichmann was tried and executed, I was embarrassingly indifferent to the whole process. These people were one single phenomenon, as far as I was concerned, and their different personalities were irrelevant. Hannah Arendt offered the counterpart to Simone Weil's reflections on goodness when she pointed to the simple fact that evil is committed in the spirit of mental dullness and narrow-minded conformity—what she called banality. Her reflections on evil caused much indignation among men, who understood, though perhaps not consciously, that this deromanticization of arbitrary violence was a challenge to the patriarchy. Perhaps women know more about evil than men, who like to demonize it.

The line moved towards an SS man who, unlike the first one, was in a good mood. Judging from photos, he may have been the infamous Dr. Mengele, but as I said, it doesn't matter. His clerk was perhaps nineteen or twenty. When she saw me, she left her post, and almost within the hearing of her boss, she asked me quickly and quietly and with an unforgettable smile of her irregular teeth: "How old are you?" "Thirteen," I said, as planned. Fixing me intently, she whispered, "Tell him you are fifteen."

Two minutes later it was my turn, and I cast a sidelong look at the other line, afraid that the other SS man might look up and recognize me as someone whom he had already rejected. He didn't. (Very likely he couldn't tell us apart any more than I had reason to distinguish among the specimens of his kind.) When asked for my age I gave the decisive answer, which I had scorned when my mother suggested it but accepted from the stranger. "I am fifteen."

"She seems small," the master over life and death remarked. He sounded almost friendly, as if he was evaluating cows and calves.

"But she is strong," the woman said, "look at the muscles in her legs. She can work."

She didn't know me, so why did she do it? He agreed—why not? She made a note of my number, and I had won an extension on life.

Every survivor has his or her "lucky accident"—the turning point to which we owe our lives. Mine is peculiar because of the intervention of the stranger. Virtually all those still alive today who have the Auschwitz number on their left arm are older than I am, at least by those three years that I added to my age. There are exceptions, like the underage twins on whom Dr. Mengele performed his pseudomedical experiments. Then there are some who were my age, but who were selected at the ramp to be sent immediately on to the labor camps, and who were thought to be older because they wore several layers of clothing, by way of transporting a wardrobe. They were not tattooed because they weren't in the camp. To get out of the camp, you really had to have been alive longer than twelve years.

I have always told this story in wonder, and people wonder at my wonder. They say, okay, some persons are altruistic. We understand that; it doesn't surprise us. The girl who helped you was one of those who likes to help. A young American rabbi says that after my buildup he expected a more heroic tale. Maybe he has seen too many action films or read too many Bible stories, the kind that tout male virtues, muscle over mind, noise over quiet resolve. But don't just look at the scene. Focus on it, zero in on it, and consider what happened. There were two of them: the man who had power he could exert on a random object, for better or for worse. He probably didn't believe that the labor of a starved little girl would promote the German war effort considerably or retard the final solution to a noticeable extent. He had to decide the case one way or the other, list or not list my number. Just then it suited him to listen to his clerk. And she is the other. I think his action was arbitrary, hers voluntary. It must have been freely chosen, because anyone knowing the circumstances would have predicted the opposite, or at least shoulder-shrugging indifference. Her decision broke the chain of knowable causes. She was an inmate, and she risked a lot when she prompted me to lie and then openly championed a girl who was too young and small for forced labor and completely unknown to her. She saw me stand in line, a kid sentenced to death, she approached me, she defended me, and she got me through. What more do you need for an example of perfect goodness? Never and nowhere was there such an opportunity for a free, spontaneous action as in that place at that time.

It was moral freedom at its purest. I saw it, I experienced it, I benefitted from it, and I repeat it, because there is nothing to add. Listen to me, don't take it apart, absorb it as I am telling it and remember it.

But perhaps you are of the opposite camp and claim that there is no such thing as altruism, that every action is motivated by some kind of selfishness, even if such egotism is no more than the consciousness of free choice. In that case, of course, freedom itself is a mere illusion as well. And perhaps you are right, and there is no absolute in these matters, but only approaches to goodness and to freedom. The main characteristic of freedom is its unpredictability. And no one has been able to predict human behavior with the same accuracy as, for example, the behavior of amoebas. Dogs, horses, and cows are semipredictable, but with humans there is never more than a certain degree of probability. People can change their minds at the last moment, and even if we knew everything about a person and stored it in the most advanced computer system, we could still not foresee the mental moment of a woman whom I didn't know, whom I never saw again, deciding to save me and succeeding.

And therefore I think it makes sense that the closest approach to freedom takes place in the most desolate imprisonment under the threat of violent death, where the chance to make decisions has been reduced to almost zero. (And where is the zero point? The gas chambers are zero, I believe, when the men in their final contortions are forced by a biological urge to step on the children. But how can I be sure?) In a rat hole, where charity is the least likely virtue, where humans bare their teeth, and where all signs point in the direction of self-preservation, and there is yet a tiny gap—that is where freedom may appear like the uninvited angel. If a prisoner passed on the beatings he received to those even more helpless than he, he was merely reacting as psychology and biology would expect him to. But if he did the reverse? And so one might argue that in the perverse environment of Auschwitz absolute goodness was a possibility, like a leap of faith, beyond the humdrum chain of cause and effect. I don't know how often it was consummated. Surely not often. Surely not only in my case. But it existed. I am a witness.

Somehow we survived. We came to America in 1947, and I enrolled at Hunter College, a branch of the New York City College System. I was lonely and haunted by history, until I made friends with three other Jewish Hunter girls, each with her own checkered past, two of them converts to Christianity, one a veteran of a Swiss sanitorium for bone tuberculosis. All of us mavericks in the increasingly restrictive atmosphere of the late '40s.

I fell on my feet and found my bearings because of these three. I could talk to them. They listened and answered, for or against, but always weighing what they had heard, unlike my mother, who used language for manipulation, not to express an opinion or state a fact. What sounded like a fact might be a lie, and every opinion was tailored for the moment. Language to her was like the makeup of an actress—you choose what your respective role requires—and so she listened for what might lurk beneath the surface, always speculating about the unsaid. But words will take their revenge when thus misused and played havoc with her mind.

She was jealous of my new friends. I invited them over and she disapproved: "With cripples and *geshmate* [baptized Jews] you hang out." When she said that I was sitting in a bathtub full of cold water, a tried-and-true remedy against the New York heat. (Since no one had air-conditioning as yet, you didn't have to feel bad about not being able to afford it. Who would have suspected that New York would ever be able to attract tourists in summer, of all seasons!) My mother is next door, in the kitchenette. She wants to spoil the new friendships that I am proud of. For no reason, just for the hell of it. I start screaming, I hate her. Another remnant of trust is gone.

We four took in whatever New York had to offer that was free or inexpensive. I learned what a joy it was to live in a city that has never been bombed. I loved going to museums and listening to Liselotte tell me what she liked about a painting. She would encourage me to dislike certain famous painters and to admire certain minor ones, in other words, to drift wherever my minimal understanding of art would take me. Museums convey a sense of permanence, the idea of "collection," as opposed to separation and loss. In a museum I feel that I belong, though nothing belongs to me. I lay claim to what my eyes take in. Libraries convey a similar sense of accumulated history and culture, but it's more a kind of promise, since you can't read all the books at once, whereas a museum offers you a ready-made feast. I can't be rejected by museums and books, except when the police interfere, forbidding me to enter the museum or burning the books. Of course that happens. But short of violence, that is, short of the ultimate abolition of meaning, art and literature can be a home for those without citizenship, because they remind us of our common race, the human race, and they sop you up, yet simultaneously feed you, like a magic sponge. They make you part of what you see and hear and yet let you stand back and choose.

The various Shoah museums and reconstituted concentration camp sites do the exact opposite. That's why I find them so hard to take: they don't take you in, they spit you out. Moreover, they tell you what you ought to think, as no art or science museum ever does. They impede the critical faculty.

In 1950, at the age of nineteen, I graduated. Hunter had given me a heap of advanced credits for stuff I never studied and didn't know. Presumably Hunter was trying to process as many students as possible as fast as possible. No one bothered to take a good look at my record. Nor did they think I was much of an intellect: in the students' counseling office, where I mentioned that I might want to go to graduate school, they strongly discouraged me because I had such poor grades, except in English, my major.

My mother had a better job now, as a physiotherapist in a doctor's office. She had gotten some money from her prewar Austrian property, had paid back our Long Island relatives the cost of our fare on the *Ernie Pyle* ("In America we pay our debts," they told her self-righteously, as if she planned to do any less), and with the rest had made a down payment on a pretty little house in Forest Hills. She thought it would be an enticement to make me stay with her. But it wasn't. I yearned to get away, the sooner the better. Just after I graduated, I learned that I had won a prize from the English Department for one of my poems. It may have helped me a year later to get admitted to the University of California at Berkeley with a waiver of the out-of-state fee. I was going to do comparative literature or English. American publicly funded schools have been good to me. I wasn't going to go back to New York, to my mother, ever, that was certain.

I worked for a year. I was a waitress, I worked in a factory, in an office, for a wigmaker, in a department store. The variety suggests that I wasn't a success at any of it, nor did I save much money. Most of what I earned went into the household. Since we never kept track of expenses, I still had to ask for money. My mother was not stingy. She just wanted me to depend on her, even if she was handing me the money I had earned. Whatever belongs to me belongs to you, was her motto. I interpreted this as "You belong to me, and therefore cannot own anything on your own." She spread a rumor among her friends that I was preventing her from getting married again. I would have been relieved to have a stepfather and to be able to leave with a good conscience. She must have felt that not finding a husband reflected poorly on her. Maybe for once she wasn't even lying, but sincerely believed that as I got older, I needed her more. I came home from work in the evening, and as often as not, I would turn around and get on the subway again, back to Manhattan, to see my friends who were still attending college. Though I was younger than they, I had graduated first due to the vagaries of the advanced credit system.

She went through my things; she never knocked at my door; she smelled my underwear. Later in life, when she came for a visit, she would often go through my wastebasket and read any papers she found there. I would confront her with this indiscretion, and she would defend herself: "What do you mean? If it's been thrown away anyone may look at it. At my place you can look through all the garbage."

No one is as dependent as mothers are on the dependency of their children.

THE BODY GEOGRAPHIC

MARGO PERIN

❖ ❖ ❖

The last time I saw my mother, I was on my way from San Francisco to Italy to teach a writing workshop. I stopped over with her for a few days in London, where I grew up and where she still lived. My father had disappeared into the ether years earlier, and I had long ago moved back to the United States, where I'd been born, seeking warmth from the cold of England—and my mother.

She was on her way back from a cruise that day and had left a key with the doorman. As I opened the door, I felt as though I'd been pitched underground. The material of her life was strewn about everywhere; every surface of her rosewood cabinets and onyx side tables, glass coffee tables, television, and windowsills was littered with vials of nail polish, small change and souvenir bells from the various countries where she had cruised, along with magazines, nail files, false eyelashes, lipstick, and perfume. Crusty ten-year-old shampoo containers and bottles of pills and suntan lotion were scattered on top of her bathroom cabinet. The same went for her two bedrooms; her desk, chest of drawers, and pink velvet vanity table were concealed under the mess. Everything was viscous and grimy, a mound of artifice under which she lay buried.

Holding my breath in fear she'd suddenly walk in and catch me in her bedroom, I reached over and opened the two drawers of her vanity table. Inside lay scores of plastic boxes holding false eyelashes, so many she'd have to live for two hundred years to use them all. I thought of her panic, like that of a smoker caught without cigarettes. What exactly was she hiding?

My mother had always masked herself. She wanted to look like Elizabeth Taylor and would make herself up to look like Cleopatra, with thick turquoise eyeshadow, heavy face powder, fake eyelashes, and red lipstick. The rare times she spoke of her past, I would scrutinize her like a detective, searching for clues. I thought if I knew her, I would *have* a mother.

"My mother's family was from the South," she said, sometimes meaning southern Italy, other times the southern United States. The bare offerings of her childhood that I tried to stitch together quickly unraveled into no more than that, strands of loose thread leading nowhere. One day when she was ten years old, she said, a social worker had turned up at her class at school and removed her, along with her three sisters. "They took us to a halfway house that housed prostitutes while the state figured out what to do with us," she said with a look of dulled confusion.

In one version of her story, my mother said that her mother had been taken to the hospital. "I don't think she knew we were in that place with prostitutes," my mother said, her brown eyes flat. She told me that when a few weeks later her mother died, my mother, the oldest, was allowed out of the halfway house to go to the funeral. My mother laughed a short laugh when she said this, a helpless, wounded sound indicating the pain she normally concealed.

"That must have been terrible," I said sympathetically.

"Yeah, it was," she said coldly, tightening her lips. She knew I wanted more, and she wasn't going to give it to me.

In another version of the story, she would say, "My mother died, and then we were taken away." She and her sisters were never allowed to go home again but instead were sent to an orphanage from which the state farmed them out to various foster homes until they came of age. According to my mother, she and her sisters were taken away because their father "had a fight with the landlord. He was carrying groceries home, and when the landlord came out and tried to get him to pay the rent, my father hit him over the head with a shopping bag," she said with her high, breathless laugh and expressionless eyes. "He was an English parson," she added, her eyes suddenly lighting up as if she had adored him. "He died of liver cancer when I was fifteen."

Then again, she told my brother that her father was Irish.

"Was he born in Ireland?" my brother asked.

"No, he never was in Ireland," she said.

"So his parents were immigrants?"

"No, his parents never came to the States."

"Mom," said my brother incredulously, "how could your father be born in the States if his parents were never there?"

I could imagine the glazing over of her eyes as she answered vacantly, "Oh yes, you're right." My brother kept quiet after that to protect himself, as we all did, from her stinging anger and icy detachment.

On a tip from my sister, I found some photographs of my mother's family, buried in a black plastic garbage bag in her closet.

They were scattered among the detritus of our childhood: old report cards, greeting cards, and tattered drawings. At the bottom was also a stack of photos of us as children, stuffed into the dusty plastic bag of a toilet-brush holder. Among these was a photo of my mother's father, who, with his pale face and downturned fleshy nose, looked Eastern European, possibly Jewish.

There was no picture of my grandmother in the garbage bag. She was supposed to have died at forty from a stroke, but I knew from one of my mother's rare admissions that my grandmother had repeatedly tried to kill herself. "We would come home from school and find her with rat poison on her lips," she once confided. "Sometimes she would be standing on a table trying to hang herself."

I struggled to turn my gaze inward, to imagine how my mother had felt when she found out about her mother's death. I couldn't tell if she had cried. There had been no tears in her eyes as she told the story, no lines of mascara running down her cheeks, no furrow in her brow indicating she had felt anything at all. There was only the way she held her shoulders erect and tilted her chin forward as if warding off the next blow.

She lied about everything. I couldn't even be sure where she came from. When I asked her where she was born, she said, "I don't remember."

"It was New York, right?" I prodded, confident of what she had let slip years earlier.

"Tsk! You're not going to start that again, are you?"

But it was my mother's cruelty, not her lies, silence, neglect, or violence, that hurt the most. Yes, she slapped me time and time again when I was a child, making my head snap to the side, her bony fingers leaving their mark on my cheek. And yes, she refused to take me to the hospital when I broke one arm at two and another at four, and during all those other childhood and teenage mishaps and infections. And, yes, I did come home from nursery school at four years old to find my family had moved out without telling me, leaving a family friend whom I didn't recognize in their place. I thought the man was the bogeyman she always warned me about, a man who prowled around the neighborhood raping and killing little girls.

And she did say we were going on vacation when I was seven, eight, nine, eleven, and thirteen years old, when, in fact, we were really moving. And yes, how dirty I was all through my childhood, making my sixth-grade teacher recoil in disgust at my gray feet when I had to take my shoes off to be measured. And she did draw away from me when I tried to hug her, no matter what age I was.

It wasn't any of that. It was her look of satisfaction and self-righteousness as she kicked me in the ribs when I was ten and lying on the floor listening to the radio in a dreamy haze instead of helping her in the kitchen. It was the glee on her face as she watched my father paddling our bare toddler backsides with a hard red Ping-Pong paddle when he came home at the end of the day ready to punish us for the crimes she had listed. She was obviously enjoying our punishment. "You're lucky you have a father," she would say, stabbing her finger in the air accusingly. And the way she stood at the door of the living room when I was a teenager while my father punched me in the abdomen and yanked my hair hard. Her face was hard and cold, her eyes smoldering black with hatred as she stood guarding the door so I couldn't escape. Her look was spiteful, her lips tight in a grimace of gratification at his throwing me on the floor and kicking me. "You should see your father's hand," she had said when I tried to get sympathy from her for my black-and-blue ribs the following morning.

And it was when I was nineteen and diagnosed with cancer. I called her from the hospital where I'd gone to get the results of tests. After my appointment with the doctor, a hospital volunteer found me wandering around the hollow blue reception area in a daze and led me to the telephone near the entrance.

"Mom, it's me," I said, bursting into tears. "The doctor said I have tumors!" The doctor had called it Hodgkin's disease. I didn't know what Hodgkin's disease was, but I knew tumors meant cancer. "Can I come and see you?"

"No," she said, her voice cold over the telephone wire. "I think it's better for you to go to your place."

Was she remembering her father, who was supposed to have died of cancer? Was she in so much pain that she couldn't think beyond herself? Or was she so damaged by her childhood that she didn't have feelings?

My mother couldn't always have been like that; she couldn't have been born that cruel, that cold. I had to close my eyes and remember that girl with the same curly brown hair as mine and a shy smile in the photograph of her standing close to her father that I had dug out of the garbage bag. I had to see in my mind's eye the six-, eight-, ten-year-old coming home from school and finding white powder on her mother's lips, a cardboard box of rat poison on the kitchen counter labeled with a skull and crossbones, or the rope strewn across their dinner table. I had to imagine the frigid stiffening of my mother's back when a social worker turned up in her school classroom, her head lowered as the social worker picked up one sister after another and led them out of the school-yard as if they were no more than criminals. I had to conjure her never being able to return home again.

When did my mother's unspoken cry begin: "Why should you have what I never did?"

Once, years earlier, I asked my mother if she cared about me. We were going down the escalator in London's Waterloo train station to catch the tube to my sister's flat, the cold, smoky air casting a gray shadow on the passengers rushing to and from the platforms. I was trying to catch her by surprise so she'd answer the question.

Standing below me on the escalator, my mother looked even shorter and more egg-shaped than usual. Sixty-five if my birth certificate was to be believed—the birth certificate she'd "lost" along with those of her other children—my mother was now per-oxiding and teasing out her hair. One of her false eyelashes lay unglued at the corner of her eye as she turned to look up at me from the metal step. "Of course I care about you. I've known you since you were born." She gave a short disbelieving laugh, that burst of breathless laughter.

Her laugh was so easy, her response so immediate, she caught *me* by surprise. I didn't realize what a strange answer that was. I was relieved she said she cared about me; I was happy.

As we dipped into the tunnel leading to the tube platform at Waterloo, she changed her sunglasses to large red-tinted eye-glasses. "I just bought these on the ship," she said, adjusting them firmly on her thin nose. "I want to see the world through rose-colored glasses." She turned her head, laughing defiantly.

On one of her cruises she met Bob. She didn't tell him she had seven children. She would have told him she didn't have any, as she told everyone else, except that when he came to her flat he asked about the photos Scotch-taped to the wall that showed her three youngest children with her grandchildren. I could imagine her laughing superficially and changing the subject. Why she had them up there I didn't know. It would have been so easy to take them down before he came over. When Bob saw me during my visit, not one of the children up on the wall, perhaps he became just as confused as I was. She had given me strict orders to indicate I was ten years younger than I was. "He doesn't have to know how old I am," my mother said, tossing her hair. Apparently, neither did I. She never revealed her age to her children or to anyone else.

As I stood in her bachelorette kitchen, she laughed, "I'd rather tell Bob I don't have children. It's none of his business." She expected me to laugh along with her, and I almost did, but at her, not with her. I wanted to throw my mouth wide open in an uproarious, murderous laugh. I wanted to humiliate her, make a mockery of all her plastered makeup, scream that she was nothing but an *old* bitch. I wanted to tear her hair out because she was so selfish and insensitive that she could deny my existence to my face and expect me to empathize with her.

My mother carried on obliviously, layering more nail polish on her already painted nails. "If you tell people you have children, that's all they want to talk about."

❖ ❖ ❖

It was early as I packed the final things in my case in the living room the last time I saw her. All the furniture was faded pink and sagging, with dents in the armrests and fluffy fallout on the floor. She appeared at the top of the stairs, disheveled in an old terry-cloth bathrobe. A few days earlier, she had been concerned about where her money would go when she died. "I don't want it all to go to death taxes," she'd said with an anxious look.

"What about your kids?" I asked, grinning foolishly at her.

She flapped her hand and stood up, moving toward the sink with her breakfast plate. "I don't believe in leaving money to children," she said over her shoulder. "It's better for them to be independent."

No matter how long I'd known my mother (ever since I was born, after all), she still had the power to stun me into silence.

"When are you leaving?" she asked. "I want to take a bath."

"In ten minutes," I said, instinctively raising my head as I used to when I was a child before leaving for school in the morning. I would try to get a kiss, but she would turn away.

"Okay, I'll take my bath now," she said and headed for the bathroom.

"Don't take a bath," I called out after her, stung, forgetting I had told myself not to expect anything. Whatever kept me seeing her—tenacity? stubbornness? denial?—whatever kept me trying to get her to love me, kept me trying to understand who she was, turned to resentment. After that would come anger, then guilt, then hope, and then it would start all over again.

It wasn't just love or understanding I was looking for. I needed a mother. A black saw worked its teeth through my gut, mangling my thoughts, twisting my desire for her into a thirsty pit of need, as empty as her heart.

"Come and sit with me until I leave," I begged.

"Okay," she said and shuffled down. She sat in the armchair, her feet not touching the floor. She looked off into the distance with blank eyes, as if she had hung up a sign saying "Closed," until I brought my cases to the front door and said good-bye. Then the veil lifted, and she peered out the door, smiling and waving at me as I walked down the long hallway until I reached the elevator.

I was confused. Why would she want to take a bath while I was still there, then stand at the door waving? Why wouldn't she come to the doctor's to hear I had cancer? I couldn't understand why she didn't care about what happened to her children after she died. Let her keep the money for herself when she was alive, I thought numbly, but it would make no difference to her when she was dead. She neglected me, lied to me, denied I was her child; now her money after she died.

Three months later, I was diagnosed with breast cancer, caused by the radiation that had cured me of Hodgkin's disease. My breast had been changing shape, and I thought it was due to age. As my mother grew older, her body had lost its shape, and I thought mine would, too, as if our mother's body naturally carves out our future. After the diagnosis, in the depths of my despair, my thoughts crowded in on themselves, running circles around each other. My mother was my body, and I was her body, and even if my mother didn't feel connected to me, we were connected. My mother's breast had given me life. The breast was life. The breast was love. I was to lose my breast. I could lose my life. Where was my mother?

But the adult part of me knew that, like the cancer itself, my mother was toxic. I felt hopeless, angry, and sick when I had anything to do with her. I was petrified of dying and devastated by losing the most beautiful, womanly part of me, the most sexually desired part of me, the home of safety and nourishment. I had to think about nurturing myself, protecting myself, being my own mother, so I could get through it. But *she* was my mother. My breast, her breast. It was a spiral I couldn't get out of.

My grandmother, according to my mother, was forty when she died. My mother said that she herself was ten. That meant my grandmother gave birth to my mother at thirty. Like my mother, I, too, was born when my mother was thirty, according to my birth certificate. In my delirium, I thought that made us a holy trinity of sorts. My grandmother abandoned my mother. My mother abandoned me. My grandmother felt so much pain she killed herself. My mother felt so much pain she died inside. And me? Just as self-destructive, I thought: cancer, the preying of cells upon cells, the festering rot of cellular memory.

In my darkest moments, I fixated on this trinity, a shining light at the very tip of my consciousness, convinced that the amount of pain I felt was not just my pain, but also my mother's pain and her mother's before her, and maybe my great-grandmother's and her mother's before that. I felt deep in my bones that my body was no more than the receptacle of what they had lived through and that I was no more than a deposit of all the pain that had gone on before me. A whole lineage of women whose pain split them apart like so many burnt trees, exploding in me in a firestorm of cancer. My grandmother and mother had bent under the weight of their pain. Now I was terrified I would bend under the weight of mine.

Just like truth, pain will seep out; it will find a route, a channel, an isthmus to release itself. I lay in my bed, curled in fetal
position, too paralyzed with fear to get up before and after the surgery, the curtains drawn, the green reflection of the digital clock
clicking away in the mirror. I squeezed my fists together, praying
that all the rivers inside me would rise up in a huge tidal wave and
crash right out of me to the sea. But the pain was so immense, the
rivers desiccated into quarries of dust. There was no hope the flow
would force its way to the ocean and finally release the pain of all
the generations of women before me. There was just too much of
it. I lay rigid, buried.

wanted to call my mother. I didn't want to call her. I dialed
once, and her answering machine picked up. I put the phone
down again, her cold words from when I was nineteen echoing in
my mind: *I think it's better if you go home*.

I didn't know what to do if she called me, whether I would tell
her about the cancer or not. But it didn't matter, because she
never called. I turned to my partner and sisters, a brother and
friends for help as I struggled to keep afloat. I tried to force my
thoughts away from her, thoughts like black freighters moving
across the night horizon.

But on my birthday, three months after my breast had been
removed, she did call.

"Marci?" I heard her voice at the other end of the line. That's
my partner's name. "No, it's Margo." I kept my voice even, hard.
"Who's that?" One good turn deserves another, I thought bitterly,
feeling the walls of my heart lock together. She doesn't even remember my voice.

"It's Mom."

"Oh, hi, Mom," I answered casually, leaning against the white doorframe of the room as I cradled the phone.

"I just wanted to call you on your birthday," she said, her voice high and thin.

I took a breath. "Thank you. That's nice of you."

"How are you?" Always that breathy faintness.

"I got breast cancer." I said in a nonchalant tone. The worst of it was over, I thought, feeling unsteady in my legs. I got through it without her. She could do nothing to me now.

"What?" The shock in her voice echoed through the wire.

"I had to have a mastectomy," I said. I kept my voice light, but I felt spiteful, like I wanted to rub it in her face. Maybe the shock would catapult her into caring. Maybe I could pay her back for every time she had hurt me. Maybe she would care so much, she would *feel* hurt.

She sounded astonished. "Oh, my God. You're kidding."

"No, it's been terrible." My voice broke, and against my will I heard myself begging for sympathy.

She gave her small breathless laugh. "I've been sick myself. I've had shingles for six months."

I staggered, then stiffened back to attention. "I'm sorry," I said bluntly. "I can't listen to anyone else's health problems right now."

Her voice was surprisingly sympathetic. "No, of course not. How awful." She paused. "Are you okay now?"

I struggled to remain reasonable, unemotional, but I felt something cracking. "I was lucky it didn't spread, but there might be something going on in my other breast. I'm going to have a biopsy next week."

"When?" she said.

"Wednesday. I'll get the results on Friday." I started crying silently, unable to stanch the torrent of fear. If I lost my other breast, my panicked reasoning told me, I wouldn't be a woman at all. I would be as good as dead.

"I'll call you Friday," she said.

"Thank you," I choked, feeling the floodgates widen another inch. "That was nice of you to remember my birthday."

"Sure," she said. "Why not?"

She didn't call again until two weeks later, a week after my results were back. She left a message on my machine while I was at the hospital having the stitches removed. "Hi, Margo," she said breezily. "Give me a call sometime."

I returned her call as soon as I heard the message, but she was out. "The biopsy was inconclusive, and I have to go back into surgery," I said to her machine. I felt warm, almost happy. She had called. That meant she was worried about me. That meant I had a mother *to* call. "I'll ring you with the results," I added, saving myself from the pain of waiting for her to telephone me again.

The night I got the results of the second biopsy, her machine picked up. "You have reached . . ."

"Hi, Mom, it's me," I spoke clearly into the machine. "They found irregular cells, but thank God they didn't find more cancer."

I didn't hear from her for another two weeks. She called while I was at a follow-up appointment. "Hi, I'm in Spain," her voice rang cheerily on my machine. "I've come with Bob. It's been so cold in England."

I punched the stop button, then kicked the small wooden table on which the machine rested, sending the phone and machine flying. I would never speak to her again, I resolved. I was better off without her. I would make her not matter. I would make her disappear altogether.

I never called again. But eighteen months after that last phone message, an insistent ringing broke through dinner at the rose-covered, stone-walled Tuscan villa where I was, once again, teaching.

"Margo, it's for you," someone called. Still smiling at a student's joke, I moved to the telephone, which was perched on top of a blazing fireplace in the cavelike living room that adjoined the dining room. My sister Ava's voice sounded deliberately cool and formal, as if she didn't want me to get upset. My throat swelled with nervousness, and I clasped the phone to my ear, straining to hear what she was saying.

"Mom is in a temporary residential care unit," Ava said. "She has something called atrophied muscular syndrome, and she fell down and cut her face. If she can't take care of herself, she'll be moved to long-term care until . . ."—she paused—"the end."

I stared at the black marble mantelpiece. No one had told me she was sick. All my old feelings staggered through me: guilt, anger, betrayal, love. I wanted to call right away, then I didn't want anything to do with her.

"What if she dies?" I blurted to Ava. I felt a tangle of love and guilt winding itself around my throat and heart. I hadn't gotten rid of her at all. I had merely put my feelings on hold, fobbed them off as she had so often fobbed me off.

After I hung up, I squeezed into a dark corner of the living room until I could still the anxiety rolling through me. Mom, dying, deadly disease. She could hardly walk. Her words were slurring. Should I catch the next plane? Should I run to her bedside, take care of her? I looked down at my hands, bony and dry, with protruding veins, so like my mother's.

Early the next morning, I picked up the phone before I could change my mind, a wall of cold air in my chest. My mother answered from her bedside after three rings. "Hello?" Her voice sounded surprisingly firm, considering what my sister had said.

"Hi, Mom, it's Margo," I said.

"Margo!" she exclaimed, as if I had been the one to reject her. "How are you?"

"I'm fine," I stammered. "How are you?"

She told me about her fall and the disease she'd been diagnosed with. "It's like Parkinson's, but it's not," she said, her voice getting weaker and shakier the longer she talked.

"Are they treating you okay?" I asked hesitantly, seeing her lying limply in her nightclothes, pale under her makeup.

"Yes, it's fine," she said.

I heard a muffled sound in the background. "I have to get off the phone now," she said. "The nurse has come to give me some medication. Call me sometime."

Call me sometime.

"Okay," I began to say slowly. Then I paused. "Lots of love, Mom."

A DAUGHTER OF ISIS

NAWAL EL SAADAWI

❖ ❖ ❖

Her face had the roundness and the whiteness of her breast. Her eyes were big and full of light. They were two circles of pure white around two honey-coloured circles breathing warmth. They were tender, touched my face like milk flowing from her breast, which filled me up with sleep, so that my lids closed by themselves. I floated over expanses of white light. I swam in the sea, never reached the land, then woke up on my mother's breast reaching shore at last. It was the only shore I knew in this vast expanse. Beneath its smooth surface I could feel her heart. It beat with mine. She and I were one heart beating in the body which was us.

On the sea-shore she taught me how to walk. My eyes searched the ground as I felt my steps. My head, now lighter than my body, was held up. My eyes took in the sea, a broad expanse of blue floating in the sun. I filled my lungs with air, breathed in the odour of sun, of salt and seaweed and of mother's skin.

My mother's breast was smooth like sand on the sea-shore. Our breathing rose and fell in a movement that was one. The air went in and out between her chest and mine, carrying with it the smell, the tang of salt and fresh sea air. I lay on the shore wearing a swimsuit with shoulder straps. It was green, with blue and red and orange bands, but in the photograph the colours change to black and white.

My mother used to hold me up on the surface of the sea, teach me how to jump or float over the waves. I thrash the water with my arms and legs, and laugh. I drown under the waves with laughter. My mother pulls me out, laughing all the time. Our laughter rises in the air above the waves. The waves rise up, then break into white surf. The white of the surf melts into the blue of the sea, and the sea fuses with the sky, travels to where they meet far away at the horizon. My mother's arms carry me high up, and my head touches the heavens.

My mother used to swim alone like a wave in the sea. I imagined she was the daughter of the sea who, born of its waters, had given birth to me. She and I had emerged from its warm blue depths, on to the smooth white sands, under this pure blue sky, bathed in this golden sunlight. This was our air, our sun, our sea. This was our land, and it belonged to her and me. When we laughed our voices were carried by the air, transported through the waves from one wave to the other, from one country to another, on and on, endlessly.

Her arms embrace me, hold me high up over the waves, leave me free to swim alone, then encircle me again, so that her body becomes my body, before she lets me go once more, her body separate from mine. Over the waves and under them we continue this never-ending game of becoming one, fusing and separating from each other again.

Against this white sand, the contours of my father's body were well-defined, emphasized its existence, an independent, solid existence in a world where everything was liquid, where the blue of the sea melted into the blue of the sky with nothing between. This independent existence was to become the outer world, the world of my father, of land, country, religion, language, moral codes. It was to become the world around me. A world made of male bodies in which my female body lived.

When I was a child, I thought the God they talked about belonged to my father and my brother and that I had nothing to do with him. I also thought that the sky with its stars belonged to them. My father would point with his finger to a trail of stars and say, "That is the Milky Way," then to single stars and say, "That is the planet Mars, that is Venus, and that, over there, is Jupiter." With his finger, he would name each star for my brother, just as God taught Dad the names of things. God did not tell us in His book that he taught Eve anything. God did not address women in his book.

My father often told us about Adam, how God elevated him above the angels and ordered Satan to kneel down and worship him, and how the sun and the moon and the stars and the heavens bent low before the Prophet Joseph. I used to listen to my father, my mouth open, my eyes staring wide at him. The world of the Qur'an was like the world of my father, the affair of men only. I dozed to the sound of my father's voice as he told us these stories, slipped into sleep, as though drowning in the sea, sunk deeper and deeper until I touched bottom and swallowed bitter salt water. My mother was now absent. Her arms were no longer there to pull me out. There was no-one to reach down and lift me out of the deep waters. I woke up in the morning with the bitter taste of salt in my mouth. Under my body the sheet was wet with salty water that smelt like urine. I would get out of bed, my body shrinking with shame. I wrapped my arms around my breasts to hide the stigma budding out. I pulled the heavy covers over the wet sheet so that nobody could see, but Aunt Ni'mat was there to pull them off, to run through the house shrieking my shame to the universe.

Gradually, my mother was withdrawing from my life. I no longer saw her except in the kitchen. I no longer heard her speak. Most of the time she sat listening to my father's stories as he moved from Allah and the Prophet Muhammad to the British and the king, then he would go on to the headmaster of the school in which he taught, for at that time we were in Alexandria and my father was a teacher in the Abbassieh secondary school for boys. The headmaster of the school was called Al-Nazir (superintendent or inspector).

The distance between my mother and me grew bigger and bigger, and the distance between my father and me smaller and smaller. My mother began to sit at the far end of the couch. Year after year the gap between us increased. My father stretched out his long legs and occupied the whole space. The space taken by my mother was shrinking all the time. She sat there, her body hiding in her clothes, her breasts hanging down as she suckled one child after the other. Her waist disappeared as her belly became swollen with child. Fat crept around her body, showing pale through her skin. She no longer belonged to the world which I shared with my father and my brother. Her world was another world which made me shiver every time I thought of it, the world of the kitchen, smelling of onions and garlic, filled with smoke or soot rising from a kerosene-burning stove.

As soon as I reached the age of seven my mother started to teach me how to light the primus stove, and my father began to show me how to pray. Was there some relationship between the primus stove and praying? I soon discovered that there was. The body movements were similar. To light the stove I had to bend my back in a movement which resembled bowing down in prayer. When I cleaned the blocked hole with a needle sometimes it broke inside, then in order to extract it with the help of another needle I would have to bend even more so that my nose almost touched the *tarboush* in a movement very much like prostration.

The hole was always getting blocked, either with a small particle of smoke or soot, or some impurity in the kerosene. The kerosene was adulterated, and at the bottom of the tin there settled a dark sticky sediment like tar, or pitch.

The smell of kerosene gave me nausea. If my mother discovered a louse or nit in my hair she washed my head with kerosene. When I stood over the kerosene stove to light it, a flame would often shoot up in my face, making me take a quick step backwards as I had seen my mother do, to prevent it burning the ends of my hair, and filling my nose with its smell and that of singed hair which made me vomit.

Little by little I trained myself to light the stove without breaking the needle, to clean the hole when it became blocked without bending down or stooping, to stand in front of it with an upright back and with my head held up.

My mother now left the task of lighting the primus stove to me. Every night when I went to sleep I would dream that the stove had exploded, see my mother in the midst of the flames, and rush to save her, but too late, for she had already burned to death. They would wrap her in a white silk shroud and lay her body down on the brass bed. In my dream, the shroud was her white silk wedding gown.

The dream kept repeating itself in different forms and accompanied me throughout the years of my childhood and youth. It left me only after I graduated from medical college and became a "distinction" resident doctor in the university hospital of Kasr Al-Aini. At the beginning of April 1955, for the first time in my life

I cashed a monthly salary. It was nine pounds, each pound as big as the other.

In the month of April the flowers open their petals. I walked down the street, my head held up to the sky, my bag clutched tightly under my arm. Thieves' eyes were capable of penetrating anything, their noses able to detect the aroma of banknotes kilometres away. I walked into a big store called Shaher on Fouad Al-Awal Street, next to the Rivoli cinema. I was looking for only one thing, a butane gas stove with an oven and four burners of the make known at that time as Master Flame. The first instalment I had to pay was five pounds, and the monthly payments would last for another thirty-six months.

The day I became a medical doctor my mother looked like a flower in bloom. She recovered her childlike laugh, the sparkle in her honey-coloured eyes. I could see them shine as she read through my certificate of graduation.

"May it be a blessing to you Nawal, Dr. Nawal."

"I owe it all to you, Mama."

The word "Mama" burst out of my lips in a gush of suppressed love. The conventions running in my mother's family did not permit expressions of love, even if it were love for one's own mother. Children once they were weaned were no longer kissed. This was the tradition in middle- or upper-class Turkish families, in which not to express warm feelings, to be cold, was considered a sign of distinction.

In my mother's eyes, I could see maternal love burning like a flame but held back, surrounded by a barrier like an iron cast through which it could not break. I, too, behaved in the same way, put up the same barrier like a partition of glass behind which smouldered my emotion.

That day in the first week of April I slipped into the house accompanied by three men from the store carrying the butane stove. They crept into the kitchen, placed the stove under the window next to the pantry, then tiptoed out. Rays of afternoon sunlight fell between the walls of the houses and penetrated through the iron bars on the window into the kitchen. They landed on the butane stove as though guided by some celestial will to make its white surface radiant with light.

My mother walked into the kitchen. Her eyes opened wide in amazement. "Where did this butane stove come from?" she asked.

"From heaven," I said.

Her eyes shone with the joy that belongs only to children. Like me, from her earliest years she had dreamed of the day when the primus stove would disappear. Like me, she had looked at the shops and stores, seen the butane gas stoves which burned with a pure blue flame, were lighted with a single strike of the match, needed no needle to clear away particles of smoke or soot. She would gaze at the price fastened on the stove, heave a sigh, and walk on.

I wanted to put my arms around her, lay my head on her breast, and cry. I wanted to let out the tears suppressed within me ever since I had been born. She, too, wanted to put her arms around me to free the feelings of motherhood imprisoned within her for so long. But we stood there unable to embrace one another, to exchange a single kiss, separated by barely a finger's breadth of air yet which seemed like a vast ocean, like a thousand years of time which neither of us could cross.

My mother lived for thirty-four months after that day. She died two months before I paid the last instalment.

HOME IS WHERE
YOUR STUFF IS

HELEN RUGGIERI

❖ ❖ ❖

During World War II my father worked for a company that manufactured parts for bomb sights, and we moved on the average of every year and three quarters. Because housing was scarce we took whatever we could get. We went from an eight-room house to three furnished rooms over a drugstore, to a place that had been a private hospital and had rooms off a central hallway and a bathroom with the tub placed dead center.

Home was wherever we were living at the moment. Things were problems. Things were materials to be catalogued into piles for discard or for storage. To get into the storage pile, the thing had to have value. Value was assigned by my mother usually, although on occasion I would hear my father yell about some article she had deemed worthless and discarded which he considered valuable. I usually didn't have a say. I didn't collect stuff, because my mother would only make me throw it out when the next move came. She liked to travel light.

When we finally settled into what looked to be a long-term residence, our own place, my mother went to the furniture store and bought a new living room suite. All the old dinged, burned, and scratched mismatched collection of odds and ends we dragged around the country with us disappeared. I came home from school one day to see her new matched set aligned in the front room.

"An ensemble," she said. I looked around from the mat in front of the doorway. I made a big show of wiping my feet. That would please her. There was a plain gray rug covering the floor and a gray and maroon three-pillow couch centered on the south wall. Approximately one and a half feet in front of the couch, dead center to the middle cushion, was a mahogany coffee table with a silver cigarette lighter and a large maroon leaf-shaped ashtray perfectly centered.

On either side of the couch, a round, matching mahogany table held an identical lamp of watery blue porcelain. The white shades were securely wrapped in cellophane, and I don't think the cellophane was ever removed from them. In fact, for years I thought that was how lampshades were supposed to be.

To the north was a matching gray-and-maroon chair and to the west a gray-and-blue overstuffed chair with a matching gray footstool. This was my father's chair and was accompanied by an old table already marked with cigarette burns. Catching my glance stopping at the old table, she said, regretfully, "He'd only burn the new ones." No matter how large the ashtray, my father always managed to place his cigarette precariously and leave the area. He'd return to find the cigarette long since gone to smoke and, under the ash, a long scar burnt into the surface. He'd brush the ash off and step on it and use the toe of his shoe to grind it into the rug. "Kills moths," he'd explain to anyone watching. He'd spit on his finger and trace the burn as if spit would erase it.

"Oh, Jimmy," my mother would sigh in a voice thick with exasperation. "You'll burn down the whole house one of these days."

This was our new living room. It was the first time I could remember that we had furniture that matched, all new, all at once, and I could already sense the guardianship in my mother's stance. I looked around. I admired it. "It's great," I said.

"What do you think of this," she asked, shoving a swatch of cloth toward me. On a background of pearl gray was a big green banana leaf with red and blue flowers climbing across it.

"It matches," I said, hoping I'd guessed the answer she wanted. She nodded, turned slowly in a circle holding the swatch out in front of her. I went upstairs to my room carrying my books. We'd never be able to sit on a couch again, I thought. We'd have to stand in the doorway. Maybe we'd have to detour to get to the stairway so as not to walk on the rug. She wouldn't put down a path of newspapers for us to follow, would she? I had been rather fond of the old couch, where I might even put my feet up if I took my shoes off.

My mother was a meticulous housekeeper. She went at it with wax and mops and vacuum cleaners and, worst, a schedule. She would clean on Friday, just when you'd be around to use the place, and she'd moan at every opportunity, "I just cleaned that." She actually moved the furniture once a week to clean underneath. Nothing was ever out of place. Books were not piled on the dining room table, newspapers were not tossed under the coffee table, glasses were not allowed in the living room. If you wanted a snack you ate in the kitchen. Certainly you could sit in the living room, but you had to do it properly. You had to lower yourself into a chair, not drop. Ladies did not drop into chairs as if they were trampolines. You lowered yourself, gracefully.

This new living room suite would only intensify her scrupulous guardianship. She would be like a mother bear guarding a cub. To mess up her intentions for this room would be dangerous. Cruising for a bruising. Calling for a mauling. Or, at the very least, a tedious lecture, which you already knew by heart.

I went down to the basement, where my father was gluing a dinner plate he'd broken. "Good as new, eh?" he asked, holding it up for inspection.

"Looks great," I lied. I automatically picked up the cigarette that was burning a groove in the edge of his worktable where he'd rested it, momentarily, ten minutes ago. I flicked it onto the cement floor and stubbed it with the toe of my shoe, careful to make sure I got all the tobacco and ash off the sole. "Should you smoke while you're working with the glue?" I asked. He just shrugged. This was his place, filled with old radios and other broken appliances. He packed them up and moved them from place to place in case he needed parts to repair something. This was something even my mother dared not interfere with. With these spare parts he would fix whatever needed to be fixed and so save money. This seemed to pacify her or convince her.

And so, we had a collection of appliances that worked, but in unexpected ways. We had a mixer you had to push the off button to start; a toaster you had to set on its side to heat; a radio that would only play if you kept your hand on top of it. He repaired all our appliances, and they worked, yes, but with conditions.

"Do you think we'll ever be able to sit up there?" I asked.

"What can she do?" he replied.

I interpreted this to mean that eventually we would be able to sit up there because, logically, that's what the furniture was for. I went back upstairs. She was sitting back with her legs crossed posed in the corner of the couch reading the paper. She looked at me carefully, assessing my intentions as I approached. I kept walking, upstairs to my room. I knew that the time was not yet. I'd let my father go first, and I'd follow him. After the first spill of ashes, the first burn, we might be able to visit.

I entered my room, flopped on the bed, got up, folded down the spread in case she came upstairs, reflopped. I kicked my shoes off, then grabbed them quick before she heard them hit the floor and called up to see if I had changed my clothes. I set them on the floor facing out, just like all good little shoes should be. They were Girl Scout shoes: brown, laced up the front. I'd wanted saddle shoes, but my mother wouldn't buy them because she would always have to be cleaning the white part, polishing them, because she would nag me and I would refuse. I tried to explain that you didn't polish them, but that was something she refused to understand.

I yanked a book from the pile on my desk. It was a new one from the library. I read the first page. Yes, it was going to be a good one. This girl loved animals and wanted to be a veterinarian, but her family was poor and wanted her to get a job at the five-and-ten. My mother would never let me have a pet. She was afraid of dogs, and they got hair all over. I pictured myself behind the candy counter at Woolworth's, the smell of chocolate and sugar. Not a bad job, I thought. I wasn't sure about caring for injured dogs and cats, but perhaps there would be horses later, after the bird's wings healed and she made a splint. Straws would work, I thought. Straws and gauze, that airy bandage stuff in the medicine cabinet. You could lay the bird on its side, hitch it into place. I could picture the process, feel the tiny thump of the bird's heartbeat. Perhaps you hired people to clean up, clean out. You had to keep the place clean, like a hospital. We could use our kitchen. My mother liked to brag you could eat off the floor. I amused myself imagining a horse with a broken leg being taken care of on the kitchen table. My father would rig a sling. I would care for it, feeding it hay and oats.

"Helen," she called up, "did you change your clothes?"

"Yes, Mom," I lied.

"What are you doing?"

"Homework," I yelled. I flipped the page. It began to get dark. I turned on the light. It took a few minutes until it warmed up and began to glow faintly. I changed my clothes, hung my skirt up, and put the blouse in the hamper. Finally, the bulb came to life. I flopped on the bed again, careful not to bounce so hard the springs would make noise and give me away. The girl in the book was befriended by a veterinarian who thought she had talent. The light went off, but if you waited a few minutes it would come back on again. It was one of my father's fix-ups. In the dark, I thought that this was my place. Even in the dark I knew where everything was. I could picture the vet: a tall, pleasant man, soft-spoken. I was sure he'd eventually come up with the money to send her to veterinary school. My place never got dirty and everything worked right, came out right, the way it was supposed to, and everybody was comfortable in it.

"Helen," she called, "Come set the table."

I closed my book, marked my place with a scrap of paper, set it on my desk. She didn't care about that, but I hated to read books with other people's dog-ear folds in them. It seemed rude, a tacky way to treat a book. I didn't like the thought of others having been in the book before me, getting potato-chip crumbs in the bindings or making chocolate thumbprints in the margin. I turned the light out. One did not leave the lights on in unoccupied territory—that was a rule. The lamp ignored me and continued to shine in the early darkness. It took a while to get warmed up, but when it did, it was reluctant to stop. You had to know how things worked. In our house we each had our own place, and we guarded it with a congenial ferocity.

was always being asked to forgo something or other that had previously occupied my leisure time, and then something or other that was essential (my schooling), to take care of these small children who were not mine. At thirteen, at fourteen, at fifteen, I did not like this, I did not like my mother's other children, I did not even like my mother then; I liked books, I liked reading books, I did not like anything else as much as I liked reading a book, a book of any kind. My youngest brother was two years old when one day he was left in my charge, my mother placed him in my care while she ran errands; perhaps I knew what these errands were, but I no longer do, I cannot remember what it was she had to do and so left me alone to care for him. Mr. Drew, our father (though his father, not really mine), was not at home. But I liked reading a book much more than I liked looking after him (and even now I like reading a book more than I like looking after my own children, but looking after my own children is something I cannot describe in terms of liking or anything else), and even then I would have said that I loved books but did not love him at all, only that I loved him because I was supposed to and what else could I do. All day I was left to look after him, and all day, instead of doing so, I read a book, a book whose title and plot or anything else about it I cannot remember just now. The day must have passed in the same rhythm as the pace with which I turned the pages (and I recognize this way of phrasing this event as romantic, even literary, for the day must have passed with its own usualness and did not care about me in particular or in general), and so when I finished reading the book I realized the day was ending and my mother would soon return home.

Between my coming to the end of the book and the time my mother should return home there were not many minutes remaining, only minutes were left for the chores that should have taken me an entire day to complete. I did the things I thought my mother would notice immediately; changing my brother's diaper was not among them. This was the first thing my mother noticed, and only now I can say (because I can see) "Of course." My brother, the one who was dying, who has died, who while dying could not take himself to the bathroom and freely control his bowel movements, then as a little boy, two years old, wore diapers and needed to have someone change them from time to time when they grew soiled. That day (and I cannot remember if it was a Monday, a Tuesday, or a Wednesday, but I do know with certainty that it was not a Saturday or a Sunday) when I had been reading instead of taking care of him, I did not notice that in his diaper was a deposit of my brother's stool, and by the time my mother returned from her errand—and she did notice it—the deposit of stool had hardened and taken the shape of a measure of weight, something used in a grocery store or in the fish market or the meat market or the market where only ground provisions are sold; it was the size of that measure signifying a pound. And in it, this picture of my brother's hardened stool, a memory, a moment of my own life is frozen; for his diaper sagged with a weight that was not gold but its opposite, a weight whose value would not bring us good fortune, a weight that only emphasized our family's despair: our fortunes, our prospects were not more than the contents of my brother's diaper, and the contents were only shit. When my mother saw his unchanged diaper, it was the realization of this that released in her a fury toward me, a fury so fierce that I believed (and this was then, but even now many years later I am not convinced otherwise) that she wanted me dead, though not in a way that would lead to the complications of taking in my actual existence and then its erasure, for she was my mother, my own real mother, and my erasure at her own hands would have cost her something then; my erasure now, my absence now, my permanent absence now, my death now, before her own, would make her feel regal, triumphant that she had outlived all her inferiors: her inferiors are her offspring. She mourns beautifully, she is admirable in mourning; if I were ever to be in mourning, this is the model, the example, I would imitate. At that stage of my life I was fifteen, my brother was two years old—I was unable to help her make sense of her life. The man she had married was sick and could not really build houses anymore, he could not really make furniture anymore; she might have loved him for a moment, she might have loved him for many moments, I never knew, but there was a child almost two years old, there was a child almost four years old, there was a child almost six years old. These were all his children. I was not his child, I was not part of the real debacle of her life, and then again, worst of all, I could not help her out of it. I insisted on reading books. In a fit of anger that I can remember so well, as if it had been a natural disaster, as if it had been a hurricane or an erupting volcano, or just simply the end of the world, my mother found my books, all the books that I had read, some of them books I had bought, though with money I had stolen, some of them books I had simply stolen, for once I read a book, I could not part with it, no matter its literary quality. (I then had no sense of literary quality, literary quality being a luxury, luxury being absent from my existence unless I saw an illustration of what this might be on a tin of cheap powder imported from England, and this picture of luxury only demonstrated what it might look like if one did not have to work at all, and so luxury was presented as contempt for working and any association with the dullness of the everyday.) A cauldron of words, even a world perhaps, may have passed, but not between us, though by then it would have been only one way, for I could make no response. But there was a moment when in a fury at me for not taking care of her mistakes (my brother with the lump of shit in his diapers, his father who was sick and could not properly support his family, who even when well had made a family that he could not properly support, her mistake in marrying a man so lacking, so lacking) she looked in every crevice of our yard, under our house, under my bed (for I did have such a thing and this was unusual, that in our family, poor, lacking a tradition of individual privacy and whether that is a good thing, whether all human beings should aspire to such a thing, privacy, their thoughts known only to them, to be debated and mulled over only by them, I do not know), and in all those places she found my books, the things that had come between me and the smooth flow of her life, her many children that she could not support, that she and her husband (the man not my own father) could not support, and in this fury, which she was conscious of then but cannot now remember, but which to her regret I can, she gathered all the books of mine she could find, and placing them on her stone heap (the one on which she bleached out the stains and smudges that had, in the ordinariness of life, appeared on our white clothes), she doused them with kerosene (oil from the kerosene lamp by the light of which I used to strain my eyes reading some of the books that I was about to lose) and then set fire to them. What I felt when this happened, the exact moment of the burning of my books, what I felt after this happened, shortly after it happened, long after it happened, I do not know, I cannot now remember. In fact, I did not even remember that it happened at all, it had no place in the many horrible events that I could recite to friends, or the many horrible events that shaped and gave life to the thing I was to become, a writer. This event, my mother burning my books, the only things I owned in my then-emerging life, fell into that commonplace of a cliché, the repressed memory, and there it would have remained forever if one day, while paying me a visit, while staying with me in my home, a place whose existence seemed especially miraculous—her presence only served to under-line this—she had not said to a friend that if it were not for her vigilance, I would have ended up not in the home and situation that I now occupied but instead with ten children by ten different men. And she had a story to illustrate this fact: apparently, when I was about the age at which my brothers' existence—all of them— became also my responsibility (even though they were not my children, I had nothing to do with them being in the world), a boy named Lindsay used to come to our house and ask if he could borrow some of my books. This boy only pretended to love books (my mother knew this instinctively then, and she knew this with certainty at the time she came to visit me); what she believed he wanted was to seduce me and eventually become one of the ten fathers of the ten children I would have had. One day, she said, when she grew tired of his ruse, she said to him that I had no books, that I was not a library, didn't he know. The person to whom my mother had told this story only repeated it to me when she thought my judgment of my mother had grown too harsh, had only repeated it to me to demonstrate that my mother had done the best she could and was only acting in this way to prevent me from experiencing a harsh life, to make it possible for me to have the life I had when my mother was then visiting me. I had forgotten the burning of my books, I remembered it when my friend told me the things my mother had said.

When I was young, younger than I am now, I started to write about my own life and I came to see that this act saved my life. It was because I had neglected my brother when he was two years old and instead read a book that my mother gathered up all the books I owned and put them on a pile on her stone heap, sprinkling them with kerosene and then setting them alight; I cannot remember the titles of those books, I cannot remember what they were about (they would have been novels, at fifteen I read only novels), but it would not be so strange if I spent the rest of my life trying to bring those books back to my life by writing them again and again until they were perfect, unscathed by fire of any kind.

HOW I LEARNED
TO COOK

HILLARY GAMEROW

❖ ❖ ❖

I was an incurious child. The questions other children asked often startled me: who cared why the sky was blue or the grass green? They just were, weren't they? When it rained, water fell from the sky and I stayed indoors. When I was five, my mother's belly swelled like the silver foil on Jiffy Pop popcorn. Then she had a stomachache and disappeared for a few days. I was packed off to my grandmother's. I didn't give the visit another thought because I already spent a lot of time at my grandmother's. Then my mother came home. No stomachache. No popcorn belly either. She had exchanged them both for a squalling, red-faced bundle tightly wrapped in a blue blanket: my new brother, Ethan. If there was some connection between these two events, I managed to miss it.

There was not much grass where I grew up in Brooklyn. We lived in one of three apartment buildings that stood shoulder to shoulder in quiet solidarity against a neighborhood jammed with small houses. Neighbors tended tiny plots of flowers in front of narrow red brick homes. And although East Twelfth Street was overhung with trees whose roots pried up the concrete squares of sidewalk, I reached college with an excellent grasp of photo-synthesis but could not tell trees apart. They were just trees. In freshman year, this gap convulsed my roommate. Hiking together that first autumn, she pointed out a blaze of color roaring in the unnatural-to-my-city-girl-ears silence of gray Long Island woods: a magnificent red maple. I stared, amazed. "Trees have *names?*" I asked. For all I know, she's dining out on that story to this day.

So food appeared on the table, and I never questioned its origins. Why bother? I already knew all I needed to know. Eggs came in cardboard cartons from Henry the Grocer. Fruits and vegetables came from Saul the Vegetable Man. Our neighborhood was a regular medieval village, name-wise. John the Butcher wrapped meat in tidy brown paper packages. Larry the Soda Man delivered seltzer right to our apartment door, grunting under the weight of a wooden case filled with thick green-glass bottles tipped with heavy silver nozzles. Blackout cake came from Ebinger's, and my father brought home Wonder Bread from his job as a delivery man. There were two kinds of milk that tasted the same: the kind in the toy-like red-and-white wax containers at school and the kind in clear-glass bottles delivered by John the Milkman, a stocky, smiling Italian, who would learn to fear Ethan, an ankle biter from the moment he could crawl.

In kindergarten, when they showed us a cartoon about happy cows and friendly farmers and I finally made the milk-cow connection, I was horrified. Milk came out of an *animal?* Ugh!

"Just drink it," my grandmother advised, tapping her cigarette into her half-empty coffee cup. "Or I'll beat the crap out of you." I giggled. The only hand she ever laid on me was a gentle one. On the days my mother went to work as a fabric designer, Gramma and I watched game shows together on her plastic-covered gold couch. While Ethan played on the floor, I curled up with my head on her lap as she smoked an endless chain of Marlboros and shouted instructions to the contestants.

When I was in first grade, Mrs. Caputo beamed as she handed out reading primers printed on cheap thick paper, already disintegrating around the edges. Their powdery yellow smell made me sneeze. "Reading is magic!" she said enthusiastically. "It is a magic carpet ride that will take you to wonderful places. How I envy you the adventures waiting for you!"

She must have handed out the tickets to the magic carpet ride on one of the days I was home sick with one of my frequent, disabling stomachaches. I was not one of those prodigies who taught themselves how to read before they could walk. Today I would probably be diagnosed as dyslexic. In 1966, my mother found another word to describe my problem: *stupid*. I couldn't recognize the shapes of letters with any regularity. Worse, I transposed them, transforming English into a mysterious foreign tongue that existed only in the slice of air between the page and my eyes.

"Just work with her," Mrs. Caputo suggested in response to my mother's frantic query. Vibrating with anxiety, my mother had hauled me in front of the teacher. Every now and then she shook me to make a point. Stunned with the shame of my violated invisibility, I pulled into myself and lost track of the conversation.

"Of course she's not retarded!" my teacher exclaimed, bringing me back with a start. I knew right then I would always love her for the surprise in her voice. "Give her time," she said, smiling at me. "She just needs a few extra sessions at home; she just needs a little more patience."

, ❖ ❖ ❖

Patience was not one of my mother's virtues.

Every evening, when the dishes were done, my mother and I grimly sat down at the kitchen table for an hour of mutual torture. The evil primer lay open between us, and the pain in my stomach grew exponentially with each page. Just looking at that book jump-started a small animal clawing to escape from behind my belly button.

After endless weeks of fruitless struggle with the incomprehensible, we were both ready to snap. "And" was the worst, my nemesis. It slid right off the surface of my mind. One winter night, my halting recitation stopped dead at a mysterious three-letter word lying smack in the middle of the page. I had never seen this word before. I would have bet anything that it had never even existed until this very moment. I had no clue what it might be. Brows knit together, I frowned at it with my mouth open. A? N . . .

My mother screamed, a long, wordless "Aaaaaaaahhh" that shocked me out of my concentration. She woke Ethan, in the next room, who screamed right back. She slapped my face so hard that she knocked me from my chair, and I curled into a ball on the floor. She threw the book at my head; a sharp corner of its cardboard cover stung my cheek.

"And!" she shrieked. "And! And! And! And! And! You fucking retard! It's AND! Get to bed. I don't want to see your stupid, ugly face until you learn this word! You're a moron! You're as stupid as your fucking father! Stupid stupid STUPID!" I uncurled myself, grabbed the book, and fled to the room I shared with Ethan. He stood uncertainly, clinging to the bars in his crib, dirty diaper falling from his hips. The sharp, sickly sweet reek of his urine filled the room and stung my eyes. I threw myself on my bed but quietly, as quietly as I could. My throat was so tight I started to choke, but I stopped myself. If I cried, that just made her angrier. When she was *angrier*, there was no telling what she would do. At times like this, silence and invisibility were not enough. The best thing was just to go away. So I erased myself. I could blend into my surroundings better than the chameleon in the tank at school. I melted into the green flowered coverlet so I wouldn't have to breathe. Breathing too loud was something else that sent her over the edge. In the next room, she paced like a caged tiger, talking furiously to herself. Then she started crying. I caught my already held breath. How could I have made my mother cry? My heart hammered against my chest.

"And," I mouthed silently. "And, stupid. You are so stupidstupidstupid." If I could just learn "and," my mom would be happy again, and this angry stranger who shared her body would go away. I waited until the noisy sobbing subsided. I waited until the apartment was quiet. Then I slowly changed back from blanket to girl.

It was nice to have hands again. I retrieved my flashlight from under my bed and wrapped myself in my coverlet. Ethan had gone back to sleep, blanket pulled over his head, leaving his pale feet bare. They shone in the dark. In the wavering cone of yellow light, I stared at "and" until my eyes staggered out of focus. And.

I burned "and" into my stupid, stupid head by sheer force of will. And.

The round, black letters smoked against my brain. A-N-D. I ate *and*. I swallowed *and* until the dull cramping in my gut went away. Andandand.

Finally, I knew it. I was sure. I did know it. I filled the hole in the page. Those three letters were no longer a blank spot: they formed the word "and." The apartment was cold. Shivering, clutching my book, I crept from my room and slipped into my parents' room. My father worked the night shift. The bedstand light was on. My mother was asleep, fully dressed, under the covers. She hadn't washed her face before going to bed, and her makeup was smeared crazily over puffy cheeks. She looked so tired that my heart contracted with love and guilt. Why did I have to be so stupid?

"Mommy?" I whispered. Her eyes flew open and focused on me immediately.

"What is it baby? Are you okay?" I heaved a sigh of relief. My real mother, not that bad stranger. The stranger never looked at me directly.

"I learned the word, Mommy," I said proudly. "Can I show you now?" She sat up, rubbing her eyes. "You didn't need to work so hard tonight, Sarah." Sometimes she called me by different names. I answered to almost any girl's name, although she had her favorites. Hillary was not one of them. "But I'd love to see what you learned." Trembling a little, I opened my book and laboriously sounded out that impossible sentence: Dick AND Jane . . . She laughed and hugged me. We both laughed. I was giddy with relief. Learning "and" made my mother happy. Learning "and" made my real mother come back. I could breathe again, and the air made me giddy. Reading was magic. Mrs. Caputo was right.

became insatiable. Suddenly, I was a starving creature, and words were what I hungered for. That whole winter, as long as I didn't need her, as long as Ethan didn't cry, as long as my father kept some kind of job, my real mom stayed with us. Oh, she had lapses, but these were usually my fault, or the baby's. I could ignore them because I was convinced that reading was the glue that held our fragile juggling act together. And even when the glue failed, and my mother flew apart, I could escape. Reading could take me farther and more completely away than anything else I'd found so far.

I caught up to my classmates, and then I passed them. I read everything I could find. I didn't have to understand it, I just had to run my eyes over the page, sounding out the words. I was indiscriminate. I was powerful. Reading muted my parents' constant fights to a dull roar in the background. Reading was more than magic: I finally found something that could keep me safe.

By the time I was seven, no book, no box, no magazine, no cereal carton was safe from me. One day my mother carelessly left *The Joy of Cooking* on the kitchen counter. I greedily snatched it from the countertop and fled like a thief to my room to devour it. I planned to read it methodically from cover to cover, just like I read any other book. I hadn't yet noticed the differences between them. They were just books, a medium for words, delicious words. Lovely, anesthetic words.

Other children carried their toys around with them everywhere they went. I carried *The Joy of Cooking*. My mother laughed and shook her head, but she let me. I was at my grandmother's house when I reached the section on spices. When I read about spices, something clicked into place. Neither my mother nor grandmother kept many spices in the house, but I knew I'd seen some of those words before. I asked my grandmother to show me cinnamon. She looked at me curiously but obediently handed the tin to me. Sure enough, it said, "Cinnamon." Just like in the book. The congruence astonished me; I, who could not afford astonishment. Astonishment was too close to surprise, and surprise was too often painful. I didn't like being surprised. But when I read about cinnamon, I could hold it in my hand. I could twist the plastic cover to expose the holes in the spice can, shake out the contents into the palm of my hand. I could touch cinnamon; I could taste it and smell it. Cinnamon was more real than I was. I felt like Helen Keller in that movie the family had watched on TV, in that part when she figures out the connection between Anne Bancroft tickling the palm of her hand and *water*.

That was me. And here was more magic: origami words expanding into three dimensions, unfolding with a breathtaking suddenness into something more than an abstraction. Cinnamon. My first link to life took root in a can of cinnamon. The world became more than an ill-defined concept seen indistinctly from the corner of one nervous eye. Oregano. Allspice. Garlic. Cinnamon.

What the hell do you think you're doing?" my mother snapped, charging into the kitchen to find me dreamily swirling together Worcestershire sauce, wine vinegar, black pepper, paprika, and cloves in a Flintstones jelly glass. I couldn't tell her. I didn't know myself. I stared at her, frozen in mid-swirl. "Just clean this mess up," she snarled over her shoulder, charging back out. I emptied my concoction into the sink, orange flecks of paprika spiraling slowly and silently down the drain. I ran the water to clean the sink and slunk back to my room. I sullenly returned to *Little House on the Prairie*. I felt sure that Laura's Ma would not have wasted such a fine mixture.

Then I stumbled upon the recipe for applesauce.

In our house, every night had its own dinner, and the schedule never changed. Thursday night was pork-chop night: pork chops and Rice-A-Roni, served with applesauce. Wednesday night was meatballs and spaghetti with tomato sauce, and a wedge of iceberg lettuce served with Italian dressing. It was easy: tomato sauce was for spaghetti. Applesauce was for pork chops. Period. And everything came from the supermarket in a glass jar whose label had to be soaked off. The empty jar was then carefully stored under the sink, just in case any of the 325 other glass jars stashed around the house were shattered when the Russians dropped the Bomb on Brooklyn.

The Joy of Cooking, however, claimed that applesauce came from apples, long before it ever reached the supermarket. In my entire life, I'd never taken a line of reasoning that far before. But if it was in a book, it had to be true. Books did not lie, they did not change, they always said the same thing no matter how many times I read the words, and that was why I liked them. If there were surprises in store, they came slowly enough not to wound me. And—*and!*—we had apples. Just yesterday, I had been allowed to walk by myself around the corner to Coney Island Avenue to buy apples from Saul the Vegetable Man, a quarter clutched so tightly in one fist that it embossed my palm. I was still basking in my great achievement. Perhaps it was this feat that imbued me with such unusual courage . . .

Because a feeble light had slowly dawned, somewhere between my mind and my heart, and by its glow, I examined *The Joy of Cooking* with a new eye. Cookbook: a book for cooking. Applesauce: a sauce made from apples. And sugar. Water. Cinnamon. I could *cook* applesauce. I could make some now, if I wanted to. Even though it was supposed to come from the store . . .

"Ma!" I yelled. "What does 'peel' mean?"

Ensconced on the couch, engrossed in her book, my mother

probably didn't give my question a second thought. After all, she was my own personal walking dictionary. She knew everything. I could ask her what any word meant, and she always knew, no matter how many syllables it had. Better yet, when I looked them up, she was always right. Words were our bond, our secret, the most pleasurable bridge between us.

We didn't have a fruit peeler or an apple corer, so I used a steak knife. When I was done, the chunks of fruit from my carefully counted pile of apples looked like miniature Easter Island sculptures, softened and browned around the edges. To me, "one cup" was the little plastic orange cup with the chewed-up rim that I drank milk from. I used that to measure sugar and water. My mother kept her pots and pans in a cabinet to the right of the kitchen sink, just east of the glass-jar collection. I picked the first one, which happened to be a frying pan. Pulling it out by the loose wooden handle, I had a bad moment. I was not allowed to play with the pots and pans. But I would not let myself think about it or, worse, consider the consequences of using the stove. On the Forbidden Scale of one to ten, the stove was an eleven. Even though my mother's mood had been exceptionally mellow that day, I just knew that if she caught me playing with these things she would kill me like she always said she would. Well, I wasn't playing, was I? I was cooking, and that was different from playing. But the truth was, I didn't care. I, the good girl, the quiet one, the obedient one, the invisible one, was so absorbed in my project that I didn't care. I'd gone too far. Now I had to see it through to the end. Bring it on. I'd go down fighting in a cloud of *cinnamon*.

I dragged one of the chairs over to the stove and didn't even flinch at the noise it made scraping across the linoleum floor.

❖ ❖ ❖

What surprised me was the smell. The Rombauers didn't mention odors in the book. The last thing I expected was perfume. After a couple of terrifying false starts, I had figured out how to regulate the gas flame, and the sweetly seductive scent of simmering apples and sugar and cinnamon wafted around me. I stood on the chair, hypnotized by this amazing sludge I'd created. Bubbles slowly swelled and burst on the thickening, heavily textured surface, releasing that incredible smell. I bent my face over the steam, dazed with pleasure and ownership. So this was Applesauce!

"You were so quiet, I got worried. You still alive in here? What are you up to?" My mother wandered into the kitchen with her book. An unlit cigarette dangled from the corner of her mouth. I flinched and nearly fell off the chair. She strode across the room and steadied me. "Applesauce," I squeaked defiantly. She glanced around the kitchen, took in the carnage of hacked apple skins and spilled sugar and cinnamon that dusted the counters and floors. I looked with her. Where had this mess come from? I certainly hadn't noticed it before. My mother hated messes almost as much as she hated my father. Holding my breath, I cringed against the chair. The black metal bit into my back. My mother looked at me as if she'd never seen me before, an odd expression in her brown eyes. The silence made my stomach hurt again, a throbbing, icy pain that zigzagged down my middle. I bit my lip so I wouldn't cry out. She frowned a little and then shook her head, as if to clear it.

"Smells great," she said finally and grinned at me. "Hey, I know! Tell you what, even though it's not Thursday, what the hell, why don't we have pork chops tonight?"

❖ ❖ ❖

filled jars and jars with applesauce. I decimated whole orchards. Saul the Vegetable Man, white apron straining across his belly, taught me how to choose the best ones: "By the smell, Hilly-girl, by the smell. First make sure they're nice and firm and they don't got no blemish. Next, they oughtta smell like wine, yeah, right here by the stem. Whaddya mean you don't know what wine smells like? Shi— Excuse me, sweetheart. Well, if your mouth don't water when you smell it, it ain't a good apple." I depopulated the community of glass jars under the sink, filling even the dustiest, tomatoey-scentedest Ronzoni jars for posterity and all our cousins. I was a pioneer woman, keeping company with Laura Ingalls Wilder, putting stores aside for winter, never mind that spring was on its way. Applesauce would never replace books, but it came a close second.

"At least she doesn't have her nose buried in a book all the time," my mother sighed to my grandmother over coffee cake. She ran a slender hand through her light brown curls.

"First you bitch about how she can't read, and now you bitch about how she can. Will you for Chrissake make up your mind?" my grandmother demanded. "I for one love applesauce!" she said, and winked at me.

It was something of a minor miracle, then, that applesauce was not on the menu the first time my mother decided to poison us.

It was Saturday, Tuna Casserole Night, but we were having meat loaf instead, because my father was at home, having just lost another job. Daddy refused to eat anything but meat loaf.

Mommy didn't like anything that interfered with her schedule. The atmosphere in the kitchen was as charged as the air before a thunderstorm.

"You gotta stop telling people about the laser, Arnie," my mother said, slamming his plate down in front of him. Meat loaf, mashed potatoes, peas, and carrots. "They get nervous when you talk about killing people." He shrugged broad shoulders. For almost a year, my dad had had a steady gig as a chauffeur. He was a good driver, but to say he lacked social skills was a gross simplification. Worse, he always told the truth. When clients, making small talk, asked him about his plans for the future, he told them. His hobby was electronics. He wanted to buy a small island and build a big laser that would destroy the world. I'd heard it often enough so the concept no longer bothered me, but sometimes his voice took on the same gloating tone as when he talked about killing gooks for the U.S. of A. in Korea, a tone that still sent a stream of ice down my spine. His almost-black eyes—my eyes, everyone said—glowed with moist enthusiasm. It was easy to imagine how some stranger meeting those eyes in a rearview mirror would feel. I shivered and chewed some meat loaf, which suddenly tasted like cardboard and ketchup. The potatoes were a warmer, saltier version of the library paste my best friend, Gina Brunetti, dared me to eat the week before. Everything grew flat and strange and one-dimensional when my father was around. My skin itched to be away. But I'd never be excused from the table if I didn't finish what was on my plate.

I risked a glance around the table. Head down, my father shoveled in his food. My mother leaned back in her chair and stubbed out her cigarette in the potatoes. Ethan had finished his meat loaf and was busy crushing the library paste and tiny cubes of carrots into his soggy paper plate. My father pushed aside his plate and stood. "Good dinner, Di," he told my mother. "Yeah, good dinner," I echoed, and started to get up, too.

"You wait," she said. I sat back down and started shredding my paper napkin. In the living room, the television blasted into life.

"I put rat poison in the food tonight," she said.

"I didn't taste anything different," I said.

"Rat poison doesn't have a taste," she reassured me. "In a couple of hours, you'll start getting pains in your stomach and you'll start foaming at the mouth like a rabid dog. You know what 'rabid' means, right?" She leaned across the table and stroked my cheek. "I love you so much, and I can't stand it that your daddy's so crazy." Her voice broke. "I can't stand living this way anymore. I hate borrowing money from my family. They never let me forget it." She started to cry, and her tears froze me in place. "It'll be better when we're all dead, believe me."

"Mommy, I—" My stomach spasmed. Or was that just my usual stomachache?

"Or maybe you'll just die in your sleep. You won't feel anything," she said. She sounded happy. "Wouldn't that be nice? Just go to sleep and not wake up in the morning? Never see your father again?" She leaned across the table and wiped the ketchup from Ethan's face with a white paper napkin. "Good boy! Good job finishing your dinner! Wanna go play?" He nodded vigorously and wiggled from his chair.

"Ma, did you poison Ethan, too?"

"Yeah, everyone." She got up and started clearing off the table. "You gonna help me or are you gonna sit there?" I sat there. I didn't know what to do. This sort of thing never happened in *All-of-a-Kind Family*. "C'mon," she teased. "You know the rules. If you don't clean, you don't watch TV. Don't you want to watch TV your last night on earth? Rat poison works fast. I'm not sure how much time you have left. Do you want to waste it sitting there?"

I was still working out how I felt about being dead. I wasn't sure exactly what being dead meant, but after a minute or two decided I didn't like it.

"I don't wanna die, Ma." I whimpered. She came over to me and hugged me.

"I know you don't, baby, and I'm sorry it has to be this way. You can blame being dead on your father. It's his fault for being such a lousy, rotten, crazy bastard who can't keep a single fucking job. Now clear the table, and we'll have ice cream for dessert."

I couldn't eat the ice cream. I tried to concentrate on *Get Smart* but not even Max and 99 could make me laugh. I thought briefly about telling my father about the rat poison and dismissed *that* thought immediately. Talk about stupidstupidstupid. Good thing it didn't take a genius to guess how that would turn out: my mother would deny it, and he would punish me for lying. Then they'd fight. Again. More smashed furniture. I kept thinking about what it was going to be like, being dead. But I couldn't imagine it. Being dead was a concept that slid right off my mind, just like "and" used to.

My family sat together on our scratchy blue couch, bathed in the flickering blue light from the TV. I huddled on one end, curled around the pain in my gut, and ripped tiny pieces out of the *TV Guide*. Ethan climbed onto my mother's lap and fell asleep. I couldn't tell if the poison was working or not. My stomach hurt, but it seemed no worse than usual. I kept touching my face, to see if I'd started foaming at the mouth yet. Would it be like shaving cream? Or would it be like the dirty yellow froth the Atlantic Ocean left on the edges of Brighton Beach?

When it was time to go to bed, we were all still alive, and I didn't have to brush my teeth. Mommy grinned and whispered to me, "It's a treat because you-know-why!" I stayed awake all night, waiting to die, waiting for the rat poison to take effect. I stayed awake all night, listening to Ethan's adenoidal snores, waiting for them to stop. I wondered if he would cry when his stomach started hurting or what kind of noise he would make when the foam came from his mouth. I had learned not to cry, not to bring any adult into my room at night, but he was too little to know about that yet. I stayed awake all night, watching the light from the street lamp, wondering what happened to dead people who were, after all, too big to fit down the toilet.

Gina's grandfather died the year before last. She said they put him in a box and the box went into the ground. If I was stuck in the ground, I would never have new books. I would never smell cinnamon again. I would never see my grandmother again. When I thought about never seeing my grandmother again, the griping pain in my belly rose up through my chest to flower into a strangling tightness in my throat. The tightness melted into tears, tears that scalded my eyes when they leaked out. "Maybe that's the rat poison burning," I thought and stuffed a corner of my blanket into my mouth so no sound would escape. It was a relief to be dying at last.

In the morning, I asked my mother about the poison. She stood barefoot at the stove in a yellow-and-pink flowered housedress, scrambling eggs and humming. "Oh that," she said. "Well, you never know. I could do it anytime, right? So maybe it's in the eggs," pushing a mound of them onto a plate and handing it to me. "Or maybe not. Life's a crapshoot. Maybe it'll be in the tuna casserole tonight. Maybe I'll wait a while, and you'll forget about it. Then I'll slip it in when you least expect it." The thought seemed to make her happy, the way the thought of reading made me happy. I thought, then, that maybe she needed to be invisible sometimes, too.

I played with my eggs, and I thought about tuna casserole. If I made the tuna casserole, I'd know exactly what went into it. Also, I'd watched her make tuna casserole before. If I could peel apples to make applesauce, I could open cans of tuna and cream of mushroom soup. I could boil water for elbow noodles. I could mix it all together and sprinkle corn flakes on top. The oven couldn't be harder to work than the stove, could it? If I asked, maybe she would help me turn it on. Right after breakfast, I promised myself that I would find tuna casserole in *The Joy of Cooking* and I would learn how to cook it.

Rat poison was not even in the index of *The Joy of Cooking*.

from

FIERCE ATTACHMENTS

VIVIAN GORNICK

❖ ❖ ❖

Mama went to work five weeks after my father died. He had left us two thousand dollars. To work or not to work was not a debatable question. But it's hard to imagine what would have happened if economic necessity had not forced her out of the house. As it was, it seemed to me that she lay on a couch in a half-darkened room for twenty-five years with her hand across her forehead murmuring, "I can't." Even though she could, and did.

She pulled on her girdle and her old gray suit, stepped into her black suede chunky heels, applied powder and lipstick to her face, and took the subway downtown to an employment agency where she got a job clerking in an office for twenty-eight dollars a week. After that, she rose each morning, got dressed and drank coffee, made out a grocery list for me, left it together with money on the kitchen table, walked four blocks to the subway station, bought the *Times*, read it on the train, got off at Forty-second Street, entered her office building, sat down at her desk, put in a day's work, made the trip home at five o'clock, came in the apartment door, slumped onto the kitchen bench for supper, then onto the couch where she instantly sank into a depression she welcomed like a warm bath. It was as though she had worked all day to earn the despair waiting faithfully for her at the end of her unwilling journey into daily life.

Weekends, of course, the depression was unremitting. A black and wordless pall hung over the apartment all of Saturday and all of Sunday. Mama neither cooked, cleaned, nor shopped. She took no part in idle chatter: the exchange of banalities that fills a room with human presence, declares an interest in being alive. She would not laugh, respond, or participate in any of the compulsive kitchen talk that went on among the rest of us: me, my aunt Sarah, Nettie, my brother. She spoke minimally, and when she did speak her voice was uniformly tight and miserable, always pulling her listener back to a proper recollection of her "condition." If she answered the phone her voice dropped a full octave when she said hello; she could not trust that the caller would otherwise gauge properly the abiding nature of her pain. For five years she did not go to a movie, a concert, a public meeting. She worked, and she suffered.

Widowhood provided Mama with a higher form of being. In refusing to recover from my father's death she had discovered that her life was endowed with a seriousness her years in the kitchen had denied her. She remained devoted to this seriousness for thirty years. She never tired of it, never grew bored or restless in its company, found new ways to keep alive the interest it deserved and had so undeniably earned.

Mourning Papa became her profession, her identity, her persona. Years later, when I was thinking about the piece of politics inside of which we had all lived (Marxism and the Communist Party), and I realized that people who worked as plumbers, bakers, or sewing-machine operators had thought of themselves as thinkers, as poets, and scholars because they were members of the

Communist Party, I saw that Mama had assumed her widowhood in much the same way. It elevated her in her own eyes, made of her a spiritually significant person, lent richness to her gloom and rhetoric to her speech. Papa's death became a religion that provided ceremony and doctrine. A woman-who-has-lost-the-love-of-her-life was now her orthodoxy: she paid it Talmudic attention.

Papa had never been so real to me in life as he was in death. Always a somewhat shadowy figure, benign and smiling, standing there behind Mama's dramatics about married love, he became and remained what felt like the necessary instrument of her permanent devastation. It was almost as though she had lived with Papa in order that she might arrive at this moment. Her distress was so all-consuming it seemed ordained. For me, surely, it ordered the world anew.

The air I breathed was soaked in her desperation, made thick and heady by it, exciting and dangerous. Her pain became my element, the country in which I lived, the rule beneath which I bowed. It commanded me, made me respond against my will. I longed endlessly to get away from her, but I could not leave the room when she was in it. I dreaded her return from work, but I was never not there when she came home. In her presence anxiety swelled my lungs (I suffered constrictions of the chest and sometimes felt an iron ring clamped across my skull), but I locked myself in the bathroom and wept buckets on her behalf. On Friday I prepared myself for two solid days of weeping and sighing and the mysterious reproof that depression leaks into the air like the steady escape of gas when the pilot light is extinguished. I woke up guilty and went to bed guilty, and on weekends the guilt accumulated into low-grade infection.

She made me sleep with her for a year, and for twenty years

afterward I could not bear a woman's hand on me. Afraid to sleep alone, she slung an arm across my stomach, pulled me toward her, fingered my flesh nervously, inattentively. I shrank from her touch: she never noticed. I yearned toward the wall, couldn't get close enough, was always being pulled back. My body became a column of aching stiffness. I must have been excited. Certainly I was repelled.

For two years she dragged me to the cemetery every second or third Sunday morning. The cemetery was in Queens. This meant taking three buses and traveling an hour and fifteen minutes each way. When we climbed onto the third bus she'd begin to cry. Helplessly, I would embrace her. Her cries would grow louder. Inflamed with discomfort, my arm would stiffen around her shoulder and I would stare at the black rubber floor. The bus would arrive at the last stop just as she reached the verge of convulsion.

"We have to get off, Ma," I'd plead in a whisper.

She would shake herself reluctantly (she hated to lose momentum once she'd started on a real wail) and slowly climb down off the bus. As we went through the gates of the cemetery, however, she'd rally to her own cause. She would clutch my arm and pull me across miles of tombstones (neither of us ever seemed to remember the exact location of the grave), stumbling like a drunk, lurching about and shrieking: "Where's Papa? Help me find Papa! They've lost Papa. Beloved! I'm coming. Wait, only wait, I'm coming!" Then we would find the grave and she would fling herself across it, arrived at last in a storm of climactic release. On the way home she was a rag doll. And I? Numb and dumb, only grateful to have survived the terror of the earlier hours.

One night when I was fifteen I dreamed that the entire apartment was empty, stripped of furniture and brilliantly whitewashed, the rooms gleaming with sun and the whiteness of the walls. A long rope extended the length of the apartment, winding at waist level through all the rooms. I followed the rope from my room to the front door. There in the open doorway stood my dead father, gray-faced, surrounded by mist and darkness, the rope tied around the middle of his body. I laid my hands on the rope and began to pull, but try as I might I could not lift him across the threshold. Suddenly my mother appeared. She laid her hands over mine and began to pull also. I tried to shake her off, enraged at her interference, but she would not desist, and I did so want to pull him in. I said to myself, "All right, I'll even let her have him, if we can just get him inside."

For years I thought the dream needed no interpretation, but now I think I longed to get my father across the threshold not out of guilt and sexual competition but so that I could get free of Mama. My skin crawled with her. She was everywhere, all over me, inside and out. Her influence clung, membrane-like, to my nostrils, my eyelids, my open mouth. I drew her into me with every breath I took. I drowsed in her etherizing atmosphere, could not escape the rich and claustrophobic character of her presence, her being, her suffocating suffering femaleness.

I didn't know the half of it.

One afternoon, in the year of the dream, I was sitting with Nettie. She was making lace, and I was drinking tea. She began to dream out loud. "I think you'll meet a really nice boy this year," she said. "Someone older than yourself. Almost out of college. Ready to get a good job. He'll fall in love with you, and soon you'll be married."

"That's ridiculous," I said sharply.

Nettie let her hands, with the lace still in them, fall to her lap. "You sound just like your mother," she said softly.

That's ridiculous. Sometimes I think I was born saying, "That's ridiculous." It shoots out of me as easily as good-morning-good-evening-have-a-nice-day-take-care. It is my most on-automatic response. The variety of observations that allows "That's ridiculous" to pass from my brain to my tongue is astonishing.

"Adultery makes modern marriage work," someone will say.

"That's ridiculous," I'll say.

"Edgar Allan Poe is the most underrated writer in American literature," someone will say.

"That's ridiculous," I'll say.

"Sports have an influence on people's values."

"That's ridiculous."

"Movies have an influence on people's fantasies."

"That's ridiculous."

"If I could take a year off from work my life would be changed."

"That's ridiculous."

"Did you know that most women refuse to leave the husbands who beat them?"

"That's ridiculous!"

Three years ago I ran into Dorothy Levinson on the street. We hugged and kissed many times. She stood there repeating my name. Then she smiled and said, "Do you still say, 'That's ridiculous'?" I stared at her. She hadn't seen me since I was thirteen years old. I felt the blood beating in my cheeks. Yes, I nodded, I do. She threw back her head and nearly had a heart attack laughing. On the spot she invited me to have dinner in a restaurant that night with her and her husband. What an evening that was.

Dorothy Levinson. So beautiful it twisted your heart. Now here she was, fifty, slim, lovely, full of shrewd Jewish wit and crinkle-eyed affection, her face looking remarkably as her mother's had at this same age: soft and kindly, slightly puzzled, slightly sad.

The Levinsons. I had loved them all—Dorothy, the four boys, the mad parents—but most of all I had loved Davey, the youngest boy, when we were both twelve, and how I had suffered because he hadn't loved me at all. There he'd been, thin and athletic, with a headful of glossy black curls and brilliant black eyes (every little girl had wanted him), and there I'd been, pudgy, sullen, superior. The whole thing had been quite hopeless.

The Levinsons were our summer people. Between my tenth and thirteenth summers we were in residence at Ben's Bungalows in the Catskill Mountains. Two contingents dominated this bungalow colony: people like ourselves from the Bronx and people like the Levinsons from the Lower East Side. Or, as my mother put it, "the politically enlightened and the Jewish gangsters."

The Jewish gangsters had it all over the politically enlightened in the mountains. They learned quickly where good times in the country were to be had, and went after them as single-mindedly as they pursued their share of the action on Grand Street. They swam out farther in the lake than we did, roamed farther afield in search of wild fruit, trekked deeper into the forest. They danced in electric rainstorms, slept on the open mountainside on hot nights, persisted in losing their virginity wherever possible, and in making everyone else lose theirs as well.

The darkest and wildest of them all were the Levinsons— from Sonny the oldest son, to Dorothy the only daughter, down to my beloved Davey. They were so beautiful it was hard to look directly at them. Two summers in a row we shared a double bungalow with the Levinsons, and I was in a continual state as they slammed in and out of the screen door that hung on the same thin frame as ours. I remember those summers as flashes of black silky curls whirling by in the noonday sun, or quick darting glances in the bright shade from a pair of black eyes filled with scheming laughter. They were always going somewhere, planning something. Whatever they did it was the thing to do. Wherever they went it was the place to go. I longed to be asked to join them, but I never was. I stayed behind in the bungalow with my mother or read on the grass nearby, while they ran out into an intensity of sweet summer air to catch salamanders and frogs, explore abandoned houses, plunge repeatedly into the lake, feel sun burning into bare brown flesh, long after I had been called in to supper.

Dorothy and her husband and I went to a restaurant in the Village, and the talk plunged headlong into the past. Dorothy's husband, an accountant, knew he didn't have a chance and settled good-naturedly into playing audience for the evening. Dorothy and I, absorbed by every scrap of memory—Grand Street, the Bronx, Ben's Bungalows—talked over each other's voices, shrieking with laughter at everything, at nothing.

Dorothy kept asking if I remembered. Remember the abandoned house in the forest? Remember the berry-picking on the high hills far away? And the scratched asses from lying on the thorns to neck? Remember the warmth and vulgarity of the women on the porch on Sunday night? Dorothy's memories were richly detailed, my own sketchy. It wasn't just that she was eight years older. She was a Levinson. She had lived it more fully than I had.

Meanwhile, I kept asking, How's Sonny? How're Larry and Miltie? And your father. How is he? (I didn't ask for Mrs. Levinson, because she was dead, and I didn't ask for Davey, now a rabbi in Jerusalem, because I didn't want to know.)

"Sonny?" Dorothy said. "All we do is analyze. Analyze, analyze. When Sonny was in the army Mama got sick. Papa had run out on her. Sonny came home. He got down on his knees beside the bed and he said, 'I'll take care of you, Ma.' She said, 'I want Jake.' Sonny walked out of the apartment. Later he said, 'When I realized she loved him more than she loved me I said to myself, Fuck her.' But he never got over it. He's got a nice wife, good kids, lives near me. You know we all still live downtown, don't you? Sure you know. So now Sonny comes in the apartment, a friend is sitting on the couch, he looks the situation over, jerks his head in the direction of the bedroom, says, I gotta talk to you; my friend starts laughing. But that's it. We don't really share anything. He comes over, gets analyzed, goes home. Larry? He's 240 pounds now. Got a girlfriend, but he still lives in the old apartment on Es-sex Street, she shouldn't think he's getting involved, he's only been with her six years. Davey! Don't you want to know how Davey is? Davey's wonderful! Who would have thought my baby brother would turn out spiritual? But he has. He's *spiritual*."

I nearly said, "That's ridiculous." Stopped just in time. But I couldn't let it go, all the same. Silent throughout the recital on Sonny and Larry, now I felt I had to speak. "Oh, Dorothy," I said, very gently I thought, "Davey's not spiritual."

Dorothy's eyes dropped to the table, her brows drew together. When she looked up again her eyes were very bright, her mouth shaped in an uncertain smile.

"What do you mean?" she asked.

"If Davey had left Essex Street at eighteen he wouldn't be spiritual today," I said. "He's looking for a way to put his life to-gether, and he's got no equipment with which to do it. So he turned religious. It's a mark of how lost he is, not how found he is, that he's a rabbi in Jerusalem."

Dorothy nodded and nodded at me. Her voice when she spoke was unnaturally quiet. "I guess that's one way you could look at it," she said. I laughed and shrugged. We dropped it.

On we went, falling back repeatedly to stories of the bungalow colony. Dorothy did most of the talking. As the hours passed Dorothy did all the talking. She talked faster and faster, the sentences tumbling one after another. A mosaic of emotional memory began to emerge: how she had seen me, how she had seen my mother, how she had seen my mother in relation to her mother. I began to feel uncomfortable. She remembered it all so vividly. She had been so intent on us. Especially on my mother.

She laughed heartily as she spoke, a strong rocking laughter. Suddenly she turned full face to me and said, "You never really enjoyed it like we did. You were always so critical. For such a little kid you were amazing. It's like you knew you were more intelligent than anyone else around, and you were always seeing how silly or pointless or ridiculous—your favorite word—everything was. Your mother, also, was so much better than anyone else around. And she was, she was. Your father adored her. She used to walk beside him, his arm around her and she holding on to him, God, did she hold on to him, holding on for dear life, clinging like to a life raft, and looking around to make sure everyone saw how happy she was with her lover-like husband. It was as though she wanted to make every woman there jealous. And *my* mother? My father came up once during the whole summer. She used to cry over your mother: 'Look how good he is to her, and look how Jake treats me. She's got everything, I've got nothing.'"

Dorothy laughed again, as though she was afraid to speak without laughing. "My mother was kind," she said. "She had a kind heart. Your mother? She was *organized*. My mother would sit up with her own kids when they were sick, and she'd sit up with you, too. Your mother would march into the kitchen like a top sergeant and say to my mother, 'Levinson, stop crying, put on a brassiere, fix yourself up.'"

More laughter, by now the taste of iron in it. Dorothy struggled with herself to stop, to get off my mother and her mother. Abruptly she took her memories back to a time before my time, and began to tell us of the Jewish mystics traveling around on the bungalow-colony circuit when she was eight or ten years old. "All the women would sit around in a circle in the dark," she said, "with a candle on the table. The medium would close her eyes, tremble, and say, '*Habe sich, tischele.*' Lift yourself, little table." ("And would it?" "Of course!") "Women would start to scream and faint. 'Is that you, Moishe? *Oy gevalt!* It's Moishe!' More screaming, more fainting."

Dorothy threw me a sharp look and said, "Your mother would have marched in, turned on the light, and said, 'What is this nonsense?'" Dorothy's husband and I both stared open-mouthed at her. Before he could stop her she leaned toward me and hissed, "She never loved you. She never loved anybody."

The next morning I realized that although I had not said "That's ridiculous" before I scored off Davey, Dorothy had nonetheless heard the words. The mother in her had heard the mother in me.

was seventeen, she was fifty. I had not yet come into my own as a qualifying belligerent but I was a respectable contender and she, naturally, was at the top of her game. The lines were drawn, and we did not fail one another. Each of us rose repeatedly to the bait the other one tossed out. Our storms shook the apartment: paint blistered on the wall, linoleum cracked on the floor, glass shivered in the window frame. We barely kept our hands off one another, and more than once we approached disaster.

One Saturday afternoon she was lying on the couch. I was reading in a nearby chair. Idly she asked, "What are you reading?" Idly I replied, "A comparative history of the idea of love over the last three hundred years." She looked at me for a moment. "That's ridiculous," she said slowly. "Love is love. It's the same every-where, all the time. What's to compare?" "That's absolutely not true," I shot back. "You don't know what you're talking about. It's only an idea, Ma. That's all love is. Just an idea. You think it's a function of the mysterious immutable being, but it's not! There is, in fact, no such thing as the mysterious immutable being . . ." Her legs were off the couch so fast I didn't see them go down. She made fists of her hands, closed her eyes tight, and howled, "I'll kill you-u-u! Snake in my bosom, I'll kill you. How dare you talk to me that way?" And then she was coming at me. She was small and chunky. So was I. But I had thirty years on her. I was out of the chair faster than her arm could make contact, and running, run-ning through the apartment, racing for the bathroom, the only room with a lock on it. The top half of the bathroom door was a panel of frosted glass. She arrived just as I turned the lock, and couldn't put the brakes on. She drove her fist through the glass, reaching for me. Blood, screams, shattered glass on both sides of the door. I thought that afternoon, One of us is going to die of this attachment.

MY TWO MOTHERS

NAHID RACHLIN

❖ ❖ ❖

How did it happen, I have often wondered, that I survived my mother's inadequate and sometimes even hostile treatment but my oldest sister, Pari, did not? Now living in the United States, with a child of my own, I attribute my strength to my aunt, who raised me during the first nine years of my life, before my father took me away from her to live with him, my mother, and other siblings.

My mother had promised me to her sister when I was a mere fetus inside her. Her sister had been unable to have children from her husband, a man much older than she was, who died soon after they got married. She had begged my mother to let her adopt what would be my mother's fifth living child (two had died before me and two were born much later). My grandmother had stayed with my mother to help her with the pregnancy and birth. When my mother went into labor my grandmother sent for the midwife. After helping deliver me and cutting the umbilical cord, the midwife put ashes on the wound for antiseptic purposes.

My grandmother thought it best to wait six months before transporting me from one daughter to another. They lived far apart: my mother in Ahvaz, my aunt in Teheran. This gift must be protected and delivered in health. I needed to be a little older to stand the arduous fourteen-hour train ride.

The Shah's attempts at modernity and beautification of the country hadn't gone far. The train from Ahvaz to Teheran was old, the tracks bumpy, needing repair. I had been sleepless on the long ride. After I finished the bottle of my mother's milk, my grandmother bought some goat's milk at a station where the train stopped. Other families in the compartment asked her questions about me, were amazed at the task she had taken on. The women tried to help my grandmother, holding me so that she could sleep a little. When we reached Teheran, there were no taxis waiting by the station, so we had to take a horse cart.

I can imagine my grandmother getting off the horse cart at the end of a long dirt alley and walking slowly with an infant in her arms. She walked faster as she saw her daughter, Maryam, squatting by the door of her house. Maryam jumped up as we approached, and my grandmother put me into her arms. "This is the happiest day in my life," Maryam said excitedly.

A few days later my grandmother left to go back to the village, where she lived with her widowed sister. But during her future visits, when I was old enough to understand, she told me, "Maryam loved you from the moment she laid her eyes on you."

During the years I lived with my aunt as her child, my mother was a shadowy figure to me. We lived in a house in an alley set in a maze of other interweaving alleys, in an old neighborhood of Teheran. The house was one of three attached houses my aunt had inherited from her husband. We occupied a row of rooms in the biggest house. Another one of my aunts and her husband and three sons lived in the same house on the other side of the courtyard. One of the other two houses was occupied by a third aunt and her husband and three daughters, the other by a family, distant relatives of Aunt Maryam from her husband. Our neighbors were uneducated, poor, and observant Muslims—a milieu very different from that of my parents', I found out later. There were mosques on almost every street in the neighborhood. The voices of muezzins calling people to prayer filled the air three times a day. I had a sunny corner room with a mantel on which I kept my toys. A rug with designs of flowers, leaves, and peacocks was spread on the floor. Two large embroidered cushions were set on the rug against the wall. My aunt's bedroom was next to mine, and she always closely attended to me. None of the rooms had any furniture other than rugs on the floors and some cushions to lean against. At night we rolled out mattresses on the floor. The Muslim religion requires that people, poor or rich, live simply. If they have more than they need they should give it to the poor. This helped to bring people closer to each other, created a supportive environment around me.

She took me everywhere with her, to the public baths, to the market to shop, to visit a neighbor. She served me my favorite food, was indulgent with me. I went to bed when I wanted, threw my toys around, roamed through the courtyards freely. She was also full of praise for me, something that motivated me to do well at school, made me more courageous than most girls in the neighborhood.

The three sisters' lives meshed together closely. They all were relieved when the men left the house and they were together without them. For one thing they could do their tasks without covering up (something they would have to do in the presence of the husbands who weren't theirs) and also were able to talk freely. The day in the household started at dawn, when the adults got

out of their beds at the sound of the muezzin, washed ritualisti-
cally in the pool, and then prayed. Aunt Maryam saying the
words "Allah o Akbar" aloud in the midst of silent prayers woke
me if I hadn't already been awoken by the splashing of water
in the pool. I was still too young to pray, but had I lived with
her longer than the nine years, I probably would have been encouraged, maybe even pressured, to do so. After prayers was breakfast, with each family eating in their own quarters—the only meal
that the sisters ate separately, with their immediate families. After breakfast the men left, and my aunts began their household
chores.

At noon the men returned home and we ate lunch, all of us
together, in Aunt Maryam's living room and, on warm days, outside. Females sat separately from men around *sofrehs* (cloths for
food to be arranged on), spread on rugs. A variety of food was always served at each meal—two kinds of rice dishes, two or three
kinds of bread, lamb stew and chicken, green salad and a yogurt
salad, halvah, fruit, and pastries for dessert. The air became aro-
matic with spices—turmeric, mint, saffron. My aunts collected
what was left of the food in plastic bags and gave them to beggars
who came to the door every day. The men left, and the women
continued with their tasks or sat and talked with visitors who began to come in again. Then there were evening prayers. After
prayers we had dinner, which again we all ate together.

Because we had no baths, once a week my aunts took us female cousins to the public baths for women which was near our
house on the other side of the Little Bazaar. (My middle aunt's
three sons went to the baths for men with their father.) A visit to
the baths lasted for hours. With loincloths wrapped around our
naked bodies, we sat on the tiled-covered ground with pans of

steaming water before us. As we scrubbed our bodies and washed our hair, women talked and children carried on their games.

The main topic of conversation among the women was men. How cruel they were, how selfish. All the Shah's claims of equality for women were nonsense, they said. In reality the laws were the same as before, giving all the power to men. Didn't sons inherit twice as much as daughters when their parents died? Wasn't a man allowed to marry more than one woman? Didn't fathers automatically get custody of the children in case of divorce? Wasn't it the simplest thing for a man to divorce his wife, whereas if a woman wanted a divorce she had to give up everything, money, children. The Shah had changed nothing, other than giving women freedom not to wear the *chador* if they chose—but what good did that freedom do when nothing else was right for them, when it was the husbands who could dictate to them whether to wear the *chador* or not. Some of the women had bruises and scars on their bodies. "He comes home angry at the world and beats me up," one woman said. Someone would start crying, and others tried to comfort her by massaging her back or giving her *sharbat* to drink. As the day wore on, everyone became cheerful and laughed a lot because of the sweet intimacy, all the support given.

Once a year, my mother came to Teheran to visit her relatives, my uncles and aunts, and stayed with us part of the time. But she paid no particular attention to me. There was no bond between us. I called my aunt Mother and my own mother Aunt Mohtaram or nothing at all. The fact that she was my biological mother did not have much relevance for me, did not register anything significant. I was afraid of my father, whom I had met once when he came to visit with my mother, a fear I caught from my aunt. "He's very powerful," she told me. My father was a judge (later he had a successful private practice as a lawyer). In addition he owned a cotton-thread factory. His being wealthy and educated made him more powerful in my aunt's eyes than even my other aunts' husbands. And in reality he was. Her worst fear of men, of him in particular, came true later.

When I was nine years old my life changed suddenly. I remember that day vividly. It was an autumn day with a pale, cool sunlight shining on everything. I was playing with a friend in the yard of our elementary school when I saw a man standing on the steps of a hallway, looking for someone. He was thin and short, with a pockmarked face and a brush mustache, but gave the impression somehow of strength, power. He was wearing a fancy-looking suit and a tie, a contrast to the plain clothes that men in the neighborhood, even the male teachers, wore. His face brightened at seeing me, and he began to walk over to me. "Don't you recognize your father?" he said as he reached me. "Let's go. I'm taking you to Ahvaz. I'll explain later."

I stared at him, fear rushing through me. He took my arm firmly and led me outside. "I already spoke to the principal; you aren't coming back here any more. You're reaching an age when you need me to look after you."

I was silent, in shock. I looked back and saw my friends standing by the door of the school, but before I could say anything, my father prodded me forward. Finally I asked, "Does my mother know about this?"

"You mean your aunt. By the time she knows we'll be in the airplane. I sent a message to her through your uncle."

"I want to talk to my mother myself, now."

"Don't call your aunt mother any more. You're going to live with your real mother."

"I want to talk to my mother."

"Your aunt you mean. You'll have a chance to talk to her when she comes for a visit. If she loves you, which I know she does, she'll understand it's better for you to live with us."

"I want to go home and talk to her, let me go, let me go."

"Your home is in Ahvaz from now on."

From the corner of my eyes I saw a woman in a *chador* looking like my aunt. I screamed, "Mother, Mother." Then as the woman came closer I realized she was not my mother-aunt.

"Don't try to put up a fight. It isn't going to do you any good," my father said, raising his hand to hail a cab. "It's all for your own benefit I'm taking you back. You need my supervision."

It was all swift, getting to the airport, on the plane, then riding another taxi to a house that became my second home, one I never adjusted to as long as I lived there.

"You'll like it here, I'm sure," my father said as we entered the house.

We went into a hallway and came into a palm-filled courtyard with a pool at its center. I saw my mother sitting by the pool talking to an old man. She looked at me in a perfunctory way and said distractedly, "That dress doesn't become you." I was wearing a dress with floral designs my aunt and I had picked together from a store. I did not like her own dress, mainly because it was different from the way my aunt dressed. It was in bright pink, which I thought belonged to children's clothes. My aunt's dresses were brown, black, green, navy. My mother was also wearing makeup on her face. It made her seem artificial to me; my aunt never wore makeup.

She got up and embraced me tentatively. Her embrace was weak compared to my aunt's strong one. No, I couldn't think of her as my mother; my aunt was my mother. Then the woman, who was supposed to be my mother, looked at the old man, who turned out to be the live-in servant, and said, "Ali, show her to her room." Her cool reception of me, which did not change during the time I lived with her, was painful.

I followed Ali up the steep stairway to the second floor and then to a room. He left and came back in a few moments with a bundle of clothes, a robe, slippers, a dress, some underwear, which he put on the bed. "I'll come and get you for supper." He left, shutting the door behind him.

I sat in the unfamiliar room, shivering, even though the temperature must have been above ninety degrees. Then I lay down on the bed with my own clothes still on. My body curved uncomfortably in the soft springs, being used to a mattress against the hard floor. The spikes of the palm tree in front of the window were threatening. In my aunt's house we didn't have palm trees, Teheran was a much cooler city. We had a plum tree, cypress trees, rose bushes.

Finally I fell asleep and kept dreaming about my aunt.

My aunt had no legal right to me, but even if she had, my father would have been able to take me back. My aunt came to Ahvaz soon after to take me back. She cried and begged, but my father was adamant in keeping me. My mother, who perhaps found me to be a burden, would have complied. My aunt and I parted tearfully, and soon it became clear that the home my aunt had made for me was shattered forever. I saw her only for holidays, when I was allowed to go for a visit or when she came to visit us.

My parents' house was large and had all the modern conveniences—phone, refrigeration, city-supplied water, showers—but to me it was a cold place, because of not sensing any love from my mother. Also it seemed chaotic, not arranged around any steady rituals as my aunt's home had been, something that I missed. My mother already had two boys and two girls before me (three came after me and one of them died), and we all interacted in random ways. Even though we were one family, the connections were loose, it seemed to me.

Scenes from my parents' home come to me. I am in the kitchen. It is eight o'clock in the morning, and sunlight, already harsh, is pouring into the room as some of us siblings and our parents sit around the long wooden table to eat breakfast. I feel cut off, neglected by my mother, who doesn't look at me once, who keeps complaining about the day ahead; there is so much to do: shopping, cooking for so many children, buying one thing for one child and something else for another, taking care of so many needs. It is as if I am the one she is mainly complaining about, since the others have always been there. A little later we all disperse. I need school supplies. I go to my father's office, a room in the house, to ask for money. I am afraid of him, his stern aura, his volatile manner, but at least he doesn't ignore me like Mother does. He is standing on the balcony outside of his study looking out, contemplating something. "I need a new notebook and a new pen."

"That's your mother's territory. Go and ask her. And remember, call her Mother. Since you have been here, you haven't addressed her once."

She isn't my mother, I think to myself. She doesn't treat me like her child. But I don't dare say it aloud because he slapped me when I said that to him before. She is on the terrace putting pieces of ice into a pitcher. I go and stand silently beside her, not addressing her in any way, until she looks at me. "I need money to buy a notebook and a pen."

She doesn't answer. Her hair, which she has set in a perma-nent, and the tight jersey dress she is wearing remind me how dif-ferent she looks from my aunt. Her paying so much attention to her appearance is upsetting to me at that stage of my life. I can't help it, I shout, "I want to go back to my aunt. She's my mother."

"Manoochehr," she calls out to my father. "Manoochehr."

"What's going on?" he comes over to us.

"You must talk to her. She's giving me trouble."

"I want to go back," I say.

"This is your home. Apologize to your mother, and every-thing will be fine."

"I won't." I didn't do anything, I think to myself.

He grabs my arm. "Go on, say 'I'm sorry, Mother.'"

I say nothing.

"Say 'I'm sorry, *Mother*.'"

I start to run to my room. He catches up with me. "Go back there and call her Mother."

"I won't, I won't," I say as I get into my room and lock it from the inside.

At other times, too, whenever I need something my father sends me to my mother. Her answer to my requests is mainly no rather than yes, which I was used to with my aunt. No, you can't buy a new dress. No, you can't invite that friend over. No, no, no. My responses range from a slam of a door, to bursting into tears, to saying, "Why, why can't I?" None of that changes anything.

It is late afternoon on another day. I am miserable and lonely for my aunts, my cousins, friends. I go over to my father in his study and say once again, "I want to go back home, to my aunt. She's my mother." I persist though it has not worked so far.

"I told you not to ever say that." He holds my hand and brings me to my mother, who is fretting with Ali in the kitchen. "Say 'Mother, I love you . . .' Go on, say 'I love you, Mother.'"

I remain silent. My mother is silent, too, and is avoiding looking at me.

"Say it now," he says.

"Get her away from me," my mother says.

My father walks away briskly, maybe hoping my mother and I will have an easier connection when he isn't present.

Instead my mother mumbles, "Get out of my sight now."

The cough I developed since I came to live with my parents has become chronic. Pressure builds in my chest, and I cough and cough as I run into my room.

It is a few days later. My cough has become worse. My father takes me to a doctor. The doctor asks me a few questions and examines my ears, throat. Then he says, addressing my father, "Nothing is wrong with her, it's all nerves." He gives my father a prescription to fill for me.

Outside Father says to me, "You heard what the doctor said. Your cough doesn't have a real basis. If you try to relax and view your mother as a mother you'll be fine."

"My mother doesn't love me."

"If you show her that you love her, she'll show you that she loves you."

"She won't." I know that instinctively because I don't sense even the tiniest spark of love from her.

I was lonely in my parents' home until my oldest sister, Pari, began to become my friend. She had been lonely in the middle of her own family, she said. She was five years older than me, and she remembered when my grandmother took me away. She had missed me for days.

We both came to the conclusion that our mother's degree of attention, of love, for her children was unequal and not easy to understand. Pari, the daughter who came after my brothers, was neither the target of our mother's hostility, nor the focus of her attention. Whereas I had a feeling that my mother deliberately tried to obliterate me, Pari felt forgotten. She had to shout to get my mother's attention. Finally Mother would sigh and say something like "All right, I heard you. . . . Go get what you want. Leave me alone now." In my case she just looked away in anger or irritation or called my father over to say to him that I was acting too demanding. "You say she already needs another pair of shoes." "How many notebooks a week does she need?" She lavished a great deal of attention on one sister, the one who was two years older than me and three years younger than Pari. If we challenged Mother about her favoritism she would try to justify it. She preferred her oldest son to her younger one, she said, because he survived after two, who had been born before him, had died of childhood illnesses. She claimed that Pari was strong enough not to need much attention, whereas our middle sister needed more attention because she was weak and sickly. Of me she said, "It's her own fault; she's always giving me trouble." Perhaps her feelings toward me were the most complicated and irrational because

she had given me away to her sister. It could even be out of loyalty
to her sister that she did not want to love me; she did not want to
compete with her sister for my love.

When I think back, I see my mother as a child playing
house, treating her children like dolls. She made a great deal of
our looks. Pari was "healthy looking." Indeed her skin glowed as if
there were light behind it, and her expression was vibrant. I was
"too thin."

Perhaps Mother never had the chance to grow up, become an
adult. She was only nine years old when she got married and had
her first child at fourteen. She gave birth to a total of ten, three of
whom died: two boys, the first ones born, and one girl, who came
after me. The legal minimum age for a girl to marry at that time in
Iran was nine. (That could have had something to do with the
fact that my father took me back when I was nine; he saw me as
reaching adulthood, needing his supervision more.) As soon as
Mother reached that age, she was married to him, a man selected
for her by her parents. Father was her second cousin on her
mother's side. He was twenty-five years older than she and was already a lawyer. They were married in Teheran, where their parents lived; then he took her to Ahvaz.

He was not ashamed of the fact that people often took her to
be his daughter. It was common practice at the time, and to some
extent now, too, for husbands to be much older than their wives.
In fact he talked openly to us about how on their wedding night
Mother had been so small that he had had to lift her off the
ground and, holding her in his arms, put her into the carriage that
would transport them to the wedding reception. Their relationship was like father-daughter: he often treated her as one of

us children. He corrected her vocabulary, explained to her the proper way to act with guests. He even put her on his lap and read to her as he did sometimes to us.

My mother learned to read and write only after she got married; my father hired tutors for her. He wanted her to be educated (at least to some extent) and dress in a modern way. So she read books and magazines; wore clothes imported from the United States, put on makeup and nail polish, set her hair in a permanent.

But the fact that my father wanted my mother to be modern did not mean that he wanted her to be an independent woman, have a career, have strong opinions on her own. He still was a traditional Iranian husband and father. That meant that his wife had to devote herself to her domestic chores and her children.

He was in charge of the big decisions. Mother went along with him on all issues. (If she disagreed she did not say so.) Their goal for their daughters was to marry us off right after high school (if not sooner) to men they selected. Then we were to become good wives and mothers, giving up any individual ambitions and settling for a life of domesticity and subservience to our husbands. My brothers though were to have professional careers and be good providers for their own families, when they had them. (They both went to America to attend universities soon after I came to live with my parents. It was fashionable for parents who could afford it to send their children, mainly sons, abroad for their education.)

It was not only because we had similar feelings toward our mother that drew Pari and me close together. It was also because we rebelled against our prescribed roles. We did not look to our mother as a model. By then, even though I still loved and missed my aunt and thought of her as my mother, I did not see the way she and my other aunts lived as ideal either. They were in constant fear of men, had no aspirations other than running the household.

Instead Pari and I searched for models in the more independent, glamorous women we saw in American movies, dubbed into Farsi, and read about in books by American writers available in Farsi translation. Ahvaz had a large oil refinery with some American employees. So there were movies and shops catering to their interests. The Shah, also, encouraged Westernization.

Pari loved movies; the two of us would go to see whatever was shown—they were usually a decade old—in the two cinemas in town. Then we would stop on the main street at a shop that carried photographs of actors and actresses, and she would buy a few—of Elizabeth Taylor, Paul Newman—to add to an album she kept. She also had an interest in acting. I can still vividly see her standing on the stage of our high school's auditorium (a school for girls only—a high school for boys stood in another part of the town), wearing striped pajamas, a mustache, and dancing and singing along with other girls dressed similarly, doing an imitation of an American musical.

My interest was mainly in reading, and then I began to dream of becoming a writer myself. "I wrote a story today," I would say as soon as I found Pari in one of the many rooms in our large, outlandish house. I would sit next to her on the rug and read to her. She always lavished me with praise, the same way I praised her when she practiced the part for the high school play and then parts she would copy from movies and act out. I dreamed of writing something that she would act in.

Our father was critical of Pari's aspiration to act, calling her "foolish and impractical." He said, "An actress is a whore," following a common belief that actresses slept around, did sexual favors for directors and producers. His attitude toward my writing was not as negative, though he was afraid of the written word, the "wrong" kind of message it could convey.

I lost Pari's support in the household when she was forced to get married. Although our parents were not fanatical in their practice of the Muslim religion—we did not have to cover up when we went out, we did not even pray—they still embraced many of the values of the culture, an amalgam of Western ideas and old-fashioned, traditional ones, some dictated by religion. They believed in arranged marriage, for instance. Pari, being the oldest daughter, was expected to get married before all of us sisters. One afternoon, when she was eighteen and I thirteen, I came home and found her sitting in her room, crying.

"What's wrong?" I asked.

"A suitor is here with his mother. They're in the living room. Do you want to see what he looks like?"

The two of us walked softly, slowly, to the living room. We took turns looking through the keyhole. Our parents were sitting with a man and a woman on the maroon velvet sofa and the two matching armchairs and having tea. The suitor was thin and tall and had a desiccated, humorless face. We walked back to Pari's room. "Did you see his ears? They were sticking out," she said.

In a moment our father came to the door of the room and said to Pari, "Come in now; his mother wants to talk to you."

Pari got up reluctantly and followed him.

An hour or so later, from my room, I heard an argument going on the porch. The suitor and his mother must have left.

"I don't want to marry him," Pari was saying.

"Be sensible," Mother said. "When you have your own children you'll be happy to have a husband who can provide well
for them."

"You want to marry a poor teacher who can barely support
himself?" Father said. He was referring to a high-school teacher, at
the boys' school, on whom Pari had a crush. He, too, liked Pari
and had once sent his mother over to ask for Pari's hand. My parents had said no.

A little later Pari said to me bitterly, "They're selling me. He
has nothing but money to recommend him." We both blamed our
mother more than our father. Pari said, "She's a woman; she
should understand her daughters better," and I agreed.

She argued with them, day after day, and they kept insisting
how foolish she would be to give up such a candidate. She finally
gave in but partly because she hoped she would be able to pursue
acting after getting married. The suitor, Mohajelli, had said he
would take her to Teheran after they got married, and in the big
city she would be able to find what she wanted. Once they were
married he immediately denied having made that promise.

Before the wedding reception a Muslim priest came to our
house and, reading from the Koran, married Pari and Mohajelli.
The reception followed, in the garden of a club. The place was
decorated with bright lights for the occasion, and a musician and
belly dancer performed. The food was plentiful, and its aroma
filled the air. Pari was wearing an expensive diamond on her finger and emerald earrings and a matching emerald necklace, given
to her by the groom. She looked beautiful and rich. But my most
vivid image of her from that evening, one that lingers the most

strongly with me, is the expression on her face. As she sat in her wedding gown next to her dark-suited husband she looked a million miles away.

A few months later, on a visit home, she said to me, "Don't ever give in to marrying someone they pick for you. I feel like a prisoner."

I managed to evade the forces that trapped Pari by fighting and fighting with my parents, trying to convince them to send me to the United States. It was a long battle, full of arguments and tears, but I did not give up as easily as Pari did. My strong will finally wore my parents out.

One evening at the dinner table, with both my mother and father present, I said suddenly, propelled by a churning defiance inside me. "I didn't choose to be your child."

My father flushed. "What is this nonsense?"

"You forced me to come here, now you force me to do whatever you want."

My outburst was provoked by my father's having taken away a book in translation I was reading. It was a book called *Mother* by the Russian writer Maxim Gorky. I had been drawn to it because of its title, being preoccupied by the issue of motherhood. As it turned out it was a political book about the country Russia. Still I liked reading it and was upset that Father had taken it away from me. He was acting on his fear that I was reading a banned book and would not listen to my reasoning that I would never show it to anyone outside the family. I had bought it in a bookstore that sold books in translation secretly. Even under the Shah (and more so under the new government) books in translation were considered to be "dangerous," spreading the "wrong" ideas among young people.

"See the way she talks," my mother said.

My father got up from his seat and came toward me, his hand raised, about to hit me. I got up too and ran into my room before he reached me.

A few days after that fight, I found my father standing at the door of my school. My heart began to beat loudly, afraid of why he had come there. We had not exchanged a word since my outburst. I followed him to the park, a few blocks away from the school. We did not talk until we were sitting in the shade of the awning in the park's café. After he ordered lunch for both of us he said, "I'm going to let you go. I asked your brother to send application forms for you to fill for a women's college near him. He will look after you."

"You're sending me to America?" I mumbled, incredulous.

"I know sooner or later you're going to get all of us into trouble, the way you talk, those books you read . . . writing things . . . My license could be taken away because of you."

He was referring to the fact that anything could be interpreted as "anti-government." Under the Shah, with his huge secret police force, people were arrested and put in jail with the slightest provocation. The books in translation I read, the essays and stories I wrote and read in my composition class, all of that could make me a suspect, a "revolutionary."

He thought for a moment and added, "Besides things between your mother and you didn't turn out as I hoped. I can tell her what to do, but I can't change her feelings."

He was letting me go, and that was all that mattered to me.

Not only was I admitted, but I was offered a full scholarship that covered room, board, and tuition. My situation had changed so suddenly that for days I could not quite believe it. I went up and down in my moods, fantasizing about going away and then falling into despair that it would not happen, that Father would change his mind.

Then it really happened. Father came into my room and said, "We have to update your passport and get you a visa. You'll leave by September so you won't miss the first days of college."

On the day that I was leaving, he came to the doorway of my room and said coldly, "Go away, go, you're giving your mother so much trouble." That remark may have been meant for my mother, who must have been complaining to him about something that I might have done to displease her. He left the house, saying he had an important business meeting and could not go to the train with me. My mother left the house, too, without trying to say even a warm good-bye to me. Ali was the only one who accompanied me to the train station.

As I was descending the back stairway I thought, I will never climb those steps again. The road for me went only one way, away from home, from my parents, particularly my mother. In America I managed to go my own way. My brother was not really looking after me. He had his own life to lead, and by then he was too Americanized to follow my father's expectation that he protect me.

I met my husband on my own, in a class I was attending at the New School University in New York City, where I had come immediately after graduating from the small women's college near St. Louis, and stayed on in the United States.

I feel that having been raised by my aunt was the best thing that happened to me, a good fortune Pari was deprived of. I was an only child to my aunt, and she could pay a great deal of attention to me and she genuinely loved me.

The only benefit I had from the trauma of being torn from her home and forced into my parents' is that it made me think about things. I did not choose my aunt's or my mother's ways of life. I chose a third alternative. But I cannot say that I have not paid any price for my independence. Although I am in contact with my family by phone, letters, and visits to Iran, my aunt and Pari are not an integral part of my life, can not be because of the huge distance between Iran and America, and because of the vastly different ways we live. I am sad too that Pari got trapped while I have achieved many of my goals. The last time I spoke with her on the phone she asked me, "Are you still writing?" I wished I could have said, "Do you have a part in a new play?"

I am not angry at my mother as I used to be. I can see that her life has been limiting, difficult. But still, up to now, it is my aunt I consider to be my mother. I still address her as Mother and I have a hard time calling my mother Mother.

A LITTLE DEATH

PAM LEWIS

❖ ❖ ❖

Just before ten my mother and father go out riding. I watch them from behind the curtain as they stride across the flats to the corral. Anyone would think, seeing them, that this is the way they always are, walking in step, with purpose and authority. Anyone would think they are never any different. They are that convincing. Even to me.

On a horse, she has the rigid posture of an Eastern riding school and many years of lessons, and she sits a horse, even in those bulky, high-backed western saddles with the ridiculous phallus in the front, absolutely straight. He slouches in the saddle, but he makes up for it by taking the lead. I step out from behind the curtain and watch as they cross the plain toward the mountains. I'm sure he hums for mile upon mile.

Later I go swimming in the pond with Buddy Wilson. It has recently rained, and the water in the pond is fresh enough. I pull myself up on a rubber raft quickly and with so much force that I spill over the other side, letting Buddy see my ass. I know what I am doing without knowing for sure what I am doing. I circle under the raft and come up next to him in the water, daring him to grab me or splash me. But he really is fighting for possession of the raft and takes the opportunity to grab it and swim off with it.

Later in the afternoon, I am back in the cabin, alone in my room. I look at myself in the mirror. My hair, which is long and thick, is still faintly damp and smells of pond water. It tumbles across my face. I brush it out in long even strokes so it gleams. I pull it across one eye like the movie stars. It is wavy and dark blonde touched with gold, and I know it is extremely beautiful. Just then my mother comes in. She sits down on the bed and takes the brush from me. She brushes the hair off my face, straight back as though she is about to braid it. She's got it all caught up in her hand in back, a fat fragrant ponytail. We both turn to look at our reflection in the mirror. She's smiling at me. I look very young without my hair.

"That's better," she says.

"Am I pretty?" It's a terrifying question. One I've never thought, until this moment, to ask.

"Of course you are," she says, but it's a brusque, unconvincing answer. Then she lets the hair go. I reach up to loosen the thick knot of hair at the nape of my neck. I shake it out, and when I look up I'm glamorous again. She grabs the hair again, this time much more roughly, snapping my neck back with the force of the gesture. "Too pretty for your own good," she says and leaves.

It's been like this since my father came to stay with us for August. My mother has been irritable and angry. Angry at me. They drink more than usual. I'm having to be very careful about what I say and do. Like this business with the hair. I know it has to do with Buddy Wilson, and slithering over the raft hoping to be chased, and with brushing my hair this new way and asking questions about beauty. It's all connected, and it means I'll have to be more careful.

In the evening, the adults talk about driving into Jackson. I know the road to be long and straight and poorly lit. As they get closer to making a decision I go into the kitchen and eat a spoonful of powdered mustard from the cabinet. I drink a glass of warm water on top of that and then a glass of milk. Then I sit down outside next to my mother. I wait and then plunge my head between my knees. "I feel sick," I tell her.

She reaches over and helps me sit up, then she holds my head in her lap, stroking my hair. And soon I really do feel sick. "Please don't go," I whisper in a strangled voice before bolting for the tall grass and vomiting.

"I think we'd better not," my mother tells my father and the Wilsons, the people who have moved into one of the other cabins on the ranch. It is all I can do to keep my relief from showing. Even with my stomachache, I feel great all of a sudden. They take the liquor from our cabinets and carry it over to the Wilsons, but I don't have to worry because they can't have a car crash.

After dark, Gladys Shoor, the old, leathery woman who owns the ranch, comes to our cabin with Buddy Wilson. "Come on," she tells me. She has bearskins with her. "Let's surprise them."

Across the flat I can see them lit by candlelight through the summer screens. It is still early enough to see where the white mortar holds together the cedar logs of the cabin. Although it's getting dark where we are in the valley, the Grand Teton is still brilliant at its summit. It's a beautiful night.

We creep to the Wilsons' under our bearskins and watch

through the window. My father is standing by himself at one end of the room staring at the floor and swaying. The Wilsons and my mother are at the other side of the room laughing. It's odd to see my father off to himself like that. Gladys throws open the door and leaps into the room under her bearskin. Buddy does the same. He's like a child in kindergarten, making bear noises and lumbering around on all fours. I just stand in the door and watch, the bear head on top of mine.

I see my father lurch, lose his balance, and fall, crashing into the table of bottles and glasses. And then he gets on all fours, like Buddy. The others look at him and laugh. Someone takes the bearskin from Gladys and throws it over my father. He lumbers around under the fur, its old sparse head bobbing on his shoulder. Everyone laughs, even my mother. I run from the room and back to our cabin. I hide out in my bed, looking up at the sky through the window. It's a perfect night. The sky is black, and the stars look as though you could just sweep them together and gather them up with your hands.

Later that night, the door to my room opens. Light floods in, and I can see my parents in silhouette. My mother is leaning against my father's side. She's much smaller than he is and a little bit behind. It's the sudden intrusion of a fire drill at school. They probably only intended to make sure I was asleep before they left the house, but when I wake up, they invite me to come with them.

"We're going to swim in the Snake," my father says to me. "Do you want to come?"

"Yes." Swimming in the Snake has always been forbidden. It is a swift and dangerous river.

"Just put on your robe," he says. "And come on." It is curious, I think, that they don't tell me to get my suit. We get into the car, and I realize that something is wrong. My mother's giggling like a girl. My father weaves along the dirt road, running down sage bushes to either side. I hold tight to the door handle, ready to jump if the car goes over the edge and down to the river.

When we get to the spot, my father turns off the motor but leaves the headlights on. They shine on the thick treetops of the opposite bank. We sit in the sudden stillness. Below us I can hear the river's roar. My father gets out of the car and slams the door. He undresses right there. In order to prevent myself from watching him, I get out on the other side, hidden from him, and take off my nightgown. My mother stays inside the car.

He starts down the steep riverbank, his skin green in the half light, seeming all limbs as he picks his way down the stony bank, touching it with his hands often for balance. And then he loses his footing and slides, clutching at loose stones. From where I stand I see him fall and roll like an ungainly doll, loose and easy. He rolls away into the night, out of our sight. I lunge down the bank, falling, too, rolling down the stones to where my father lies at the water's edge.

When I pull at his arm to make him sit up, he grabs at me for balance and pulls my face down across his lap. In the dark, with my mother still screaming on the bank above us, my father claws at me like a drowning man while I struggle to be free.

Sometime during the night as I slept, my father has come into my bed, and I wake in the morning with him beside me. His white smooth shoulder rises above me, blocking my view. The smell of his back is slightly rancid, a stronger version of the smell of my parents' closet. He has scratches on his back, fine black lines dot-ted with tiny beads of dried blood. Over us muslin curtains with red rickrack billow into the room on a whiff of breeze. I watch them fill up and slacken, in and out. Grasshoppers have started to sing. It will be a hot day.

I have to get from the bed without waking him. I try to slither down to the end, but I am pinned between him and the wall. As I squirm to get out, I realize that I am naked. My breasts, still small, rub against his back, my thighs and stomach move along his buttocks. Feeling me, he wakes enough to reach out behind him and stroke my hip. His hand leaves me, returns to himself. I can see his elbow moving in a slow rhythm as he strokes his own genitals. Then he reaches back to me again. His hand feels me blindly, awkwardly flicking my nipples with the tops of his fingers, then reaching down, groping at my crotch. At first I lie frozen, waiting for him to realize who I am and what he is doing, and to stop without me having to stop him. But he is doing it in sleep. He doesn't know who I am or where he is. It is up to me to get out of the bed, to save us both from what we are doing.

I slip down to the end of the bed away from him. My pajama bottoms are twisted around my feet, and the tops lie under his legs. I pull up the bottoms, grab a towel to cover my breasts and run from the room, suddenly frightened and thinking only that I must get out, I must run and run.

I get as far as the front porch. It is very early, before anyone is stirring, the time of day I've hated ever since that morning. I sit down in one of the cowhide chairs on the porch. Our cabin is set a hundred yards back from the edge of the river. From where I am I can see the tops of the trees that grow in the river bottoms. I sit there for a very long time watching the unmoving landscape. In a while I hear my mother making coffee. I go inside, letting the screen door bang behind me. She looks up from what she is doing. I still hold the towel across my chest. It is cold in the cabin, a chill left over from the night before. I wait for her to speak, but she too says nothing. I must look guilty and ashamed to her or awful in some unspeakable way because she suddenly turns from me in anger, pulls out a frying pan, and lets it drop onto the stove. What is wrong? Not able to go closer to her and not able to go back into my room because of my father, I have to go back outside to the porch. The sun is coming in full now, blazing hot over me as only a western sun can. I sit back down. In a while the heat of the sun feels so good that I let the towel slip down so I can feel the sun's clean warmth on my skin.

My mother catches me like this. She throws open the screen door. I jump and jerk the towel up to cover myself, but it is too late. She slams the door and goes back into the kitchen.

I take a dark green cardigan from the hook next to the door and put it on to cover myself. Then, barefoot, and still in my pajama bottoms, I walk toward the river. I kick up little plumes of dust with my big toes so my mother can see where I am if she is watching. I can hear the steady wind-sound of the Snake River. I stop at the top of the bank and watch the dark blue uneven water rushing. It is so high and so fast there are white caps on it as well as the usual white water breaking around stones. I have to walk down the bank along the trail and through the soggy stretches of river bottom. I sit at the edge of the bank for several minutes, just watching the river. Once in a while I turn back to see if my mother is coming after me, but she isn't. I strain to see her, thinking perhaps she will be watching me from the window and worried about me, but the cabin windows are black rectangles against the log-and-mortar walls.

It is lush with trees here and moist as a rain forest. I make my way through the dense underbrush. In the distance I see two moose grazing in a clearing, a bull and cow. The bull picks up my scent. He raises his mammoth head, the wide, flat, foolish-looking nose lifted high, then he gives some sort of signal to the cow, and they lope off, out of sight.

I keep walking. Wet black earth squirts between my toes as I make my way. I hear a rustling near me. I stop short, holding my breath. And then I see them, a herd of eight cows that were put out to graze last summer and never returned. People call them wild cows, and until today I've never seen them. They trot past, their coats matted with filth, distended, leathery udders swinging below them like heavy genitalia. Once they pass, I scramble the rest of the way to the river.

I stay a long time at the river's edge, throwing stones, watching them disappear. My bladder presses on me, but I keep holding it back, thinking I should wait until I get back to the cabin. Finally I can't hold it any longer and I crouch at the river's edge and let go with a stream of steaming urine. Seeing how the stones at the water's edge seem to soak up water, I pick up a flat gray stone about the size of my palm and hold it to myself. It is warm from the sun and feels soothing. When I take it away I see it is darkened by urine and stained as well with something darker. I put my fingers there between my legs. It is blood. The smell is something strange, like fish. It's the curse, I think. I will have to tell my mother.

I walk back through the river bottoms unafraid. I am grateful to have something to tell my mother that will make her less angry with me. Something that is not my fault at all.

When I get back to the cabin, Buddy Wilson is there the way

he often is. He makes some remark about the way I look in my pajama bottoms, muddy feet, and green sweater, and I feel I need to defend myself to him.

"They must have had a fight last night," I whisper to him. "Because I woke up this morning, and my father was in my bed." I say it in this joking way just in case it really is funny. I watch Buddy closely for a reaction. "Oh yeah?" he says.

"Pam." My mother has that edge to her voice that she always uses for dogs and sometimes for me. It means come here, fast, now. She has heard me talking to Buddy. I go into the kitchen, where she is standing at the stove. She turns to me, and in a voice bristling with hostility but whispered in a way that Buddy can not possibly hear, she says, "I'm only going to tell you this once." She jabs at the air between us with a spatula. "Don't you ever tell anyone about anything that goes on in this family. Is that understood?" I nod. In that moment, waking up with my father beside me is no longer wrong. The thing that is wrong was the telling about it. My mother turns back to the dishes in the sink. I pick up a towel and start to wipe while she washes. She is much calmer than earlier in the morning. When we get to wiping off the counters, she is beginning to hum.

SLADJANA

GINA SMITH

❖ ❖ ❖

My mother has to be the only child ever imprisoned in a Nazi concentration camp who got to ride around it on a new red tricycle.

She's told me this story for as long as I can remember. It is 1941. She is four. The sky is gray or brown or black. She wonders what happened to the sun. To her brothers. To the little lamb and her favorite little pig in the back of the house. And what about the house? The village?

It is all gone, and there are so many other questions still left over that no one, not even her mama, even tries to answer. Why this stinky smell everywhere? In the buildings, the yards, even the grass, that stinky stink sticks to everyone. And then there are the skinny, scary people to worry about. Their dark, hollow eyes look like the eyes she used to punch out of paper dolls.

Everyone looks like this, everyone. Except the guards, her mama, and that nice German man and lady who gave her this wonderful tricycle.

The tricycle! Amazing. It is the magic of all of this. It shines and it whirs as my four-year-old mother wheels it around in dusty circles, gloriously content to be the center of everyone's attention.

There she is, a toddling half-Gypsy girl with messy brown-gold curls, just basking in it all.

My mother has the kind of luck that allowed her lovely-yet-genetically-unfit little half-Gypsy life to be saved by a childless Nazi couple. Herr und Frau Scheinlein thought she was so cute, it didn't matter that the Roma in her bright almond eyes was a pockmark on the master race.

They took her in and made sure her mother received extra bread—not the moldy kind everyone else choked down with the gutter water, but fresh-baked *Schwartzbrot* right out of Frau Scheinlein's tidy little kitchen. My mother's mother got decent food and treatment for the rest of their stay. Her workload dramatically lightened; she started gaining back weight and hair.

The first time my mother was allowed to see her mother—by then, she felt at home in the rosy, cozy main living area of the Scheinlein's little heimat right on the edge of the camp—my mother hardly recognized her. It was only when her mother called her by her nickname, Cica—pronounced "seetza"—for "pussycat," that my mother ran to a mama's hug she hadn't felt in months.

Eventually, Herr Scheinlein let my mother's mother live in the house and work as his translator for German to Serbo-Croatian and back. And after the Americans liberated the camp, my mother, her mother, and the little red trike caught the next train back to Montenegro.

Now that is some kind of luck.

Luck? Vell. I vouldn't say luck." My mother tells me this over cocktails at the Bali Hai. Her eyes, half closed, are the color of deepest amber. And I see a glint of secrecy, too, as if she's about to reveal something hidden and delicious. The truth, it is sweet, sweet as the candied cherries the bartender slips me every now and then. I scavenge for the truth in everything, why everything works like it does, how I got here, how she got here, how she got out.

By now, I have a good idea about the huge numbers of Gypsies and part-Gypsies who were shot or gassed to death at Auschwitz-Birkenau from 1941 to 1945, the same four years she lived there.

"I vas just cute," she says, shrugging. "Cute like a Shirley Temple, you know."

I do know. I am only eight, and already she has schooled me in the superb importance of looking cute at all times. This is second only to developing a "talent" that might get me into Hollywood, New York, Las Vegas, or somewhere equally glamorous. I'm wearing a blue polyester pantsuit with a wide-lapelled yellow blouse and matching blue shoes and pocketbook. I take modeling lessons, singing, jazz, tap, and ballet.

Even at eight, I am desperate to do what she has not: become famous at something, at anything. To marry a rich man with blue eyes. Or at the very least, to have an affair with one who will give me diamonds, money, blonde-haired children.

If the fame thing doesn't work out, my mother's other big dream for me is to go to junior college and become a dental assistant. That way, I can have an affair with a cute, fair-eyed married dentist, no strings attached to me or my future footloose glamorous life.

"Don't attach to vun man," she tells me. "De only ones dey treat vell are de mistresses." And above all, don't marry a doctor, because "dey all tink dey're Jesus Christ."

It is 1972, and she is in fact the consummate mistress. Wearing a leopard-print jumpsuit cut nearly to the navel, she strides on five-inch platforms and dons super-sized, sequin-rimmed tinted glasses. They are the kind of glasses Elton John will make famous two or three years later.

"So why were you saved when all those other people died?" I want to know. I can never hear enough about the terrible Nazis and what happened in Cell Block B2E, the "Gypsy family camp" where she and my grandmother lived at first. But I hate the part she tells about the two guys she saw hanging, one of them missing a shoe, a single foot hanging white and bare. It gives me nightmares.

"Oh, Gina, deez is depressing and it making me sick." She spits when she talks, an unfortunate habit I seem to have inherited. "Can vee pleeeze stop?"

A little bit of red lipstick smudges her teeth, but before I can tell her about it, she puts a little finger in her mouth and sucks on it fast and hard.

Lady's trick. The lipstick is gone.

"Vaiter!" She rolls her r's like the waves of the sea we hear rolling just under the window.

"Vaiter," she calls again loudly. More spit. More eyes on us. I hate this, I hate the attention. "Come here, pleeeze!"

It's an emergency. "I need nother martini."

One more martini. It is always another martini. They arrive early and often because we are regulars here at the Bali Hai. For the most part, I'm okay with this. I like the Don Ho–type decorations. I just plain like Don Ho.

At the Bali Hai, tikis hang from the ceiling, and mirrors shine on every wall. A giant mural of Hawaiian hula girls—it must be forty feet long—covers the entire back wall. In it, the hula girls (and some hula guys, if you can believe that) dance in a line going so far back you can hardly see the last one. That last dancer is so tiny. There are thirty-two hula people, and I know; I count them again, just to make sure.

The mural is an endless source of amusement for me while my mother hangs around the bar before dinner and after. It is a good night if the guy at the piano, we call him Big John, doesn't ask her to join him with a little tambourine and a dance. I used to think this was great and be proud of her. Now it is starting to bug me.

The same goes for the mirrors all over the place. I can't stand seeing my mother and me reflected together in the same glass slab. My face is a little mush ball compared to her bright angles, up-slit eyes, and sharp red mouth. Her teeth are wet and white, perfect squares.

She gets her martini. I get another Shirley Temple. When she's had her three, we'll order the same thing we always do: Delmonico steak with french fries for me and a prime rib (rare) for her.

Later on, I will coach her driving from the backseat as we drive the short half mile along A1A back home in her 1972 white Corvette Stingray. She has a pillow on the seat so she can reach the pedals with her tiny, manicured feet. She always drives barefoot.

"No, Mama, go left. No, not that far left! That's in the other lane . . . Make a right . . ."

We repeat this routine three or four times a week. She loves the Bali Hai.

And I love her, love her so desperately that I get nightmares about her dying in a car crash, or running away, or just disappearing altogether. I think she'd just poof into whatever weird and magical world she came from, a world I could never be a part of.

Sometimes, when she is hung over, she tells me she wishes she could run away and start all over again.

She would just leave me right here, right here all alone.

Who would take care of me?

Sometimes, I wake up in the middle of the night, my pillow just soaking at the idea.

The nights we are not at the Bali Hai I am force-fed a painfully wide variety of Yugoslavian cuisine. It's embarrassing food that I go to great lengths to hide from my friends. Runny, bloody beets. Stinky sauerkraut that my very best friend Laura says she can smell all the way up the street. And vinegary asparagus out of a can, which is the worst.

Then there's the *cevapcici*, pronounced "che-vop-chee-chee." The little rolled-up spicy sausages mixed with sharp, raw white onions remind me of cat turds. I try to feed them to Daisy, our Chihuahua, who will eat anything. But even Daisy knows enough to refuse the *cevapcici*. No one I know has to eat this gross kind of food.

As usual, my mother washes everything down with a series of martinis, beginning at "cocktail hour" at 4 P.M. By 8 or 9 P.M. she's out cold, and I can do anything I want.

I make sure none of my friends come over after 5 P.M. I can't let them see what happens here. I can always leave, though. One of my favorite things to do is walk down to the beach; it's only a few houses away. All my friends are jealous of all this freedom I have after dinner hour.

Their parents always call them home at some point. They're eating lasagna, or watching *The Waltons*, or playing Scrabble, or who knows what. But not me. I stay and build sand castles in the dark.

When I am nine years old and my daddy has already been dead two years, this wish consumes me. I just want to be a regular kid, and "regular" is something I can define by what it is not. It means your parents (and you have two) don't have accents, don't wear things like turbans and platform shoes, and don't spend days at a time conducting endless parties, leaving me to baby-sit all the other little kids there.

My best friend Laura lives exactly the life I want. She has strawberry-blonde hair and freckles and a gap between her front teeth I would pay for. Her parents are perfect. Her mother is American, wearing jeans and a T-shirt when she serves us pizza before Sunday night's *Wonderful World of Disney*. Sometimes she offers up syrup-and-banana sandwiches in her syrupy southern accent: "Girls? Would you like a treat tonight?" Her voice never rises above a certain lulling tone. My mother never stops yelling even when she is just talking to you.

I want us to be just like them. Hearing this, my mother thinks I am an idiot. We are, she says, beautiful people destined for beautiful things like rich men and diamonds and "maybe, maybe if you rrrreally lucky, maybe even you be famous!"

Plus, my mother adds, "Laura mama have fat ass. Aren't you proud of your beautiful mama?"

I am. If you are smart and beautiful, there is no end to what you can achieve, she says, and I believe it.

I do hold out hope I will be beautiful. It's a long shot, what with all the mosquito bites and the hairy legs and Dumbo-sized feet. Already twice the dainty size of my mother's, my feet even have hair on the toes. It is disgusting. I grimly wait for who knows what other features to appear out of my unsuspecting body.

But smart, I already know. I know I'm smart; I hear it all the time. And I have just learned that I am about to skip the fifth grade. It is more important to be smart than beautiful, Mama finally tells me. And it is okay if I just end up "interesting-looking" instead of the drop-dead Sophia Loren looks we had both been pulling for.

I try not to hear that. We both know it is a lie. Interesting-looking is a disappointment. It's the worst we could hope for. I worry so hard I will fail her with this.

But I do trust her. After all, she is my mama, and there is no one else.

But I worry, worry so hard that I can find relief only in picking at my cuticles or scratching my mosquito bites until they bleed and leave little white scars.

For one thing, I can't stand her constant drinking. No one else's mama does this. When I ask her why she doesn't stop, she says, "Vat else I supposed to do? Drink soda pop."

Also, I have just learned some really disturbing things.

The first thing is, I am "lucky to be alive." She told me that she was just hours away from getting an abortion in Miami before a stop on Worth Avenue in Palm Beach and "de most beautiful dress I ever saw" stopped her cold. Instead of driving two hot more hours and getting an illegal abortion, she bought the dress. It was bright red, with Spanish-looking ruffles around the top.

"I figure I need child sooner or later, so vhy not now? And dat vaz you!" I know I am supposed to be pleased about this, but I somehow can't get that feeling going.

The second piece of information is even worse: Daddy, the one who died just two years ago on Valentine's Day, turns out not to be her second husband and not my Daddy at all. She says her first husband was Clifford—okay, I know her friend Clifford—but Clifford isn't my father, either. She knows that because Clifford, who is a merchant marine, was away at sea before I was born.

My mother tells me "the trute" just before his relatives arrive from out west. Very quickly, almost as an aside, she says, "Gina, you know that Daddy didn't meet you till you were two, he not your real Daddy. Remember?"

I don't remember, but I am crying too much to make much sense of it all. And later, when my crying finally stops, I am left with only a question:

So who is my father?

And Mama won't say. She just won't. No matter how many times I ask her, she won't. It makes me so mad when I think about it that I bang the piano as hard as I can when I am practicing. But she never acts as if she notices.

Sometimes, when she is really drunk I think I can trick her into telling me, but nothing works. I am the only kid at school I know who doesn't know who her real father is.

s it . . . Vic Damone?" We are at the Bali Hai again, same martini and Shirley Temples in front of us as usual. I am ten by now, and I want to get the answers out of her while there is still enough of her left to answer.

This had been the day of the president's physical fitness test for the sixth grade, and some girl on the field asked me if I'd ever heard of Vic The Moan. She is the same mean girl who, a year ago, started calling me Regina in a way that rhymed with vagina. In the same way my mother's name, Sladjana, can be made to rhyme with vagina. Regina Vagina, Sladjina Vagina. We are the Vagina family. I pray every night this will pass, this will pass . . .

But on this day, the girl on the field told me that her mother told her that he was a singer my mother went out with, and that the whole town knew I was his "bastard" child. I'd heard the word before, but only when my mother was referring to one of her boyfriends. Or sometimes, she might say it to someone playfully, like, "Oh, don't be a bastard . . ."

"Don't be ridiculous, Gina," my mother says, and she has that rising tone in her voice that says she could start yelling at me any minute.

But the next day she sits me down next to her dusty collection of Twist and Presley LPs. And there, among them, is one by Vic Damone, signed on the cover with a thick magic marker: To Sladjana, Love and Kisses, your Vick-y.

My heart pounds like a happy rabbit. I have a father, yes! And he's famous! Yes!

"Oh, Gina," my mother says, stirring a martini extra slowly with a skewered olive. Her voice is soft, and she has a faraway look in her eye, gazes just past me. "Vic Damone vaz handsome man, lovely man. Famous singer from New York. He came to visit Daytona many times, thought the beach vaz so beautiful . . ."

"But is he my father?" I know he is. I just know he is. I start praying for this as fast as I can under my breath—please, let him be my father, please let him be my father—trying to get the prayers to reach heaven faster than my mother's words will reach me. But it doesn't work.

"No." She says it abruptly, a bullet firing straight at me. It hits my heart, and I look at her numbly, stupidly, wondering maybe if all of this is just a game, some kind of trick to keep me guessing.

"He nutting to you. No more qvestions. Now eat your steak."

And dat, as she would say, was dat.

And then there is Harry Belafonte.

Here is a great story I used to love to tell at parties, especially when I had everyone's attention and was glorying in the dead center of it.

One time, sometime around fall of 1963, my mother read in some celebrity fan magazine that her longtime celebrity idol, Harry Belafonte, was playing at a club. In New York City. Barely able to speak English, but perfectly able to drive, she grabbed her mother-in-law's pink 1960 Cadillac and drove the three plus days from Daytona Beach up Highway 95 to New York City. Drove it straight.

Once she found the nightclub where Harry Belafonte was supposedly playing, she parked the car and changed into a shiny black dress and pointy heels. "It vaz the longest vak of my life," she says now. But at the door, she was refused because she didn't have a husband or escort with her. A small tip took care of that, and the host immediately seated her along the side, where the club was more dimly lit.

My mother waved the waiter over like he was the last waiter on earth. She immediately ordered two double martinis—for courage, she says—and teetered her way on four-inch spikes toward the stage, then around it to the back. She practically broke a heel off, trying to get down those stairs so quickly. But she made it, and knocked on the only door she saw.

"Who is it?"

"It's me-ee," she sang. "Sladjana. For Harry."

Unbelievably, or maybe inevitably, the door opens, and inside she sees sitting around a table of highballs and paperwork, Harry Belafonte, Diahann Carroll, and various others. I can only imagine what they must've seen: this young, dark, and exotic girl with this totally determined gleam in her eye. I have seen it many times before. It is the look of a huntress.

Then my mother half runs, half skips up to Harry, kisses him, and says, adorably: "Harry! Harry! I came all the way from Yugoslavia to meet you!"

And here is where my mother and I are as different as wine and vinegar. No way do I have this magic, this courage, and this ability to confront and not give a damn about what anyone thinks. I try to emulate her all the time, but it is just not in me. I can't walk into a room without wondering if people are criticizing my clothes or my hair or the way I walk, much less crash a party of movie stars I never met.

As for my mother, she spent the next three weeks touring with Harry Belafonte, Diahann, and the bunch.

She didn't bother to send a postcard to the mother-in-law, who undoubtedly was trying to figure out what'd happened to her car and her son's unpredictable and foreign young bride.

My mother is blurry on the details of what ended the happy little romp. Maybe a fight. Maybe it happened during a blackout.

Or maybe it was the imminent arrival of her husband, Clifford, a merchant marine, who was due back from the sea at any time.

"So is Harry Belafonte my father?"

I am eleven when I ask this, and she pulls out pictures of her and Harry, a signed Christmas card and some autographed albums. We examine each one of them, one after the other, sitting side by side on the round leopard-print couch in the living room.

She is quiet for a long moment, and then: "No. Please, Gina, please. Don't ask silly qvestions. End discussion."

I think now that maybe she intends never to tell me. That maybe it is Harry Belafonte, maybe it isn't. Maybe it is the man next door. Maybe it is some guy parking a truck across the street. Normal kids don't have this, I think to myself. Why can't we be normal?

More than anything, I just want to be normal. And if I had to trade knowing who my father is for being normal, I'd pick normal, no question. Sometimes I tell kids at school that I have a bunch of brothers, and a father who's a doctor, and a mom who teaches at the school across town. I invent a whole Brady Bunch life for myself. I don't know if anyone buys it or not. I keep kids out of the house, just in case.

Funny thing is, I actually met Harry Belafonte on the set of *Good Morning America* when I was working there as a journalist a few years ago. He was there promoting some new project, had just finished his segment, and was there on the set with his wife. I was shaking like a heart attack, but I knew I had to approach him.

When it seemed the right time, I did. I said, "Mr. Belafonte,

my name is Gina. I am a reporter for GMA." He smiled politely
and shook my hand. My mother would be happy to know that he
is still really handsome.

"I think we know someone in common," I told him. "Back in
1963, you met a Yugoslavian girl, named Sladjana, whom you
toured with for a while . . . ?"

Belafonte paused cold and glanced around for his wife, who
was talking animatedly with Joan Lunden all the way over on the
other side of the set.

"How do you know her?"

"She's my mother."

"My God," he said, and there was a little gravel in his throat.
"How old are you?"

I told him I was thirty-two, and cut it off right there. It was
obvious he'd never heard of me. It was also obvious that he only
wanted to know how old I was because I was by then so much
older than my mother was when she first met him. When his wife
walked over, I thanked them both, congratulating him for his successful appearance, and walked away.

Later, I called my mother and told her what happened.

"Did he remember me?" she wanted to know.

"He seemed to," I told her.

"Of course he did," my mother said.

"He asked how old I was."

"Oh, Gina," she said, "I know what you doing. Don't be stupid."

The whole topic got kind of depressing. I knew I'd disappointed my mother with my less than glamorous physical results.
I'm tall and brunette, slim enough to meet her approval, but I
look more like a girl next door than some sexpot who'd wander
her way into a Hollywood movie. I have this annoying round face,

for one thing. No matter how much weight I lose, I end up looking like a stick figure with a big Have a Nice Day head on my
shoulders. My mother always tells me to wear my hair around my
face, to hide my round cheeks. I look friendly but never glamorous, gorgeous, all those things I was supposed to be.

I was named for Gina Lollobrigida, perhaps the intended
heiress to all that glamour and sex appeal, but I've never come
anywhere close. Even when I was a regular face on network TV,
my mother never let me forget it. Every week after my on-air segment, my mother would call me with "advice."

"Gina, your hair look nice from front but in back like a
rat nest."

"Gina, you need more lipstick. Can't you tell someone? Your
thin lips look inveesible."

"Gina, how many time you gonna wear that same earrings?"

I begin to suspect that whoever my father is, he must be
someone really unattractive, and someone she is ashamed to tell
me about.

Clifford was the homely sort. All my life, it was "poor Clifford"
this and "poor Clifford" that. Clifford Smith. And so far, I haven't
spoken much about Clifford. That's strange, I guess, because his is
the name on my birth certificate. As if that means something.

Clifford was my mother's first husband. He must've been
around me before that, but the first time I remember meeting him,
I was probably a year and a half old or two. I was in a little plastic
pool. My mother brought him out to me, and I purposely splashed
him and then got slapped hard for it. I cried outside as she took
him away.

My mother met Clifford at a naval base in Yugoslavia; he was the friend of another sailor she'd been having an affair with. He was into lots of drinking, too, so they got on just great. "But I knew this one would marry me the minute I saw him," she said. "He just seemed shy, you know."

I do know. Shy guys are easy catches. They're grateful just to talk to you. I used that little piece of knowledge countless times in my life: when I needed a boy's notes for a class or a car to borrow or someone respectable to marry. The shy guys are the easy ones; they're too embarrassed to put up much of a fight. My husband, not surprisingly, was a shy guy. He was easy to get. I've discovered since that he was harder to keep. We've been married thirteen years, which blows my mother's longest record away by at least five.

But Clifford was shy, a mama's boy to the end. At forty he'd never married and was probably intrigued with all this attention from this attractive twenty-two-year-old. By then, my mother's beauty was getting all kinds of recognition in Yugoslavia: she'd won the Most Photogenic Girl award two years in a row. She wanted to come to America, to be discovered, to be a movie star. And Clifford Smith was the one whom she chose to get her there.

I guess because of his being away at sea half the year and my mother's penchant for bars and partying, I didn't see him or my mother much for the first couple of years of my life. Maybe that's why I don't remember Clifford so well. I know he was quiet, terribly withdrawn in an overbite, receding-chin sort of way. He was deadly quiet and a constant (but calm) smoker and drinker. He had fastidious handwriting and drove a cherry-red Mustang with a Virgin Mary statue glued to the dash.

And as he shipped around the world merchanting and marining, my mother did some of the same but in a smaller pond. She wasted no time looking for movie stars, trying to be discovered, sleeping around; she knew she was destined for big things. She had a goal and a purpose, and it was to move onward and upward.

My mother later told me I was about two when, in a darkened Miami bar called The Carousel, she and I both met Daddy.

Daddy. The first time I hear the word "Daddy," I am maybe two and a half and on a flight from Daytona to New York. I am sitting on my mother's lap. She is closing the airplane window cover and telling me to take a nap. When I wake up, I will meet "Daddy," she says.

I am very curious about who this "Daddy" is.

Daddy took her away from the dreary life with Clifford and her countless parties and the endless search for movie stars that never quite seemed to get her Hollywood dreams. Daddy's the "love of her life," she says now, and she means it. He left his wife for her, helped her get a quick divorce from Clifford, and moved her and me to his house about as quickly as he could.

Daddy taught me to read before I was three. He taught me to eat shrimp cocktails, Shirley Temples, and silver-dollar pancakes. He told me I was smart. By five, I knew how to type. He used to leave me little messages in my room with a quarter inside, so that I could buy ice cream at school. He called my mother Big Gypsy, and I was Little Gypsy. Or Tiny Mite. Or Chatter Box.

If anyone teased me in kindergarten, he'd say, "Don't take it, Tiny Mite. Just punch them in the nose!"

The best thing about Daddy was that he was awake after

dinner and that he let me stay awake, too. Cocktail hour started at 6 P.M., as soon as he got home from work. They'd drink martinis until my mother passed out, usually within a couple hours or so.

Then Daddy and I'd watch *Bonanza* or read a book or play Game of the States or Trouble. Or sometimes he'd mix a drink for me—a "Grasshopper"—with green liqueur and ice cream, and we'd dance and dance to the newest Frank Sinatra or Tony Bennett. How I loved my daddy.

Sometimes, we'd play the "clean-me-up game" and take showers and lay naked in bed, talking and playing for hours.

Sometimes, he showed me his banana, and how part of it peeled back in the funniest way.

But Daddy died of a freak heart attack when he was forty-seven and I was seven. I didn't think I would ever stop crying after the second-grade teacher sent me home to get the news.

Daddy's brother and sister-in-law came to the house soon after, asking if they could take me off her hands. I heard the whole thing. "You're a young woman, Sladjana," they said. "You can start your life again." I figured they were worried about her drinking. I was only seven, and even I was worried about the drinking. I knew that every night, once my mother really started drinking, anything could happen. She might get mad at me for nothing and chase me around the house, threatening to spank me with a wooden spoon.

Thinking about the wooden spoons, I hoped for a minute that Mama might agree, that I would go off with Aunt Yvonne and Uncle Carroll and live this great new life in Salt Lake City, where my uncle worked for a big oil company. Something about that seemed safe, a safety I have to struggle to describe even now. I mean, they were always nice; I'd never seen them drink.

But my mother smashed that idea like a martini glass in the fireplace, saying "No. No. I keep Gina. She mine."

I knew that meant I was missing something big, something as big as that giant salt lake Uncle Carroll loved to tell me about. The lake you could float in even if you were little like me and didn't even know how to swim.

I wanted to live that life, float in that salt, soak in some kind of new life that didn't involve yelling and spankings and cock-tail parties that I would never again be a part of, now that Daddy was gone.

So we moved back to Florida, and when I was twelve, she re-married Clifford, explaining to me that she'd been married to Clif-ford before Daddy and did I remember him? All I remembered was the splashing in the pool incident.

Then, one day, just a few months after they were remarried, she asked me to take a walk on the beach with her.

We lived a few houses from the beach, twenty-six straight miles of hard white sand. Daytona Beach, you might know, is one of the longest, unbroken straight stretches of sand in the world. I used to ride my ten-speed up and down the length of it—fifty-two miles in a day, sometimes—and I knew it as well or better than any kid in that town. I spent every spare minute there.

But my mother never came near the beach. That's why it was so strange that one late summer afternoon when, around 7 P.M., she asked if I wanted to take a walk on the beach. Usually, she'd be half in the bag by this time. But tonight, she was sober.

"What's wrong?

"Nutting. Let's just take a walk."

So we walked on the beach, probably a mile, not saying much to each other, until finally she came out with it: "Leesen," she said. "You don't think Clifford is your father, do you?"

"No," I told her. I mean, duh. I was twelve; I wasn't a doofus.

"Vell," she said, "Clifford doesn't know that, and it would really hurt his feelings if you told him you didn't tink he was your father."

"Who is it, then?" I was hoping that she might mention someone cool, maybe someone like The Fonz on TV.

"Daddy, it's always been Daddy. I just told you it wasn't because I didn't want you to tink I would sleep with someone while I vas still married to Clifford."

I hoped she was right, that it was Daddy. Something inside me stirred, but it was so deep inside me I barely recognized it. This constant question over my head was getting old, too old.

And that put an end to the mystery for some time, and I soon after immersed myself completely in the rock teen culture of the mid and late '70s: Aerosmith, Queen, Ted Nugent, Led Zeppelin. Smoking pot, doing drugs, just like everyone else. I guess I inherited from her a love for chemical escape. That made me more like my mother. And now, I saw why she did it. Drinking and using drugs makes the happy times happier and the sad times easier to bear.

It also helps you to forget all the things you're embarrassed about, and makes it easier to talk to people—the way normal people do.

And so finally I felt normal.

LITHIUM FOR MEDEA

KATE BRAVERMAN

❖ ❖ ❖

I walked into my mother's house, wingless, hopeless. Francine still sees me as that six-year-old, pale and puffy. By ten, I was a marshmallow woman, pasty and white, almost as tall as I am now and afraid of everything. I did not accept easily. The sky was never simply a matter of air and space and color. The flametips of stars seemed to burn. My skin felt scarred from the constant abuse of a stalled white noon or a night black as a sea of rats. Summers wounded me, too yellow and hot, too molten and unmoving. Winters were bitterly short, a brief sharp bristle above singed lawns pushing stiff lilies with fat gaping toothless white mouths.

I was a brooder, caressing demons in my nine-year-old darkness, making pacts and spinning into sleep reciting my long lists of resentments. I could not forgive. I was sly, listening at locked doors and frowning at my mother pointing a camera, making certain she would remember and later, sifting drawers, discover a girl staring at her with twisted lips and mouth snarled. I was listless, always refusing, my mouth forming an iron no while I stored invisible scars from air torn by slammed doors. I wandered alone and practiced abandonment in parks of low drained hills. I was the one wearing childhood like a rare disease, already bored by fairy tales, already knowing better. I was the one with straight A's and secrets, the one who moved slow and said no and meant it. I was cold, closed, never learning to charm or beg. I was the one who spun webs and made night a contagion.

"You look terrible," Francine observed. It's a standard greeting between us.

"What are the odds?" I asked.

I knew Francine would compute the possibilities into odds. My mother and father had spent their first three years together on the road. My father was a gambler. The thoroughbreds were his passion. My mother and father rode trains and slept in hotels while following the thoroughbred horses from New York to Florida and back again. Their map was not cities or states, but race tracks. Tropical, Hialeah and Gulfstream, Havre de Grace, Monmouth and Garden State, Aqueduct, Jamaica, Belmont and Saratoga. That was before I was born. That was before the first cancer.

"Even money says he'll make it through the surgery. But there's more involved." Francine lowered her voice. "You know those bastards." She meant the doctors. There's always more involved.

I was staring across the living room at my mother. Francine and I are always studying one another across a savage gulf of space neither of us wants or understands. It is dark. Things stir, rustle and peck. The path sinks. There are thorns. A dull wind thick with debris settles over the surfaces, the edges blur.

"Are you going to have a nervous breakdown?" Francine asked.

She walked to the bar. She sat on a stool with narrow cane legs. A mirror, round and the size of a child's globe, was perched near her elbow. The mirror was framed by small bright bulbs,

pinkish and looking hot. Francine was rubbing a bluish cream
into her eyelids. From time to time, she sucked in her cheeks and
tilted her head, studying her reflection from various angles.

"Well? Are you going to break down?"

Francine made it sound like a race horse breaking a fragile leg.
A horse that would have to be shot.

"I want to know what this is going to cost me. How many hospital tabs do I have to pick up? Just his? Or both of you?"

Francine held a small black brush in her hand. She was putting on mascara. Her cheekbones were high, rouged. They looked
as if an electric current ran through them. Her neck was thin. Her
mouth was full, expressive. I could see her thoughts float across
her lips. Her hair had been arranged into a perfect auburn swirl.
The telephone rang.

"No way," Francine said, holding the receiver lightly and
opening a tube of brownish lipstick. "My husband's got cancer."
Francine always calls my father her husband, despite their divorce.
"I don't care if they're giving it away free. I can't get to New York
now. Screw Barbara Walters." Francine hung up the telephone.

Francine's house is large and cool, elegant in an antiseptic
way. Her house is a series of tans and beiges, caramels, browns,
bones, oysters, bronzes, coppers and creams. Nothing of an earlier
Francine remains. Here the past has been completely eradicated.
There is not one single chair or table, not even a small lamp or
vase, recognizable from childhood. The new tan sofas and light-
brown rugs, the new suede chairs and camel-colored pillows came
all at once. There was no birth. The house existed fully formed
from the beginning, a house without mistakes, not even one tiny
mismatched throw rug in a rarely used back room.

Over the years, Francine has been bleaching herself of the

past and the invisible black scars it left embedded in her flesh. Francine has pronounced her past useless. Here, on the other side of the country, in the lap of the Pacific, in the land of always summer and peaches hanging big as melons on branches, Francine found her second chance. She was reborn. She ascended, white and pure, with the others, the elect, the white dazed, white bleached, white capped.

Despite her stiffness, and she is a stiff woman, Francine has a strange gaiety, a kind of unnerving optimism. I have observed her in lobbies and elevators, subtly alert, watching men out of the corner of her eye. She is waiting for the one who will take the sting out of darkness with a snap of his fingers. She is waiting for the one in particular to cross a crowded room and hold her close, hold her through everything—the childhood of orphanages, the lifetime of nightmares, hypochondria, chronic depression and the grinding tedium of endless budget meetings.

I have watched my mother straightening her shoulders when she feels a man glancing in her direction. Slowly, as if unconsciously (and perhaps it is unconscious), she rearranges the thin strands of gold necklaces at her throat. I feel her sucking in her breath, wondering, is this the one, is this him, has he finally come, at last?

In my mother's house, in the layers of tans and bronzes, brown-golds, creams and pale salamanders, I realize that this woman is not the same person I knew in childhood. Francine is something newly created, both inventor and invention. For her, the future is white and amorphous, flat and etched in something hard like stucco. The past never happened. It was savage and painful and now it is gone, over, finished, less than dust, less than the memory of dust.

"It's going to be a long haul. Months in the hospital, if he makes it. Months to recover, if he recovers. Are you going to collapse?" Francine asked me again.

"I'll try to hang on," I said finally. The ceiling looked dangerously low. The far side of the room had developed a slant.

"You'll do better than try, kid," Francine said. "We're in this one, this shit heap, together. I was twenty-seven years old the first time, alone, in a strange city. They said he wouldn't live through the winter. I had to beg the train ticket money. I didn't know a single person in this town. I had a child, an invalid husband, no education. You don't know. You couldn't know. I breathed life into him. He wanted to give up. He wanted to die and I wouldn't let him. It was August in Philadelphia, 102 degrees. He was lying under blankets, shivering. I bent down and breathed air into his mouth. Are you following me? I wiped him, washed him. I emptied bedpans. I changed bandages. I saw the blood, the scars, the horror. I went to work, paid the rent, put food on the table and clothes on everybody's back."

The phone rang. Francine held the receiver while blotting her lips with a Kleenex. "Sacramento?" She tilted her head. She lit a cigarette. "What kind of car?" Pause. "No, I'm not going to Sacramento for a goddamned Volkswagen."

Francine hung up the phone. She looked disgusted.

The phone rang again. Los Angeles is a city dedicated to the telephone. In part, everyone is constantly on the phone because they are continually making, breaking and changing their deals. They're constantly on the phone because here, in the City of the Angels, where the elect have ascended, they often find themselves perched on cliff tops, on canyon tops and hilltops, absolutely alone.

I sat down in my mother's den on a caramel-colored sofa with coral and tan stuffed pillows. For no particular reason, I began thinking about my ex-husband, Gerald. We were living in Berkeley, in a one-room attic apartment with a hot plate in the closet and a Murphy bed on the wall. The one window was small and permanently jammed shut. By April, the stiff air was unbearable. Heat dulled us into a terrible mindless lethargy.

Gerald had changed his college major for the fourth time. He had already lost his scholarship and his teaching assistant position. He said he needed entire days to ponder and reflect. A job, any job at all, would be degrading to the intellectual climate he lived in. When he spoke about his intellectual climate, I imagined he had a large fluffy white cloud inside his head.

We didn't have money for luxuries like soap and shampoo. We bathed at neighbors' houses. We ate Ritz crackers dipped in ketchup and salad dressing from the student cafeteria. I had completed one year of college. I was in the honors program, permitted to take special classes taught by visiting professors from Europe and the Orient, men and women who spent the semester dazed, in culture shock. When Gerald developed an inability to hold a job, any job, I dropped out of school.

I became a waitress in Giovanni's Italian Restaurant on Shattuck Avenue. The pasta sat steaming in big black pots and the smoke was hot against the thickening spring air. I had to wear my long reddish hair pinned up for work. I stuck the bobby pins in tight against my head each night. They felt like thorns. My feet ached continually. It didn't matter, I told myself. Wives often supported their husbands. Gerald would find himself, commit himself to some program of study, sooner or later. There would be grants

and scholarships, a sense of progression. I wouldn't be working in
Giovanni's forever.

Gerald and I hadn't made love in a year and a half. I was filled
with an indescribable sense of futility. Gerald had gained weight.
His flesh seemed oddly leaden, a heavy, awkward thing that had
to be willed, jolted and forced into motion.

When Gerald wasn't reading, he was sitting in the lotus position on his straw mat in front of the television. Each night, at six
o'clock, as if a gong had been struck summoning the faithful back
to prayer, Gerald assumed the lotus position on his straw mat and
turned on *Star Trek*. He sat there, barely breathing, rapt, as if in a
religious communion.

The program was about a star ship, a gigantic machine holding a crew of four hundred human beings who seemed to be wearing flannel pajamas. The star ship *Enterprise* was one of only
twelve such ships in the fleet. Its five-year mission was to roam
through the galaxy seeking new worlds and new civilizations and
boldly going where no man had gone before. After a while, I realized Gerald planned to watch the entire five-year mission.

Sometimes the *Enterprise* found parallel universes remarkably
similar to earth, like planets patterned on mob-ruled Chicago of
the thirties, or the Nazis, or ancient Rome with the added attrac-
tion of modern technology.

There were planets where the rulers lived in a cloud of magnificent splendor while the majority of the population suffered
cruel exploitation below, in the mines, where a poisonous gas retarded their intellectual development. There were planets of
aliens with antennae on their paper-thin white faces and the
power to alter matter at will. There were green men, horned men,

giants, dwarfs, blobs, monsters, Amazons and wayward telepathic children. There were decadent civilizations run by computers. There were witches, soldiers, merchants, kings, scholars, warriors, peasants and killers.

The *Enterprise* was run by Captain James T. Kirk. Gerald dismissed him as meaningless. Gerald was only concerned with Spock, the first officer, a scientist who was half human, half Vulcan. Vulcans had conquered their aggressive tendencies by severe mental discipline. Vulcans were freed of the scourge of unpredictability and emotion and love.

Gerald had a special appreciation for the forces and events that occasionally allowed Spock to have emotion. Once Spock was hit in the face by a kind of psychedelic plant that made him climb trees and laugh. And once Spock went back in time to an ice age generations before his people had conquered emotion. Spock reverted to barbarism, ate meat and had sex with a woman. Normally Spock had sex only once each seven years. And then the sex consisted of something like an intense handshake. The rest of the time Spock amused himself with a special neck grip that made people instantly collapse, a more than genius IQ and a form of telepathy called the Vulcan Mind Meld. Spock also had gracefully arched pointed ears and greenish skin. Gerald seemed to love him.

"It's a metaphor," Gerald would say.

"But we've seen this one before. At least three times."

"Five times," Gerald corrected, sitting in the lotus position, transfixed.

Gerald claimed each new viewing revealed another aspect of the ship's functioning or Star Fleet Command. Gerald wasn't concerned with the plots. He was interested in the details at the edges.

"This is a poem about humanity," Gerald said, staring at the screen.

"But we've seen this show five times."

"The man of knowledge is a patient man," Gerald said, dismissing me.

I came back to Los Angeles to talk to Francine. I was nineteen and vomited all the time. I was seeking guidance. There were other problems. There was the revolution. Gerald had been in the library. He stopped to watch the demonstration in Spraul Plaza, the puffs of angry white smoke rising from the tear gas canisters. He had been listening to the explosions and the screaming. An Alameda police officer, tape covering his badge number and riot gear covering his face, hit Gerald from behind, across the back of his legs, with a billy club. Gerald collapsed on the cement.

"You look terrible," Francine told me.

I was sitting inside my parents' house, the house where I grew up, a modest pastel stucco in West Los Angeles with small square rooms and a sense of sturdiness and purpose. It is the house where my father still lives.

My mother and I were whispering. Francine and I whispered together, as if my father were a foreign agent. He politely ignored us. He was standing outside in the small square strip of fenced backyard watering the avocado and peach trees, watering the perpetually balding ivy, the rubber trees and patch of wild black grapes growing up along the bamboo garden gate.

"You wanted him," Francine cried, trying to keep her voice down. We were sharing a marijuana cigarette, discreetly, a secret from my father. My father was watering the apricot tree. I could see him outside the window, his back turned, his hand directing the hose.

"I told you, no, hold out, you'll get something better. But you didn't listen. Oh, no, not you. You never listen." Francine inhaled marijuana deep into her lungs. "He's nothing. What was it? The Greek and Latin bit? Boy, oh, boy, did you sell yourself cheap. Cheap even for you," my mother added.

I began crying. There was a long period of my life when I cried and vomited almost continually.

"You've got to be tough," Francine explained. "Move out. Divorce him. Just go. He's nothing. Forget him. He's slime. Take a suitcase and don't look back. Maggots will do the rest."

Francine was getting dressed for a film premiere. She pulled a silk blouse over her head. Her arms looked like wings. She kept spraying herself with perfume. She was elated. Recently, she had crossed an invisible boundary whereby her name was now automatically included on special-invitations lists. She had joined a new, smaller, more elite inner circle. There were cocktail parties now before film premieres and dinner parties afterward. Francine showed me her new evening purse. It was made of round white beads that glistened like so many hard gouged-out eyes, or the backs of hard white insects. She sprayed more perfume on her neck. I couldn't bear her desperate optimism, her certainty of perfect ascension.

Los Angeles is like a white world, filled with ever smaller white circles, leading to some perfect white core. Los Angeles is where the angels, with their white capped teeth and their white tennis dresses, gradually edged closer to the pure center, ambrosia, the fountain of youth.

Francine swung her skirt in a peach swish against her legs. In her way she was saying, look at me, I'm not really an orphan. See the box they just hand-delivered, the big one with the fat round

red ribbon? That's for me. I'm on a list with engraved invitations.
I'm not alone.

"He isn't worth death by maggots," Francine said to the mirror. She was talking about Gerald. "You could probably get him
committed, but why bother? He's got no assets, right? Christ, he's
an embarrassment. He's garbage," she added.

My father wasn't going to the film premiere. He was going to
watch a boxing match on television. My parents never went anywhere together. Once they had quarreled violently, kicked holes
in doors and broken windows. Twice neighbors called the police.
No one on the street spoke to us. They said our shouting made the
dogs bark.

Now a strange calm had settled between them. They rarely
spoke. There was a terrible sense of finality, of bitter ends beyond
the possibility of synthesis or regeneration.

"We have nothing in common," my father explained. I stood
near his shoulder while he picked avocados. "She has no sense of
values. Her priorities are shallow." My father studied an avocado.
He put it down gently in a rounded wicker basket. "She's been
one hell of a disappointment."

"I'll call the lawyer for you," Francine said. She was walking
down to her car. She was still talking about Gerald. "We'll nail
that bastard. Maybe he doesn't have anything now, but when he
does, we'll know about it."

I watched Francine get in her car. I watched my mother disappear down the street. I never seriously tried to talk to her again.

ANYBODY COULD SEE IT

ELIZABETH PAYNE

❖ ❖ ❖

When my father betrayed my mother, he betrayed me as well, because there had been three people sustaining the marriage, not two. When your parents are in a seething, long-term lie, you are both the little wife and the little husband. You fill in the blanks, smooth things over and stand by.

It was the Mother's Day before the summer of my big swim. I was twelve. Muffled talk was coming from the kitchen; the cleaning woman was running the vacuum upstairs. The TV room door burst open. "Your mother's flowers are in the car," my father said. "Go get them and throw them at her." I stared down the TV. On a commercial, I retrieved the flowers and pulled the collar of baby's breath out and flung it under a bush by the kitchen door. Anybody knew my mother didn't like baby's breath.

Our house was on a cliff overlooking Narragansett Bay in a community called Plum Beach. I'd never seen any plums. The idea of tromping out of the bay, plucking a succulent plum from a branch and juice cascading down my chin made Plum Beach seem some kind of Eden. It wasn't. I'd figured that out.

Eavesdropping, I overheard my father say that a certain well-respected man in the neighborhood had a girlfriend, and when his wife found out, she had thrown herself on the hood of his car to keep him from leaving her. I was fascinated. Was she lying horizontal, spread like a starfish? Or straight up the center, her face smushed, slug-lipped and bug-eyed against the windshield? Did he tear up Plum Beach Road with her still on it? Did she cling to the wipers?

When I was twenty-five I found lodged behind the drawer in my old desk a letter I'd written to my best friend that year. "My parents will never get divorced," it read. "They just like different things. My dad likes to work and is angry a lot. My mom wants my dad to go out Saturday nights but he doesn't want to." I remember writing this letter, and I remember hiding it. I wanted someone not to worry.

That summer I swam laps between two jetties and tallied them on a poster in the Plum Beach clubhouse for the Labor Day "Jamestown swim." The point was to swim back to Plum Beach from Jamestown, the island directly across the bay. I prayed only that the night before there wouldn't be a storm. A storm's aftermath was the only thing to really put you off swimming, the seaweed clotting the bay and the shoreline appearing as if a million slippery toupees had washed up.

There were two important facts about this swim. First, my parents would be "spotting me," meaning that for a long stretch of time they would be confined in our dinghy, together, their knees even possibly grazing, while I swam behind. I was both pleased and deeply frightened by the prospect. I planned to awe them as my Vaselined body propelled through the water at warp speed. But I knew that anything could come out of my father's mouth. His temper was volatile and consistent. My mother and I would be stuck, unable to go anywhere but inside ourselves.

My mother and I did have one thing going for us: chocolate. After the motorboats towed the swimmers and the spotters to the Jamestown shore, the organizers dispensed Hershey's bars. I killed two and acquit my mother with five more, passing them to her as if they were tight stacks of fifties.

The whistle blew. I ran through the buffeting waves toward my parents. My father was at the oars, my mother sitting with her back to him, facing me. My mother's posture said she was spotting me but also ignoring him.

I was mostly breast-stroking because with that stroke you could dive under and play porpoise, then shoot up fast like you were super serious about making headway. I wasn't long into the swim when I'd shot up and realized it had begun. My father was irate over the current, the oarlocks, the fog. I could tell that my mother was giving me a broad smile to help keep me going, because when I sprung up when she wasn't expecting it, her face was dark with something I couldn't name. That was her way: silence.

I spent more time under the surface, porpoising for two strokes or four, depending. Underwater, I was completely free. I wished my mother would come under with me.

My father took issue when I requested some Hershey's. "She needs energy," my mother said. "She needs her teeth," my father said. My mother slipped me secret bites. I'd been underwater, taking my time with a mouthful of salt-water-marinated Hersheys, when I surfaced to hear my mother exclaiming "Oh my! Oh, no!"

An enormous, prehistoric-looking barge was coming our way. The Coast Guard had been properly alerted, and the bay was supposed to be clear of large craft for three hours.

"Christ!" my father said. My father was in a rage. My mother ripped open a Hershey's and held it two inches from her mouth like a microphone, while motorboats gunned by with bullhorn-wielding men saying, "Hold up! Remain calm! Stay with your spotters!" You were disqualified if you got in the boat. I held on to the dinghy's metal catch, panicking. Being stuck, unable to do tricks, porpoise, or otherwise distract them and myself, was intolerable. As long as we were moving forward we were fine, but stopped in the middle of the bay in a boat, my father angry at everything, my fingers welting around the catch, I felt only despair.

Three years later my mother asked my father to move out and "served him with papers."

"Your mother put me out," my father said.

Through the floorboards of my bedroom I heard my sister yell "Why are you protecting her, Mom? Why can't the little princess know the truth about Dad? She should know about the other women, that he was *cheating*." *You're lying*, I thought. I knew she wasn't.

Confronting my father with this fact of his cheating was the worst horseshoe crab, the nightmare of the bay, a bottom-dweller nailing you right through the foot. I could tread water forever.

In the following years I thought but never dared say to my father *What was wrong with Mom? She dressed nice and was a good mom. Couldn't you see that, Dad? Couldn't you see what I see?* Under these unspoken words were more upsetting words: *What was wrong with me?*

Every night around nine, after my father had eaten his late dinner kept warm in the stove, I'd bring him a large glass of orange juice with ice to his den and ask him how his day was. I'd applied the sloppy dermatitis-control creams to his back. For my mother, that was out of the question. I'd never seen a sign of affection pass between them, much less a cream application.

That summer, I looked out at the water and imagined using the cliff as a diving board, doing a sun-cresting swan dive with fifteen stunts built in. I'd heard the rumors: kids were cliff diving in Newport. You dove, but you never knew which it would be: taken by the water in a soft gulp or wind up paralyzed. Thrill seekers, that's what they were called. I was not that brand of person.

My mother and I were on weathered rocking chairs on the stone-walled porch, gazing fixedly at the bay and the lobsterman who was pulling pots. He was right where he always was every summer, in front of our house. He could be counted on. I'd taken to watching him with binoculars. My mother thought he could see me and, using the word *voyeurism*, told me to put the binoculars down. I thought the lobsterman and my mom should meet. She didn't. My mother was special, and the lobsterman would see it; anybody could see it. I put the binoculars in my lap and sipped my Crystal Light.

"Mom, we can get our suits and just swim out to him. Say hello. He's probably been wondering about us, too," I said, badgering.

"I can't swim," she said, distracted.

"Of course you can swim."

"No, I can't."

"That's ridiculous. What are you trying to say you can't swim?"

"Dear . . ." she said.

She had a zillion different "dears." This one: *I'm telling you the truth.*

"That is just so weird, I can't even deal." I got up, to get away from the bad smell of this revelation. I left her sitting there, when she had been having a lovely time with her daughter on the porch. That's what she would have said to the lobsterman if he'd asked: *Oh, I'm having a lovely time with my daughter on the porch.* The screen door snapped shut.

I sat on my bed in my bedroom above the porch, staring out the window at the water. I repeated "Can't swim" as if it were a foreign phrase I was trying to master. She oversaw four kids through the whole swimming-lesson run: tadpole to senior life saving. She owned a panoply of swimsuits and even bought us a Sunfish sailboat that we had until my sister and I didn't pull it all the way up the beach and the tide made off with it. Rhode Island was the Ocean State, making swimming almost a mandate. I raked my memory. I knew she could swim. I'd seen her swim, or had I? There is a picture. She has on a white eyelet kerchief and those seventies outsized sunglasses. Her hands are visored to her forehead, watching me swim. I am pulling tricks. Tumblesaults and back flips; handstands where I make my feet swish and spasm. I hope to appear balletic. She was ankle deep. She was always on the shore. She wasn't ever swimming. And I'd never noticed.

My mother was capable of duping us, her family. I took this revelation to my sister and brothers. They gave me a couple of "Huh's" and a "Makes sense; she never does totally get in. So?"

I telescoped in, giving examples of family trips where we had all been swimming and she had not.

They were bored; I was repeating myself.

My mother had secrets. We were a lot alike that way, grievously good secret keepers. I needed mine, but I also needed hers. Her secrets were evidence of crucial things, a chain of things, that if you followed, shadowing, on her tail, creeping slowly, so she didn't notice you were peeking, you would find a hidden mother, a mother you didn't recognize but yours nonetheless. You could claim her, bring her back. You had to; she was your mother.

At the kitchen table with the lion paws I liked to stroke with a slow, private toe, I confronted my mother.

"I don't understand you not being able to swim. Why can't you swim?"

"Fear, I suppose."

"How could you be afraid? I mean, you love the beach. I just thought you didn't get all the way in to keep your hair nice."

"I didn't want you to know. I didn't want my children to be afraid of the water."

"I don't get you at all, Mom." I meant to say *I don't know you at all, and if I don't know you, my mother, then I will drown.*

Swimming wasn't the only thing she'd duped us on. Swimming was pleasure. And pleasure was missing for my mother. There it is, sliding right under the surface of my need for her to be able to swim: the wet, the sensuous privacy of water. My mother had never plunged through necklaces of seaweed, never submerged solitary, never seen the numinous light-refracting spectacle that is breaking through a wave from below. She'd missed the pleasure of buoyancy. She'd missed this pleasure, but she watched everyone around her take it greedily. She'd pretended so that I, her daughter, wouldn't be afraid to risk for pleasure. But I was afraid.

It was late, a school night the following March. My father had been gone for a year. I'd just turned sixteen. I lived in my new bedroom, my father's knotty-pine den. The bright yellow rug, dust ruffles and eyelet had been left behind. It was a necessary move. You couldn't double-pierce your ear with ice and a needle from your mother's sewing kit or cradle a hand mirror between your legs and try to determine how you should feel, in a kiddie room. You couldn't listen to The Cure in a kiddie room. You couldn't reinvent yourself in a kiddie room. In your dad's den, anything was possible.

My mother checked and rechecked her messages. As usual, there were none.

A knock. She didn't believe the machine.

"No one called, Mom."

"Open the door, please."

"I can't right now." No one respected that my bedroom was a vault. It was opened infrequently and by appointment.

"Please, Elizabeth, open the door."

"Can't you tell me what you need? I'm busy."

"Dear, please open the door." The "dear" said *Seriously, open the door.* I undid the bolt, gave only my face.

"I need to speak with you."

"I'm here."

"May I come in, please?"

She was scaring me, so I got tougher. Whatever it was, I didn't want to know.

"I'm right here. We can speak right here just fine."

"I really wish you would let me in, but if you won't," she sighed deeply. I looked down, listened with one ear, a priest in a confessional. "Elizabeth, everything is going to be fine. I'm going to be fine. They've found some cells; there's going to be surgery, a hyst . . ."

My body pressed against the gurney of thick pine, and her body pressed back.

"What cells?" I said, pressing my cheek hard into the door's edge.

"Cancerous cells," she said, inhaling the words. I'm up on the roof, down on the porch, over the cliff.

"Okay," I said, like she'd asked my permission.

"I'd like to . . ." She drew her finger; it was coming for my cheek. I leaned harder into the dull knife of the door to say *I want to.* Her fingertip slipped to my chin. I felt it and shook my head.

"I need to . . . could you . . . I need to . . ." I said, in a blurt, withdrawing my face. I closed the door, not hard but without mercy.

I knew she was behind the door. I knew she was looking at me through the solid knotty pine.

"Go, please . . . Mom," I said, forcing a pitch of calm. She was not moving. "Please stop trying to listen to me." I lay back on my bed, my eyes wide. I darted for my closet. Camel Lights, always the box, never the soft pack, under a stack of sweaters. My father was gone, I could smoke; my mother couldn't persuade it away. I hit the stereo's volume and cranked the window wide, letting in the cold. My hands trembling, I struck a match to the sill. I inhaled hard and held, so it would burn. My eyes watered; I bobbed my head to the music to make them stop. I pulled at my cigarette and stared at the black drape of the bay, the words *She said cancer . . . she said cancer . . . she said cancer . . .* cresting and breaking.

Cancer was a ramp that lowered and you were rolled on. And then the ramp was gone and so were you. It was efficient, brutal and final. The ramp lowered for my mother's mother when she was nineteen, her father when she was twenty-nine, her brother when she was thirty-two. She barely spoke of them, as if their deaths had sworn her to silence.

Just like that, Dad, like dominoes. Can't you see the weird way she never talks about them? She's scared of the ramp, Dad. And I'm scared, too.

Flicking the ashes, I let the smoke feather around me. My mother was in her vault, letting honeysuckle-colored chardonnay feather through her. I knew my mother was grieving, and it wasn't the cancer. It was as big as the bay.

She was in her lavender silk robe, at her vanity table. The glass was empty, but she had two fingers on the stem, as if it might topple. I sat behind her on her bed, watching her back. She was not in her body. She'd left. Where was she right then, with her fingers mindlessly pressing on that empty glass? At her mother's bedside? At the altar? In the delivery room? When I left my body, I stayed around the house, but my mother? I don't know. I just felt it when she was gone. It made me want to listen to The Cure louder, to fill up the empty space. My brothers and sister would have said *She's right* there, *what are you talking about?* She didn't fool me.

She sighed and turned to me, asked if I was okay. "Fine," I said. I got up quickly. To be hugged or touched was out of the question. I would not sink in my own water. I had school in the morning. Field hockey practice. A father to, at turns, be angry with and miss. I had a whole head to quarantine.

"I'm sorry," I said. "I need to go to sleep. I need to not talk now."

Under my sweaters, in the closet, a Sucrets tin containing water pills. They were a shade of eggshell blue. They shimmied inside when I handled the tin. They were diuretics, but I preferred to think of them as "water pills"; it made them sound necessary, enjoyable even. I took them by the handful.

When the lights were out, when all the knots in the pine walls were blind, I clasped my pillow. I could find my mother through the tiny bits that no one notices, the mole that looks like a smashed peppercorn on her ankle, the pinprick hole in her cheek from trying to extract something she shouldn't have, the rubbery scar on her forearm from manning the popcorn maker at the school fair, the missing baby toenail. The bits were like a constellation I memorized to bring her close, but her distance from me was fathomless. I drew the lines from bit to bit. Someday, I would lift the scar off, plug up the hole, apply cover-up to the mole, lend her my baby nail; that way, I would be the one who could identify her, the one who knew her secrets, the one she would thank for finding her.

At nineteen, I was in college in Boston and starving myself with great success. I was still gripping a dinghy, steeling for the next barge. I resented my father's new wife, with her collapsible iridescent Christmas tree. I resented my mother's being on Slim-Fast, because I wanted her to be different from me. I resented spackling Jolen creme bleach on my upper lip every two weeks; it seemed like a tremendous failing of femininity. Most of all, I resented my round face. "Uncanny, your father's face," people would say. I wanted my mother's face. I thought that if I only had a face with angles, I would be powerful, incapable of being hurt, and everyone would take me seriously, starting with my father. It always came back to him, for my mother and me, this man who had chosen other women over us. It was our shared secret.

My mother was kind and beautiful and perfect, like she was my daughter and I strained out all the imperfections. But I didn't let on. *Mom,* I would say, *shoulder pads are* over, or *You can't wear coral lipstick with a red blouse,* or *That jacket looks like something the giant Golden Girl would wear.* My mother was a source of exasperation. I needed her to be all the things in those tiny inspiration books by the bookstore checkout: serene, centered, creative, powerful, free—and consuming three balanced meals a day. I wanted to see that these things were possible. I wanted her to fix herself first.

My mother kept a rubber band around her wrist, a rudimentary anxiety-control system she'd rigged. She snapped it every time she had a nervous thought. I didn't ask if it worked; I didn't have to. You'd hear the snapping. She was trying to improve. Sloshing about in the spilled coffee in the console of her old Mercedes: tokens for the Newport Bridge, ravaged Hershey's with Almonds wrappers and cassette tapes: *What to Say When You Talk to Yourself* and *Love, Medicine & Miracles.* Spared by virtue of living in the tape deck: *A Return to Love.* For years Marianne Williamson talked to my mother and me about returning to love. We were trying, but we'd been betrayed. I wasn't sure Marianne understood that.

I preferred reading Anne Sexton and Sylvia Plath for my instructional needs. They were really upset. I wanted to know what they said when they talked to themselves. I knew what I said; it was in my journal. I wrote declarations of new diets and brutal self-recriminations for cheating. *Stop!* my entries read. *Stop wanting ice cream! You're fat!* The invisible ink read: *Stop wanting love! He's not coming back! It's your fault! You're a big failure!* The journal was my snapping rubber band.

It was my mother's fifty-sixth birthday that year. I drove down to Providence in my light blue Honda Civic for the party. It was being held at my cousin's house, where my mother was living for the week. She'd rented out our house for a wedding party and single-handedly moved every valuable, breakable or memento into her bedroom and bolt-locked it. I didn't like the idea at all. I imagined one hundred and fifty ants, dressed in finery, crawling all through our home.

My mother's elaborate schemes centered on her house, and my elaborate schemes centered on my body. We were desperate in our efforts to fix them, shore them up and keep them standing.

I was late, but I couldn't square why my cousin was on her stoop watching down the street. I pulled in front of the house, and she jogged to my car. Her forehead was a billboard for bad news.

"You mother was just rushed to Rhode Island Hospital, her heart. . . . They don't know." I had no voice.

I would find out later that fifty-six was my grandmother's age when she died. I was nineteen as my mother had been. I talked to her as I tore over to the hospital: *You're okay. You're okay. You're okay.* I lined them up in my mind—the scar, the toenail, the peppercorn, the hole—and pulled her tight.

"How is she? Is she all right?" I said, running toward my sister in the hospital hallway.

"Take your time," my sister said and made a smart remark about my tacky purse. I knew she was okay. She had to be.

I sailed past my sister, wanting to barricade the door and keep her out. *She's my mother,* I wanted to say to my sister. *Mine. You don't know her at all.*

My sister and I stood for a moment at the foot of her bed: a raft of white with my mother's head poking out. She looked frightened and spent.

"It's okay, Elizabeth," she said, in a tone that said it wasn't. "This was just . . . an attack of . . . well, anxiety, the doctor thinks. The EKG was normal. I'm sorry. I . . . thought I was . . . not going to make it."

"But it's your birthday, Mom."

I left the music off on the drive back to Boston. I remember the sound of the Diet Coke empties rolling forward and breaking against the passenger-side ramp of carpet and then flying backward when I downshifted, like a tin tide.

I was twenty-six and living in Manhattan when my mother announced she was selling the house. I sobbed uncontrollably, in a way I never had when my parents got divorced. I was finally sinking in my own water, ten years later.

I prevailed upon her to change her mind. "I invite you to consider that I simply can no longer afford to keep it," my mother had replied. When my mother invited me to consider something, discussion was closed. My mother was land poor. She was pulling the plug and moving first to a condominium in Newport and eventually to Florida.

A month later, after having gone home for the move, I stood up at my desk on the thirty-sixth floor of the advertising agency at which I worked and, without any identifiable provocation, screamed for help. It was lunch. I was eating a dressing-free salad packed from home. I put my fork down. My brain was closing.

Paramedics placed me on a gurney and fastened an oxygen mask. I about wet myself. The gurney rolled me past the crowd and into the boardroom. The paramedic said he felt I'd had a "panic attack." "I was just sitting there though," I said, lifting the oxygen mask. "I wasn't doing anything." I took "panic attack" to be an indictment. I was certain that I was sick and was, in fact, about to die. Panic attacks were the pasttime of fragile people. Or freaky agoraphobic types trotted out on Sally Jessy Raphaël. I didn't know people who had panic attacks.

I was sent home for the day, but a wire had been tripped. I was panic-attacking like it was an obligation. My hands had slipped off the dinghy.

I had to figure out how to breathe. My mother wasn't going to go first; I had to.

My sister and I visited my mother in Florida for Mother's Day my first year of graduate school. It was during this trip that my mother told me that she had written love poems to my father when they were first married. He'd told her to stop.

"Don't ever stop," she said, looking not at me but straight ahead.

The next day at the ocean, my sister and I stripped to our suits and went for the water. We were waist deep and both turned to watch my mother in her green suit with matching wrap skirt walking toward the water. She moved from shin deep to thigh deep, splashing water on her arms and smiling at the sun. I did handstands and porpoised, to show her how fun the water was.

"Is it possible for you to not put on a recital?" my sister asked when I came up for air. It wasn't.

I skipped to my mother at the shore like I was twelve. "You look just like you did when you were a little girl. I love to see your face like this," she said.

My mother turned and announced she was taking herself for a walk. I watched her in the distance, on a vacant stretch of beach, as she flapped her arms up and down in that way she called exercising, but I called embarrassing. But I knew better. When I walked next to her I could see on her face that she flapped out of the pleasure of being alive.

She began to disappear from my view. A shrunken shadow. Somebody's mom or nobody's mom. I lay down on a beach lounger to let the sun dry me. I could see her on the back of my eyelids when I closed my eyes.

FATAL FLOWERS

ROSEMARY DANIELL

❖ ❖ ❖

In the backseat of a black limousine, my mother and I speed through darkness. Like Evelyn Mulray's daughter in Chinatown, I'm being saved by my glamorous mother from dangerous men. Pressing my nine-year-old cheek against her shoulder, stroking the cream satin of her blouse, breathing her gardenia perfume, I feel enclosed in a dark cocoon of safety. With a sigh of contentment, I flop my arm across her breasts and discover that, beneath the slippery cloth, one side of my mother's chest is hard, flat—stiff with bandages and adhesive. . . .

When I woke sobbing in 1974 in my red velour–papered room in the Virginian Hotel in Medicine Bow, Wyoming (population 450), I didn't know that, as a child, my mother had been driven to school each day in a chauffeured black automobile—just that my dream of her mutilation made me want to rush into the hallway to the hotel's one pay phone to call her at home in North Carolina. Only my fear of the miners, who were the only other guests at the hotel, and whose drunken shouts I still heard from the bar adjoining the café, stopped me. That, and the knowledge that my mother's wound was real, had long since been inflicted, and there was no longer anything I or anyone could do to save her.

A year later, I lay on a lumpy bedspread in a room in the John Milledge Motel in Milledgeville, Georgia, sipping Jack Daniel's and tap water, watching the *Tony Orlando and Dawn* show. I needed to forget, for a few minutes, the poetry workshop I had just conducted at the state prison for women—to forget fifty-five-year-old Jewell's lifelong dream of "staying in one of them motels, just once"; Chain Gang Candy's tale of throwing Clorox into her faithless husband's eyes; and black Doris's story of being railroaded into prison by the white police officer who was the father of five of her six illegitimate children. As I lounged against the cheap veneer headboard, trying to focus on Tony's cheerful sing-along, on the way he lifted women from the audience—plain, fat, pantsuited—to momentary media "life," the phone rang.

My sister Anne's voice came tiredly over the line. Mother had been found unconscious, she said; dressed in a new blue peignoir and her best white-gold costume jewelry, with her favorite bright-red lipstick carefully applied, she had left a scrawled note and an empty bottle of pills beside her bed. Anne would be traveling with her by ambulance to a hospital in Atlanta; would I meet her there as soon as possible? As I faintly registered Anne's irritation that, as usual, I was not on hand for a family crisis, I felt a mixture of relief and numbness that lasted through the minutes of making phone calls, throwing things into suitcases: Mother had finally done what for years she had said she would do. . . .

As I drove through the piny dark, my usual fears of pickups full of red-necks with rifles and a penchant for rape were overlaid by images that wove themselves with the asphalt opening before me. Photographs of Mother, pensively smiling in a black velvet dance dress, holding red roses in her plump arms, standing solemnly with Daddy outside his University of Georgia frat house, dressed in satin-faced cloche and dressmaker coat, her kid slippers fastened with tiny round buttons; or laughing, linking arms in a row of girls, theatrically jutting a knee to show the hemline of her chemise in a local fashion show—"the prettiest girl in Atlanta," I had heard time after time.

Earlier in the day, driving down the Spanish moss-and-dogwood-lined main street of Milledgeville toward the prison, I had passed the college Mother had attended at seventeen—Georgia State College for Women, now the Women's College of Georgia, best known as the alma mater of Flannery O'Connor—and had recalled another picture of her, plump on starchy school food, yet pretty in the required navy pleated skirt and white middy blouse. Grandmother Lee, her mother, had told me that Mother cried so much from homesickness that she was allowed to return home after her first year. She didn't yet know Valentino-dark Daddy, her destiny of two years later—or that he played the saxophone on the roof of the military school across the street to attract the girls.

As I neared the prison, I had recalled that Daddy, too, had visited prisoners. A tire salesman, he had sold truck tires to a warden and had brought supplies for an inmate who made jewelry. The grateful man had given him a matching set of earrings and bracelet which he, in turn, had given to his best girl. For years, after her trousseau lingerie and Persian-lamb coat were gone, the pieces had been Mother's best jewelry. As I turned into the drive leading to the institution, I recalled, through five-year-old eyes, the shiny onyx chunks echoing her jet curls, the glint of filigree as the stones fell from her wrist. . . .

The next morning, allowed into a curtained room in intensive care, I saw that, for once, she wore no jewelry at all—she had become a slight child beneath blue cotton, struggling for breath, cruelly jammed through nose, throat, arms with tubes bubbling red. As I held her small hand in mine, hopelessly whispering "I love you," I noticed that her nails were perfectly filed in her favorite pointed style—and that her face was full, round again. Around eyes as tightly closed as a newborn's, Mother's cheeks and forehead were smoothed for the first time in thirty years of the deep marks of some indescribable inner pain. . . .

wanted to understand Mother's victimization, her frustrations, and most of all to forgive her. Only a year before her death, at a family Thanksgiving at my house, she had looked venomously at me across the champagne and turkey, with a gaze in which I suddenly saw the full shocking depth of her hatred. The look upon her face was the one I had seen so often as a child in the moment before her palm unexpectedly flashed out to meet my cheek. "I've *nevah*," she snarled—here, her lip curled back, doglike—"been able to make you do *anythang*!"

She referred to the fact that a few minutes before, I had refused to give her the favorite silver bracelet I wore on my arm, but I knew that she also meant that my refusal to be policed by her into what she considered essential values had been another of her unbearable failures—that she considered the "penis" within me, my active will, as much of a deformity as I had at fourteen; that my desire for more than her passive, reactive existence was a threat and a perversion. But now I needed to think of her again as that young and innocent girl, her arms full of red roses—to at last understand, to love my mother and thus myself.

❖ ❖ ❖

We now live in a garage apartment on Oak Street. I'm three years old, lying on my back in the big bed in Mother and Daddy's room. Mother has just removed my panties, my last protection; my wrists are tied with something thin, gauzy, yet strong—Mother's precious nylons?—to the headboard of the bed.

My fat thighs burn, forced, knees bent into the air; my ankles are held viselike by Mother's best friend, Virginia, who looks, to my humiliation, at my most private parts, who now smiles as Mother approaches holding high some strange device—red rubber, metal, hose, tube—as Mother thrusts the blunt back end of it toward my exposed bottom, as, though I writhe, thrash, scream, beg her not to kill me, she pushes it into my recoiling flesh.

Yet worse than the invasion of my body is the look on Mother's face: there is no softening at my fear, rather a smirk of pleasure; her upper lip curls above a strange smile, a grimace. As my whole lower body cramps around some strange hot invasion, some animal loss of control, as I scream, "Mama, Mama, don't!" she and Virginia laugh.

Now, in this moment, I understand: never in my life will my mother be moved by my pain or fear, no matter how great it might be, that she is not only willing to watch me tortured in any way, but if necessary, to do it herself.

Even during the years of the Hot Fudge Shortcakes, the black-and-white puppies, the walks to Peachtree Street to buy the chocolate marshmallow hearts that only cost a penny, there was something dark, erratic beneath Mother's sunniness. The plump and pretty housewife holding me on her lap as she sat in a lawn chair and gossiped with a girlfriend, the round-faced young mother laughing with me at the cartoons at the local picture show gave hints of being another, less friendly being.

I had been given a book of Victorian verses, complete with illustrations designed to make children behave. Mother read and reread to me a particularly scary one of a girl burning to death while playing with matches: on the opposite page, an etching showed a skinny girl in a long dress going up in flames. As I sobbed, she giggled. At other times, precedents of the slap in the chicken yard, her upper lip would suddenly curl downward into the snarl that would later become so familiar, yet was always so like seeing a cockroach emerge from the center of a perfect magnolia, and her palm—for reasons my toddler mind couldn't fathom—would crash against my cheek or thigh or ass in an explosion that was followed by a time when her face became vacant, as though she was no longer there with me at all.

I did not know, as a child, that my mother was crazy, or, as I now understand, mad with her own contradictions; like Florence King's Southern belle, she was supposed to be "frigid, passionate, sweet, bitchy, and scatterbrained—all at the same time." Worse, it was imperative that she be as stoic as *her* mother, Lee, and at the same time deal with a husband as crazy as she was. It was simply that, at moments, she became a person I feared. The first and most painfully recalled of these was the one on the bed; it may have been the instant when my image of the embedded penis, of something within me that needed to be routed, was born.

For the next five or six years, or until I began to run screaming from the house when I saw her approach with her hands held behind her back, the enema look on her face, her perineal assaults or what seemed to be assaults, continued. My fear of them never abated, and this seemed to add to her determination; when force was needed, Daddy, looking as though he wished he was elsewhere, was called in.

Once, walking along the sidewalk in my white high-top shoes— I must have been four or five—I heard a younger child screaming from a nearby house. I wondered if she was undergoing the same torture, if this was something all mothers—no matter how nice, how kind they seemed—did to their children in secret or in collaboration with one another. If this was the case, it was truly an invasion against which there could be no protection.

When I was eight, this theory seemed borne out. At Lee's farm, I ate too many green apples. The local doctor was called in, and as my grandmother, my visiting aunts and uncles, and my parents stood around the high bed, I was given what amounted to a public enema. To me, it felt like a public rape, the ultimate humiliation, the full cooperation of other adults in a form of torture I had still half hoped was private to Mother. The doctor, I recall, gave me a stick of spearmint gum in an effort to stop my screams; he must have been puzzled at the extremity of my response.

Through my terror and shame, I was most conscious of Mother's eyes: did she enjoy seeing this happen to me in front of others? She in no way appeared disturbed—yes, there was that faint smirk playing about her lips. She looked at me as though she alone knew the secret of my inner malignancy.

A year later, Mother, Daddy, Anne, and I visited the Cancer Victim. Aunt Mary was the wife of one of Mother's stepbrothers; as young, almost as pretty as Mother, she lay dying.

Like many Southern women, Mother had a morbid enthusiasm for the details of physical mutilation (particularly those related to "female trouble"); a straightforward interest in sexuality, which was taboo, was displaced in favor of a fascination with bizarre conditions and surgical details (and sometimes crime and murder: my first mother-in-law kept hidden beneath her mattress a collection of detective magazines, the covers of which inevitably depicted a woman in underwear, bound, and perhaps bloody).

Mother didn't hesitate to describe these conditions in graphic detail. I had recently heard her tell Daddy at the supper table about a man who had fallen backward on a "Co-Cola bottle—it went right up his rectum!" Now, on the way to Aunt Mary's, I heard her say brightly, "They had to cut out the wall between her vagina and rectum."

Playing with Anne's curls in the backseat, wrapping them between my fingertips, I imagined my aunt's—and Mother's, Anne's, my own—lower body as a gruesome cavity, a cloaca, less clean than the single opening in the corpses of chickens into which I liked to stick my fist.

When I was in high school, a classmate, dressed in a matronly bed jacket thick with cheap lace, lay dying of cancer; my girl friends and I, dumb with the enormity of her situation, our first sense of our own mortality, took her an orchid corsage. As though she were going to a prom with Jesus instead of to her death, she weakly pinned it on the shoulder of the bed jacket and thanked us.

Now, as we arrived at Aunt Mary's house, we found her propped up in bed with a white nightgown that would have befitted a bride. But my once round-faced aunt had become a caricature of herself, as skeletal as the survivors of Dachau I had seen in a newsreel at the picture show. Though she was as smiling and lady-like as a hostess at a tea (I think now how trying the Southern insistence on appearances must have been for her), she barely resembled the pretty woman I recalled. As Mother complimented her on her gown, as she declared "How Rows-may-ree and Anne have grown!" I glimpsed the loathed enema bag hanging in the bathroom. On the way home, I heard Mother saying to Daddy that she thought the cancer had developed because Aunt Mary had been in the habit of taking enemas.

Something dreadful clicked in my head: my aunt lay dying because of enemas like those Mother had forced on me. *She really had been trying to kill me!*

The year of Mother's suicide became the year in which this understanding began. It was also a year during which I traveled continuously throughout the Deep South, from Atlanta to Milledgeville to New Orleans to Charlotte to Columbia to Savannah to Macon to Rabun Gap and back. Most of these travels were made because of my work as poet-in-residence, and to give readings from my own poetry.

In each place, I visited women friends and made new ones. As a feminist and a poet, my intimate friends were women like myself, women who had attempted radical solutions to our common background—artists, writers, scholars, lesbians, political activists, and entrepreneurs. Because they were like me, I understood their contradictions and the pressures. These women—all of them brilliant, charismatic—had experienced struggles similar to my own, and like me, often still lapsed into the confusion and depletion created by a lifetime of conflict. But as I met schoolteachers, housewives, beauticians, students, and factory workers, I realized that their apparently simpler choices had in no way saved them from frustration, confusion. It was simply that their responses, out of those available, had been different from those fortunate enough to have the energy or opportunity to break out.

The conflicts of all the Southern women I had met seemed magnified in the lives of the women in prison. At the time of Anne's phone call, I was deeply involved in my work at the state correctional facility for women outside Milledgeville. Because of the town in which I found myself—a town dripping with Spanish moss, antebellum charm, and a fascistic Baptist conservatism—my images of the inmates were already confused with fantasies of my parents' early lives. My poetry reading at the college Mother had attended had just been canceled as "too sensational"; each day I found myself feeling closer to the inmates I had at first feared. I had heard of the woman who had slashed another across the eye with a straight razor, of the night the administration left the building in fear of a riot—indeed, women had been shaken down for weapons on an evening of my workshop.

Yet at the time of Anne's news, in the first moments of shock and disbelief, my impulse had been to call these women—had it been possible—for understanding and support. More than anyone I had known, they knew firsthand of deprivation, fear, loss, and grief; they had truly "lost everything in the oppression," and hearing of Mother's condition, I wanted Doris's plump arms around me, Peggy's empathy, and Maybelle's sweet slow smile, Candy's passionate indignation. Instead of my drive into the night, I craved the structure of walls, even locked doors.

For weeks, I had been moved by the parallels between their lives and Mother's and mine. When Peggy described committing armed robbery to buy whiskey for her boyfriend, I recalled how Mother had gone to work as a clerk-typist to help pay off Daddy's gambling debts—and my own decision to quit school at sixteen to marry for "love." When Doris wrote, "Jealousy is when your grandmother helps your brother go to college, and now he has a house and car, and you're here in prison . . . ," I remembered Mother's upbringing as a helpless belle and my own early fantasies that I would always be taken care of by a man who loved me. At moments, it was as though the years of writing and growth had not occurred, as though I was thrust back in time to share their helplessness, hopelessness, and self-hatred.

What I had once seen as the condition of being female, I now saw as female and Southern. I perceived my mother, grandmothers, sister, daughters—and all the women whose roots I shared—as netted in one mutual silken bondage. Together, we were trapped in a morass of Spanish moss, Bible Belt guilt, and the pressures of a patriarchy stronger than in any other part of the country. (Even in the West, where men are men, and macho, the pioneering woman has long been a tradition.) I wondered what would have become of us had sisterhood, rather than feminine policing and competitiveness, been our ambience.

Like most Southern women, I had grown up feeling that only relationships with men were worth serious pursuit. Because I didn't go to college, I had not even experienced the camaraderie of dormitory life—indeed, had never seen a woman other than my mother or sister naked. (Though at nine, I had watched a teenage aunt dressing for a date; when she pulled on a crotchless girdle, I had seen her pubic hair. Since Mother had the same growth upon her body, I unhappily assumed it to be a family deformity.) The stiff corsets worn by my grandmothers, even on weekdays, had given their bodies the texture of a board and seemed metaphors for their impenetrability. But during the year of Mother's death, with an awareness intensified because of the painful shifts in my own life, in the rush of intimacy between women made possible by the decade, I sought out connections between other women and myself. My grandmothers, my mother, my sister, and I, I was learning, were not isolated sufferers. The female attitudes so often caricatured are real: the manipulative magnolia and the hysterical matron *do* exist. In attempts to escape the ramifications of my roots, I had often caricatured the stereotypes. But now, driven by a search for my own identity, cynicism no longer satisfied me. I wanted—indeed, desperately needed—to understand motivations and choices, to reveal not only weaknesses but strengths: to exonerate, at last, my mother, my Southern sisters, and thus myself.

How is it I forgive her? She means no harm.

Every morning, I come into bed with her for what my mother calls "cuddle time." I do this when I am very little. My own children will one day come into bed with their father and me when they're young, too. But for me, the practice of getting into bed with my mother in the mornings continues into junior high. Maybe longer, but my sister left home when I was thirteen, and since she is the one who remembers what happened, I only know for sure that it was still going on then.

Rona felt sufficiently uncomfortable about what went on at cuddle time that she spoke to our mother about it, she tells me later. "I told her I thought it was inappropriate," she says. Another family friend who sometimes came for visits, Ellen, told my mother the same thing. Our mother dismissed their comments, Rona says. "Joycie just can't get enough snuggling," my mother laughed. "Can you imagine what she'll be like with men?"

What I remember: my mother's dark skin and full breasts, showing through the worn, almost transparent nightgowns she sleeps in, the once luxurious but now faintly shabby hand-me-downs from her sister Celia; the smell of her and her black hair that I like to style because it's so curly, and my own is straight. She kisses me on the lips, and I kiss her back. There are names for the kinds of kisses we share. *Suction. Cutie. Movie star.*

She may comment on my body, check to see if I have any pubic hair yet, make a joke about my pink, childish nipples. She calls me "triangulo," because she says that's the shape of my bottom. "Look at your legs," she says. "People will think you've been in a concentration camp."

(Later, though, when I fill out a little, this will also be a subject of discussion. "I'm tipping the scales at 105," I write to her, from camp. "I can't come home, for sheer shame!")

Whenever my grandmother comes to visit, she brings a tin of strange green ointment called Zambuk, available only in Canada. My mother sees nothing odd or hurtful in applying Zambuk to my vagina, at night, as late as junior high. My guess is that her mother probably had done the same with her, though what the Zambuk is supposed to do is never clear to me.

For my sister, the story is different. What Rona remembers is walking past our mother's bedroom to the bathroom, listening to my mother and me cuddling, but taking part in none of it. We all knew, in our family, that Rona didn't like to be touched.

One day, when I come home, I see she has left out a copy of our local paper, turned to the sports page, which is rare in our family. She has drawn an arrow, in red magic marker, to a photograph of a high school football player in uniform. With her marker, she has drawn a circle around the boy's crotch, with an exclamation point.

"Can you believe this, in the paper?" she says. I know right away what her problem is, because I know my mother. She doesn't know football players wear athletic cups. She thinks this boy must have a very large penis—thinks he's having an erection, in fact, for all the world of sports fans to see—and she had to point it out.

My mother suffers from other frustrations. Despite her determined optimism and cheerfulness, her dreams, not only for romantic love but also for a career, were crushed a long time ago. She has her magazine career, and her teaching, but her biggest hopes rest with her daughters now, and because I am a more willing and responsive recipient, she places her most ambitious expectations on me.

She is a lifelong dieter, never wholly successful in her battle; I will be slim. I will receive the best education. I will be loved by a wonderful man. I will not have to worry about money as she does. I will see the world beyond New Hampshire.

Though my father was a champion diver as a young man, and he still possesses a surprisingly strong body and a forceful crawl stroke, he is not a follower of organized sports. In our family, we do not own a single ball or piece of sporting equipment besides our croquet set. I am twelve years old when I point out to my parents that I would like to learn to ride a bicycle—an idea that has never occurred to them. This earns me a reputation as the family athlete. My sister never learns to ride a bike.

My mother and father coach my sister and me to write. Before we knew how to form alphabet letters ourselves, we gave dictation. We spoke; our mother wrote down what we said and told us how to make it better. Soon enough, she gives us a typewriter.

Our family sport takes place in the living room. There in a circle of shabby furniture, surrounded by my father's paintings, my sister and I read our manuscripts aloud for our parents. With file cards and yellow legal pads in hand, they take notes and analyze, one line at a time, every metaphor and choice of adjective. They talk about the rhythm of our sentences, the syntax, the punctuation. My father is a careful and demanding editor, but my mother's criticism is the most exacting. Her instruction is incomparable, but it carries a price. My mother is teaching us not just how to write, but what to say. Back in that living room, I am adopting more than my mother's punctuation and sentence rhythms as mine. On the page, I could not differentiate between my own feelings and my mother's.

My sister, Rona, is regarded as the real writer in our family. I liked drawing better, and dancing, and acting in plays and playing the guitar and singing folk songs. But I'm acutely aware of my father's story, too. I know well that the fact that you love to do a particular thing doesn't mean you can earn a living by it, or that anyone will ever acknowledge your talents. Singing and dancing might make me happy, but are less likely to make me successful—something that matters a lot in our family.

Partly in anticipation of its future significance, my mother has typed what we've written, as far back as preschool days, and saved every poem and story in suitcases—one for my sister, one for me.

My childhood suitcase features not just the usual Mother's Day verses and school book reports but a three-act play, written when I was nine, chronicling the life and loves, including the sexual peccadilloes, of Henry VIII. There are hand-drawn fashion magazines in the suitcase, and tragic folk songs, and comedy routines, and the beginnings of several novels. Dozens of poems. Earnest, idealistic reflections on the Goldwater–Johnson election of 1964 (the year I turned eleven) and school busing and the Vietnam war. When I'm seven, my mother gives me a mimeograph machine for my birthday, and I begin producing a newspaper that I sell door-to-door on our street. It would never occur to me that our neighbors wouldn't be interested to read what I write. Or that I shouldn't charge a nickel for it. Later, a dime.

My mother schools me young to view my writing as valuable. She conveys another lesson too: Whatever happens in my life, I can look at it as *material*.

When my sister is thirteen or fourteen, our mother encourages her to enter the *Scholastic Magazine* writing contest. She wins— that year, and again, for years after that, collecting prizes of $25, $50, sometimes even $100.

The *Scholastic* prize money sounds to me like a fortune. As soon as I'm old enough, I also enter the *Scholastic* contest, feeling, now, the pressure to match my sister's early successes or top them. I enter in every division available to me: fiction, essay, poetry, dramatic script. Through most of junior high, and into high school, the month before the *Scholastic* deadline and the week when prizes are announced will be two of the most important times of my year. If I win only one award, I will be disappointed.

When Rona's sixteen, our mother mails a short story of hers called "Paper Flowers" to the *Ladies' Home Journal*. The magazine buys the story for $500. The story will later be named as honorable mention in the annual volume of *Best American Short Stories* for 1964. At age eleven, I'm proud of my sister, but also consumed with a need to match her achievement, and with an anxiety that I might not be able to.

In the fall of 1965, just before my twelfth birthday, I start keeping a diary. I write in it every night—entries that sometimes go on for five or six pages. In my journal, I talk about all my darkest secrets: My embarrassment that my mother is still giving me baths. The jealousy and competition I feel toward my sister. My impatience with my classmates at school, my longing for a close friend, and my sense of having no one who understands me, except for my mother. I write about my secret and shameful interest in boys, my wish that I could attend dances, and my belief that my mother would never in a million years guess that I could care about such things. I am consumed with a desire to win contests, earn money, earn recognition from the world and, above all, from my parents.

Sometimes, in my diary, I will refer to my father as being "stormy" on a particular night. So stormy, in fact, that one night he takes away my diary entirely, and sends me to bed, until my mother steps in to rescue me. "Stormy" is a code word for the word I don't dare write even in my diary: *drunk*.

SEPT. 5, 1965

. . . *Today I listened to a Judy Collins record. Oh, music excites me so. But listening to the record, and Rona playing the guitar, I feel so hopeless and far behind. . . . I never seem to get anything done or polished enough. My slow typing. My dreadfully inadequate, repetitious* choreography. Mummy would say this diary is completely without form or direction. Oh dear.

SEPT. 6

. . . I think a lot about dying these days, and how I have an image of myself as the center of things, like the universe revolving around the earth! Oh, but I am so inconsequential! I must do something. . . .

SEPT. 7

. . . I have always thought of our family as a kind of divine circle, speculating even on close friends, and their limitations—their not being wholly correct. I realize now that even Mummy has flaws! I guess truly no one can come into the "divine circle" except me. One is always so alone!

SEPT. 9

. . . I desperately need to talk to someone, but everyone I talk to is part of my depression so I can't talk to them, of course. How little I have in common with these people. . . .

SEPT. 27

. . . I must do something. I must win Scholastic Contest this year!

OCT. 6

How sad for Daddy not to have any family of his own other than us. I often notice Daddy talking about being a bachelor and REALLY PAINTING. What a lot he gave up for Mummy. It must often be sad for him to have given up the full cultivation of his talent. He thinks of art constantly! I don't think that I'll marry a man so much older, if I can help it.

OCT. 7

Reading Maria Trapp's autobiography of the Trapp Family Singers. It has a lot of religious overtones. How simple it would be to be religious. How safe. . . .

OCT. 11

. . . People are always such a disappointment. . . .

OCT. 14

I feel depressed about a space travel article I read. It talked blithely of underground living and space migration to stop the population explosion. And to think I may well live to see this day, where all purpose goes out of life, and one's goal is merely survival. To misquote Anne Frank, "I still believe all men are good." Are they?

NOV. 17

Daddy just started an awful scene. He took away my diary (it was only 9:15) saying it was too late for me to be up writing. Luckily, Mummy came to the rescue. . . . A father should be a steady person, not necessarily happy and well adjusted, but steady. If he punishes you because he's had a bad day or his shoulder hurts, no reprimand will be meaningful. . . .

NOV. 11

. . . Today in math the problem of infinity was brought up. Does space go on and on? . . . If not, does it stop all of a sudden, as people once thought the Earth did? And what would lie beyond? Nothing. What is nothing? . . . I am so little and inconsequential. . . . I must make my mark!

NOV. 28

I finished Gone with the Wind this morning. How I cried, at Bon-
nie's death, Melanie's goodness, and alas, Scarlett's alone feeling, with
no shoulder to cry on. A ruined life. I was particularly moved because,
oddly enough, Rhett reminds me of Daddy, and therefore he seemed
closer to my heart. I realize this book is sentimental, with no shape or
symbolism or form, but any book that can create such a vivid picture
of so sad an event has got to have something. It is the best book I've
ever read.

DEC. 1

Daddy is stormy tonight and wants me to go to bed so I must
hurry. . . .

A few nights later I note my father's upsetting behavior again.
This time I call it what it really is.

DEC. 8

When I came home last night, Daddy was drunk and moody—you
could smell liquor on his breath all down the hall. For some people, life
is so easy, so secure. Fathers in crew cuts, nice and dull, who bring
home the paycheck. Not so here.

The December 8 entry marks the first time I have used real language to describe my father's drinking. The next night, when I
open my diary to write again, there is a letter stuck inside the
pages, written on a yellow legal pad. My mother's handwriting:

My Dearest Joyce,

  Yes, I did look at your diary this morning. . . . Actually,
because we are so close in feeling and temperament, I haven't

learned much I didn't already know. I understand very well you longing, in a way, for a steady, crew-cut, run-of-the-crowd father. (Do you think I haven't wondered ruefully, at times, what it would be like to have that kind of husband?) But of course if you had that kind of father, you wouldn't be you. Round and round the circle goes. You really do have an extraordinary (and extraordinarily difficult) father—and in life one pays for everything. Remember the little mer-maid, and what it cost her to walk on land with little human feet? Everyone has some problem; this is ours. And it's not, after all, disastrous. When Daddy is drunk he is sad, disgust-ing, embarrassing, pitiable . . . all these things. But not mean or cruel or violent. And—this is the important thing—whatever follies he commits at midnight, he gets up in the morning, goes to work and—as you would say—brings home the paycheck—i.e., meets his responsibilities. Read around a bit in the lives of painters and poets and you'll see that this is not a bad score.

After some twenty years, I think I have as good an an-swer as possible. There is no use indulging in self-pity. ("Why did this happen to me? Other people have it so easy.") And there is certainly no use complaining, attacking, berating—or even speaking about the matter. There is nothing I could say to Daddy that he hasn't said to himself. Try to imagine what it must be like to live with the knowledge of one's own dreadful falli-bility. Positively speaking, there are just two things one can do—try to avoid situations which you know will aggravate the nerves; and accept, without struggle, the fact that this is how it is. You'd be surprised at the serenity that comes with acceptance. I used to—at awful moments—cry and accuse and attempt to *stop the avalanche. This was painful and utterly futile. Now I just turn out the light and go to sleep, knowing that tomorrow the coffee will be made and the cereal cooked as always.*

One final observation. If you work things out mathematically, our lot is not so bad. Twenty four hours a day, seven days a week—168 hours. Say, on average, six of those hours are unpleasant—I make it 3.36% of the time. And all the other times? You have a father who is highly intelligent, gifted, sensitive, witty, gentle and absolutely devoted to you. How many children can say as much?

More than thirty years later, with a daughter of my own, I reread my mother's letter to me, at twelve, with the deepest kind of sorrow. It's misguided enough for a parent to tell her child she cannot speak of her most painful feelings. But my mother goes further than that. She tells me I must not even acknowledge my feelings to myself. She requires me to support her denial. She has even provided mathematical proof: scribbled calculations in the margin, allowing her to arrive at the figure of 3.36% as the portion of my life in which I am actively affected by my father's drunkenness.

The twelve-year-old who reads my mother's letter in her diary that night recognizes none of this. I acknowledge only the brilliance and wisdom of my mother's reasoning. I am so accustomed to my mother's invasions, I don't even recognize the invasion— only her supreme and matchless understanding of me.

DEC. 9, 1965

Dear Diary,

Today I found a note in my diary that Mummy wrote me. She has read it. And, oh, how she understands me! And what use is a secret if it isn't one? She has upheld the tradition—the infallible, the God in my life, knowing all! Right now I'm crying too much to go on writing. Let me go to sleep.

As I enter my teens, my father's "stormy" times will become nightly, not occasional events—the percentage of the drunkenness rising. But after the diary episode, I will not speak of my father's drinking again to my mother or anyone else for many years, or even write about it in the most secret place.

Every now and then, some night when my father's drinking, he will stumble into our kitchen to fix himself "a spot of tea" and leave the kettle on the stove with the burner on. In the morning, we'll come downstairs to find a little silver-colored coin that used to be our teakettle. I have a collection of these. For the purpose of her storytelling, my mother transforms Daddy into someone resembling Mr. Magoo. Only with better eyesight.

I never speak with my mother about the fact that she read my diary or that after the night of December 9, 1965, I never write in it again. From now on I focus my writing energies on the kind of writing that wins prizes and makes money.

IN MY MOTHER'S HOUSE

KIM CHERNIN

❖ ❖ ❖

I heard them talking. I heard them, even before my mother was arrested.

Frank, the lawyer, came to our house. "Sit down, Frank," my father said. "Have some coffee."

My mother was on the telephone.

Frank sat at the table. He put his elbows on the table and leaned against his hand.

Frank said, "They call, they keep coming. Our own people. Terrified."

My father listened, he shook his head. I heard him jingling the coins in his pocket. I sat next to my father at the table. I pretended I wasn't listening. I looked at the comics page in the newspaper.

Frank was talking. "What do you make of it, Paul? Why would this bastard come to tell me if he wants to croak to the committee?"

My father considered. "He thought you might tell him it's all right to save his wife like this. He wanted approval."

"From me? Approval? I could wring his neck."

There were other words. People used them and their voices

had an edge. The Attorney General's List. The Blacklist. Mc-Carthy. Red-baiting. Witch Hunts. The Loyalty Oath, they said. These were words they didn't want children to hear.

I heard them talking. My father had a friend who used to stop in after dinner. When he came I brought my schoolwork out of the bedroom, I lay down next to the heater on the living-room floor. He was a screenwriter, he told stories. Actors who came drunk onto the set in the morning. People who went swimming at night in their clothes. An actress who was found naked in a place you'd never expect to see anyone naked.

One night he told another story. From this story I got the impression the committee had called someone, who was an actor, and he had trouble because he smiled. I was seven years old. And that was in 1947.

When John left I took a good look at my father. He was putting his chess set back in the drawer. I decided to risk a question. "Daddy, why couldn't Robert Taylor smile?"

My father looked surprised. "You know what the committee is?" he said. With my mother I would never confess ignorance. She thought I should know everything even before I was told. But my father liked to explain. "By 'the committee' we mean the House Un-American Activities Committee. HUAC, we call it for short. The committee is trying to intimidate Communists and other radical people. It calls people up, it asks questions."

"And then?"

"Sometimes they lose their jobs."

"What's wrong with Communists?"

"Well, from our point of view, of course, what could be wrong? I'm a Communist, Mama's a Communist, Aunt Lillian and Uncle Norman are Communists, Frank and Gene are Communists. But the committee is out to expose people, to get Communists out of responsible positions."

My father waited for me to think things over. He liked children. He rolled down his sleeves and fastened the buttons on his shirt. I thought about what he said. I considered it for a long time and he wasn't in a hurry. Finally, I had a question. "Why couldn't Robert Taylor smile?"

My father sat down at the dining-room table. "Ach," he sighed. "Robert Taylor was playing in a film about Russia. The committee didn't want people to think Russians smiled." Then he added, "About socialism."

"You were born in Russia. You smile."

"These are hard times. Things just don't make sense until you give them a political explanation."

I thought I could understand the explanation.

"Sometimes, people turn against their best interest. They don't develop the right consciousness of their political situation."

"Will they turn on *you*? Will they turn on *Mama*? Will they turn on Frank and Gene and Aunt Lillian and Uncle Norman? Will you lose *your* job?"

"Let's hope it doesn't come to that." He got up, put the queen back into the chess box, and closed the drawer.

divided my life. On the surface there was a little girl. I made a mess in my room and straightened it up when my mother yelled at me. I taught my dog Lucky to play dead. In the mornings my mother braided my hair.

But inside I had already grown old.

I figured things out. I figured out there was some new danger in the world. The fascists had gone. The concentration camps were gone. The Jews had gone to Israel. Now it was the turn of the Communists. We were Communists, it was our turn.

Alger Hiss was attacked by the committee. He was a good man, I found out, but I kept forgetting. His name made me distrust him. Hiss. I thought he was probably a snake, a stool pigeon. I was eight years old then. That was in 1948.

"That snake-in-the-grass," my mother said one night at dinner. "Would you believe it? Sam Kichle. The membership director of the entire Los Angeles County. A stool pigeon. He had the name of everyone who joined. Their Party name and their real name. Very convenient. He turned over a carbon copy of every membership list to the FBI."

Adele came over for dinner. She always brought a little bag with cottage cheese and fruit. On her way in, she'd pick a fresh sprig of mint from our garden.

One night she arrived and she was pale. She was a Negro woman, but she had light skin, and this time her skin was even lighter than my father's. She said, "We know where they came from. They went through everything. Smashing, breaking." My father looked grave. "Paul," she said, "Paul. A children's bookstore."

I didn't sleep very well at night. Sometimes, my mother would get up and sit next to me. She'd sing: *"Ticha smotret mesyats yasni."* For my sister, she used to sing in Yiddish. For me, in Russian.

One night I began to pray. I knew my parents did not approve of praying. I hid my folded hands under the covers. "God, keep my mother and father safe."

I had learned to pray in the boarding school where they sent me, after Nina died, when we first moved to California. "Jesus loves me, this I know, for the Bible tells me so." I hated that school. My mother hated religious songs. One Sunday, when they came for a visit, I sang to her. The next week they brought me home.

Then I was a Communist and at that time you could tell it to other people. It was something, my mother told me, to be proud of. We had a fur pillowcase with a hammer and a sickle.

Now it changed. It was 1950. I was ten years old. I wasn't sup-posed to open the door to strangers. I had to ask first, making sure, before I opened the door. I wasn't supposed to tell the kids at school. I shouldn't repeat anything I heard my parents say at home. The kids said they were Democrats, they were Republicans. I said nothing.

The second time the committee came to town my prayers grew longer. "God, keep Aunt Lillian, Uncle Norman, Aunt Sara Barney's safe. God, keep Lucky safe. God protect the other Lil-lian, and Dorothy, Sam and Eva, Helen and Ben."

I was horrified about my prayers. Did they work? Did they help? I began to repeat them, beneath my breath, even at the din-ner table. I took huge portions of potatoes. "Eat the string beans," my mother insisted, leaning over to take some potato off my plate. Without warning, suddenly, I picked up a glass and threw it against the wall.

After dinner, when I was helping my father with the dishes, I broke a plate. "Look at her," my mother insisted, "she's doing it on purpose."

A cup knocked against the dish in the drainer. The handle broke. My mother's nerves were bad during that time. My nerves were bad, too. "I can't stand it, Paul," my mother yelled, "I'm telling you, I just can't take any more." I ran out of the room, I slammed the door. "Hush, Rose, she's only a child." Later, my father came into my room. "Try," he said to me. "She's nervous. These are hard times."

The hard times we were living in made everyone nervous. Lillian and my mother had fights on the phone. Lillian and Gertrude and my mother stayed up till all hours talking. My father got up, he went to the living-room door. "Please," he said in a soft voice, "please. I've got to go to work in the morning." For a moment the voices got softer, then they came up loud again.

I stopped sleeping. I lay awake and kept watch on things. I kept watch on the shadows that filled up my closet. I kept watch to make certain someone had left the light on in the hall. I listened to my mother and father whispering in their bedroom.

One of my mother's comrades came over to visit. They were talking in raised voices in the living room. I opened my bedroom door, I crept down the hall.

"It's a question of conscience, Rose. I'm leaving the Party. I can't and I won't accept that from the leadership."

"Three years ago you could accept it? Something's happened to your conscience all of a sudden since the committee came to town?"

"Rose. You know better than that."

"Do I? Do I?" There was a silence. Then, my mother said: "So where will you go? Let me tell you. For us, there's a concentration camp standing ready."

I crept back down the hall. I closed the door to my room. Inside, it was dark. I opened the curtain next to my bed. The light came in from Crenshaw Boulevard. Very quietly I started packing. I put an old pair of jeans, a sweater with a hole in the sleeve, and a heavy flannel shirt into the gym bag I made at school. I added a book by Laura Ingalls Wilder. The next day I added a chocolate bar.

Every night, before I said my prayers, I checked to make sure everything was okay in that bag. I never ate the chocolate bar.

My prayers grew longer. Sometimes I would fall asleep in the middle of my list but I woke up a few hours later, in the dark. I was covered in sweat. I started reciting. "Dear God, keep Sonia and Peter and Freddie safe."

My father came into my room. He walked on tiptoe. "Are you awake? I heard you talking."

"I wasn't talking. I was asleep."

He sat down at the edge of the bed. "Don't worry too much," he said to me. "Maybe we exaggerate. Who knows? Maybe it will still blow over."

My father had a big garden in back of our house. He grew corn and radishes, cucumbers and schav. He also had flowers, roses and camellias and a large cactus, he said, that bloomed only at night.

"I want to show you something." He brought me my bathrobe and my knit slippers. We went over to the cactus. There was a big white flower. I looked at my father. I took hold of his hand. Before that I never believed the cactus bloomed at night.

One day when I woke up in the morning a neighbor was standing next to my bed. I reached up to hug her. My mind raced. Our neighbor began to speak. I knew, even before she said a word to me. They had taken my mother. I was eleven years old.

It was summer, I put on my shorts. I got my bike and rode over to my friend's house. Her parents were Communists, we went to day camp together.

"Jessie, they arrested my mother. She didn't even get to say good-bye. No, I'm not kidding, are you kidding?"

Sara Kahen came out of the kitchen. "What are you whispering about?"

"They arrested my mother. This morning. I was asleep."

She got on the phone. "Sam? Rose was arrested. This morning. No, she's fine, she's not even crying."

Jessie and I got on our bicycles. Sara Kahen made us a big lunch. She chucked me under the chin. "What's the matter? You don't miss your mother?"

"I never cry."

In the afternoon the newspapers had the headline. Jessie and I saw it when we were riding home from camp. FIFTEEN COMMIE LEADERS ARRESTED IN CALIFORNIA. There were names, pictures. I saw my mother, wearing my flannel shirt.

"Jesus, Jessie, look at that. They didn't even let her change her clothes."

Jessie Kahen used to call herself my cousin. We had known each other since grammar school, we were best friends. But the day after my mother was arrested, Jessie Kahen told all the kids at camp we weren't really cousins.

"The hell with her," I said to myself three times. Then, I rode home from camp alone, without crying.

That night Aunt Lillian came over to the house. She talked for a long time with my father.

"Paul," she kept saying, "listen to this, Paul. They need someone to take over the work at the Foreign-Born Committee. I told them, how could I take Rose's place? But someone's got to do it. They won't stop arresting the foreign-born just because Rose Chernin is in jail."

My father put coffee and cookies on the table. "Sit down, that's better, take off your shoes." He poured a cup of coffee for her. "To begin with, why shouldn't you take her place? You're a brave woman. That we know. I advise you, take over as director of the Defense Committee."

Aunt Lillian had brought dinner for me and my father. She was gathering up clothes for my mother, in jail. "What do you think?" she said, holding up a polka-dot dress. "Does she like this one?"

My father warmed up at dinner. "Lillian," he said, "you'll understand, I'm not very hungry."

I was very hungry. I ate more than they ever saw me eat before. I ate my dinner, and my father's dinner and Aunt Lillian's dinner.

"Look at her," Lillian said. "She'll eat for all of us."

The telephone kept ringing.

"Eight o'clock this morning," I said. "Sure, I was at home."

People kept coming to the house. Aunt Sara came, with a dish of stuffed cabbage.

My father gave her a hug. "Thank you, Sara," he said, "but you'll understand. Tonight I'm not very hungry."

Sara was plump. She carried a red purse. When she came in the door you could go over and take a look into the purse. There was always something, a cookie wrapped in a napkin, some chocolate, a little game.

I loved Sara. She never forgot. "So come," she said, when she saw me looking. "You're too old all of a sudden to give a look in the purse?"

In Sara's arms, for the first time, I cried. With my father, alone, I wouldn't cry. "Tell me," he'd say. "Talk to me. Why should you have all this alone? Tell me, what are you feeling?"

"I'm all right," I'd say in a furious voice. "Just leave me alone," I'd say, "I'm okay." Now he couldn't even keep my mother safe. Why should I talk to him?

One night he told me that bail for my mother and the other defendants was one hundred thousand dollars. He told me that meant they couldn't get out of jail. They had to stay there until the bail was reduced. He said, "How could we raise one hundred thousand dollars?"

"Well," I said, figuring quickly. "We'd have to divide it by fifteen, right? That means, for each one, less than seven thousand dollars." I went right on thinking. It didn't seem so bad. There was Uncle Max and Aunt Anne. They were wealthy. There was cousin Sol, who had bought the shopping center. There was Dorothy in New York, who had loaned us the money to buy our house. I became excited. I couldn't figure out why he looked so grim. "Come on, Dad. You're making a big deal. You could get on the phone, start calling, you'll have the money like that." I snapped my fingers. I began to prance around.

"Listen, listen," he said, trying to grab me. "You don't understand."

"What? What?" I was scared now.

"One hundred thousand dollars each."

"Come on." I couldn't believe it. "Just come on. They couldn't do that. It's not fair."

"Ach, fair." He sat down at the table and looked tired. "A fair world we haven't yet been able to make."

I shook him by the shoulder. I didn't want to see him like that.

"God damn it," I yelled, and my voice thundered. "We won't let them get away with that." I was eleven years old, I knew something about the law. "It's unconstitutional," I screamed. "And we're going to fight it."

We fought. The hearings lasted six months. The lawyers also thought it was not constitutional. My father said, "In these times, who's going to protect the Constitution?"

"Daddy," I shouted at him. "We're going to protect it."

We were standing in the garage, stacking up newspapers for the school paper drive. "Daddy," I yelled, and I just kept on yelling. "We won't let them get away with that shit." He looked up startled. Then he smiled. That night, he talked to his brother Max on the telephone. "A fiery one," he said, and he had the same smile on his face. "Just like her mother."

I didn't tell him I hated going to school. I didn't tell him how one day, when I walked up to the school, I saw my friends gathered together, standing in a little group, whispering. When I came up there was a funny movement. Something that had been there disappeared. And now nobody had anything to say.

Then someone was talking. "Hey," he said to me, casual-like. "What's your mother's maiden name?"

My mother's maiden name?

The kids were all smiling. Then someone was holding the newspaper clipping in his hand. Oh yeah, of course, it had to happen. ROSE CHERNIN, COMMIE LEADER, ARRESTED IN LOS ANGELES. Sooner or later someone had to figure it out.

Who cares? I walked away, shrugging my shoulders. Then it

came to me: now things were different. If I denied who we were, that was betrayal. It was not keeping her safe. I turned back. "Rose Chernin," I said. My voice was loud. "My mother's maiden name is Rose Chernin."

I never told anybody how much I hated going to school. Every day I passed through the front gate and my eyes itched. My mother said I was a fighter. I made a fist. The other kids, their gossip, that passed over. But my biggest fear was, I knew things I shouldn't know and I was afraid I might tell.

I knew the name of a man who had been deported. I knew he had come back secretly and was living in Los Angeles again. I heard them talking. He was underground, they said. If anyone found out, my mother said, he'd be sent back to South Korea. They kill Communists there.

There was a girl named Zoya Kozmodemyanskaya. I had a book about her. Adele gave it to me one night when she dropped by with her bag of cottage cheese and fruit. Zoya was a partisan fighter in the Soviet Union during the war. The Germans caught her, they pulled out her nails, they put matches against her, and they hanged her. She was only thirteen years old. Later, her brother came with a tank battalion and found pictures of Zoya. Hanging. But she never told them, she never gave them a single name.

Would they torture my mother in jail? Would they torture me? Would I tell the names I knew? Would they put needles under my nails? Would they hold a burning match under my chin?

I knew the name of everybody who came to our house. I knew if you started talking you'd tell everything. "He sang his heart out," my mother had said one night at dinner before she was arrested. "Once he started, he never stopped. He gave even his wife's name. The name of his sister."

The fascists put children in gas ovens. They put children in cattle cars, separate from their mothers.

Once a week I wrote her a letter. "Dear Mama," I said. "Everything's just great here."

I didn't want my father to find out and tell her. I didn't want her to worry about me.

At school my old friends drifted away. If they saw me coming down the hall they turned and fiddled with a locker. They went into a bathroom, they walked into one of the empty rooms. I looked back after I passed, I saw them come out again, whispering.

Then, for a while, I didn't have any friends at school. I didn't try to catch up with the other kids in the morning. At lunchtime, I sneaked out of the playground, so I wouldn't have to sit by myself eating my lunch. Tonio no longer picked me up in the afternoon. I hung around in the halls, or I sat by myself on the back staircase. That way no one would see me walking home alone. At home, in the afternoon, I clipped articles about my mother out of the newspaper and pasted them into my scrapbook. My dog Lucky and I went out for a walk in the Baldwin Hills.

But then one day everything changed. One day in class there was an incident. A boy hadn't done his homework. The teacher was exasperated. She turned away from the blackboard and she said: "Keep on like this and you'll end up collecting garbage." Before she could turn back to the board a book was flying across the room. There was a silence and then she went over and took the boy, James Grove, by the shoulder. She pulled his sweater and dragged him over to the door.

"Take your hands off him." I was on my feet, shouting. My voice cut the other voices in the room. "I threw that book."

"Sit down," she yelled back. "Don't even try. I saw him."

"I threw that book. If someone's going to the principal, it bet-ter be me."

That boy had a strange look on his face. He had light skin and gray eyes and we thought he was real cute. "Hey, hey," I saw him saying with his lips, under his breath.

It was a restless class, people whispered and wrote notes and made cootie catchers. If someone happened to know the lesson, when they stood up to read everyone else started talking. But now it was awfully quiet in the class. Everyone was looking at me and the teacher.

"Prove it," I said. "Prove he threw the book and I didn't."

"All right," she said. "If you're so eager to go to the principal, you come, too."

We sat outside in the hall, waiting for the principal. We sat in her office, waiting for her to get off the phone.

"Who threw the book?" the principal said.

"I did," said James Grove and I.

"You both threw the same book! Okay, you're both suspended. Tell your mothers to come to school."

"Hey," I was going to say to her. "Hey, my mother can't come to school. She's in jail."

But something happened to the principal's face. Before I could say a word a look crossed over it. James Grove saw it and I saw him see it.

She knew already that my mother was in jail.

She fiddled about with the charts. She looked inside and read over our records. "Well," she said, "you have good grades. Both of you. Take this as a warning."

James Grove put his arm around me when we walked back to class. James Grove opened the door for me when we came to the room. The teacher was at the blackboard and some of the Negro kids got to their feet. They stood there, girls and boys I hardly knew, cheering as we walked into the room.

In our school the white kids all left by the front gate. The Negro kids and the Mexican kids and the tougher Oriental kids went out through the back gate. James Grove was a Negro kid. And now I went out through the back gate with him. There, behind the school, were older boys from the neighboring high school. Policemen often came rushing by in patrol cars. Fights broke out. There were knives, gangs, secret clubs, violence. Once, after school, at the back gate, someone took a basketball and threw it into the gym teacher's window.

My new friends never asked me about my mother. They never whispered about me. I went to parties and the boys lined up to dance with me.

At school, the white kids stopped whispering. They just looked at me when I went down the hall, walking with my new friends. In class, I sat with the Negro kids, and the few Mexican kids and the Oriental kids.

Then, one day, the teacher called on a white boy for Current Events. James Grove stood up by his desk. "Ah shit, teacher," he said. "Ain't nothin' new 'bout this ol' world."

The next day she called on someone again. James Grove was on his feet. "Didn't I tell you, teacher?" A white girl was standing up, her newspaper clipping pasted on a piece of yellow paper. She looked at James Grove. "You hear?" he said. And she sat down again.

It was late by the time we got home from school. We stood around at the corner, shifting our books and kicking pebbles. The boys smoked, passing the cigarette behind their backs. The girls

wore two pair of socks, one color turned down over the other. The
boys had their shirts open to the waist. We didn't talk much, we
were cool. But when I went off to go home alone, a girl said,
"Don't worry, honey. You got friends."

The next day and the day after and then every day for a week,
the teacher called for Current Events. But each day one of my
friends stood up. "Teacher, don't you know by now? Ain't nothin'
new in this ol' world."

One day a boy kissed me. He put his arm around me at the back
gate, we walked all the way home from school. His name was Roni
Takata, he was a beautiful boy. He had black curls, he had dark
eyes, his lips smiled even when Roni Takata wasn't smiling. At
home, in the living room, we sat down on the gray couch with the
long shag. Roni Takata put his hands inside my pants. A feeling
came and I hid my face in his chest embarrassed.

When I went to the bathroom I saw blood. I didn't want to
tell my father. I waited for him to come home. There was more
blood, I rolled up toilet paper and held it tight with my legs.

"Daddy," I said, when he came in the door. "I have to tell you
something."

"So, tell."

"I'll write it on a piece of paper."

He read the paper. "You're a woman," he said. "Don't worry."

"Dear Mama," I wrote, "I got my period. Dear Mama, here
everything's just great."

But my father said something was building. At night, the covers were never tight enough. At night, I recited my mother's name
two hundred times in prayer.

He said it to Aunt Sara on the telephone. "Something's building in that girl," he said.

He was right, something was building. It couldn't be fought down anymore. Once, I almost started crying. My father and I were doing the dishes. "You worried about Mama?" "I'm not worried. I know she's okay." "Tell me," he said, drying his hands on the apron. "Why should you have this all alone?" "It's nothing, I mean it. Just some dumb boy at school, you hear?"

Sometimes I had to call out for my father at night. He came and sat next to me on the bed. He didn't know any Russian lullabies. "What's wrong with you?" I yelled. "Is something wrong with you? Didn't you have a Mama? Couldn't she sing?"

At my uncle's house, where my father and I went for dinner on Sunday nights, I yelled at my father. "You old goat," I shouted, for no reason at all.

I ran out of the room, no one came after me. I ran into the bathroom and locked the door. "You old goat," I screamed again. But that time I was crying. I sat right down in a heap on the tile floor, my shoulders started shaking. "It's not fair," yelled a hoarse voice. "It's not fair, it's not fair, it's not fair, it's not fair . . ."

I stayed in that bathroom for a long time. After a while, I heard them talking. "How can you blame the child?" my father said. "Six years ago she lost her sister. Now, her mother's in jail. Did you ever think," he said to his brother, "how the world must look in the eyes of this child?"

One day he came home early from work. He parked his car in the front of the house and he came up the driveway practically running.

"She's coming home," he said. "She's coming home."

"Hey, what happened? She escape from jail?"

"The bail's been reduced. She's coming home."

My father had bought me a new dress, organdy.

"Come on, Daddy, I'll wear jeans."

He bought me a pair of patent-leather shoes.

"You kidding, Daddy? I'm twelve years old."

"You're happy?" he said, and touched my hair.

"Sure I'm happy, what d'ya think?"

The day my mother got out of jail I wore the organdy dress and patent-leather shoes my father bought for me. I smiled and I kept on smiling, letting my father hold my hand as the elevator door opened and a group of men and women came down from the Federal Building, and one of them was my mother.

She was different than I remembered. She was not taller or shorter, or plumper or thinner. Her face was, I suppose, the same. But something inside me, bravely smiling, was saying: Who is she? What does she want of me?

This woman with gray hair, wearing a neat dress with a belt, walking with a good, firm, dignified stride into my father's arms; taking my hand to draw me along beside them; this woman, who spoke my name twice and pulled me against her, was an acceptable person to be proud of (and I was). But the woman who had gone away to jail six months before had taken my feeling along with her. And now, having by this time forgotten how to feel, I had lost my mother.

We could hold hands, we could walk cheerfully down the street, waving good-bye to the others. We could get into the car the way we had always done, my mother in the front, I kicking my heels in the back. But it was only pretending. This woman, coming home with us, was not my mother.

During the six months my mother was in jail my father and I had roast beef every night for dinner, except for the nights we had dinner out. We had roast beef warm, roast beef warmed over, roast beef in cold pink slices, roast beef cut into small pieces and stirred in the pan with onion. For six months we had roast beef. And that night, in celebration of my mother's homecoming, we had roast beef.

I set the table, putting out rye bread and butter, the tomato juice in little glasses. My mother went in to change her clothes and when she came back into the kitchen I could tell from one look at her face that she wasn't happy to be at home with us.

"Good to be home?" my father said, taking her hand.

My mother stiffened. "Of course, Paul, what do you think?"

I watched her. I kept my eyes on her all through dinner. She liked it better in jail, I thought to myself, she can't fool me.

There was, without doubt, a strain in our little family gathering. The conversation just couldn't get going. My father talked to her about the prospects for the trial.

"They'll have paid witnesses, what else?" my mother said.

We heard the sound of knives and plates. My dog came over to beg at the table. I threw him a piece of roast beef.

"You feed the dog now at the table?"

My father put out his hand to touch my mother on the arm.

"All right, Paul," she said, impatiently.

I saw what I shouldn't see. That was the problem. Before, when she was in jail, I knew what I shouldn't know and I felt what I shouldn't be feeling. But now, I just could not stop my eyes from seeing. They saw the way my father jingled the coins in his pocket all the time. They saw he was afraid to lose his job. He smiled too much and when he said something he put his hand to his mustache and stroked the hair back from his lips. He did that a lot; before he only used to do it when he was nervous.

My mother didn't like roast beef. I could tell. She was cutting irritably at the tough meat.

"It's great, Dad," I said, in a false voice. I always defended my father.

"Rose," he said, with his smile, "if you would count six months and then multiply by thirty, you would know, give or take a few days, how many times she ate roast beef while you were away."

My mother tapped her spoon against the coffee cup. "Years ago, I told you, Paul, shouldn't you learn how to cook?"

I heard myself shouting. "I love roast beef," I yelled, and these words were so loud you could feel them hit the wall and come back, vibrating. "I hate fish. I hate chicken. I like roast beef and potatoes and string beans and salad. And if you don't want to eat them, you can just go back to jail."

There was a silence after this outburst. My mother sat with the spoon in her hand. My father looked at his plate. And then I knew for sure she was not really my mother.

"All right," she said, "sit down." She spoke in a whisper. "I'm on edge," she said, and my mother never would have admitted that. "You think it's been easy?"

After dinner Aunt Lillian and Uncle Norman arrived at the same time as my father's brother Max. Gertrude came later, with her inevitable bag of delicatessen food. The phone kept ringing and our comrades started dropping in.

My mother sat in the living room, on the gray shag couch, her feet curled up beside her. We turned on the television to watch the news story about the release of the Smith Act Defendants from jail that morning. My mother and Dorothy Healey came out of the elevator. They were handsome and smiling. If you didn't know better you would think they were dignitaries returning from a European tour. I watched them and thought it was funny the way they were, and were not, the women I knew so well. Then, even before the news was over, my mother started telling stories. She had a cup of coffee in her hand and it just stayed there and got cold while she was talking.

My father and I sat across the room from her, watching. That was when she became my mother again.

"I used to think," she said, "about being arrested. These days, who doesn't? I used to ask myself: Will I be able to take it? Will I be able to overcome the fear of going to prison? Will I break down under the strain?"

My father held my hand. He had a certain look on his face when he looked at my mother. He loves her, I thought to myself, seeing things I would only understand fully years later. He would not have found it difficult to come home to us. For him, she was the great love of his life. His work, chess, his friendships, even his relationship with me or with the Party, would always come second. It was a fierce passion for such a gentle man.

Of course, she was spellbinding. No one could ever resist her. I fell in love with her all over again that night. But I went right on seeing.

She would always find it hard to step back into domestic life. We limited her, we tied her back down to the earth. She was made for larger confrontations, for crises and battles. And I, seeing this, knew I was exactly the same. Someday, when my time came, I would be just like her.

She said, "So we're driving away. I was nervous. Who knew what to expect from the FBI? And certainly, I was worried about my daughter. Well, I know myself. When I get nervous I talk. When I start talking, who knows what I will say? Sooner or later, I thought, they're going to question me. The only thing for me to do is to shut up my mouth now and not to open it again."

She clenches her fist. "I am a determined woman," she says, "as you know. I had made up my mind. I would answer no questions. So now the nurse says to me, 'Rose, would you like to borrow my lipstick?' Because you can believe me I looked a sight. I was wearing clothes my daughter had thrown away a year before. I didn't have a chance to comb my hair or put on make-up. These are the clothes you put on for cleaning up around the house in the morning. They are not, I assure you, the clothes you choose to be arrested in. Then the interrogation proceeds. 'Rose, would you like some coffee?' But I had decided to keep my mouth shut and that's exactly what I did. I was arrested at about ten minutes past eight and from that time until twelve o'clock, when they came for me, I didn't say a word. I don't remember any other time in my life when my mouth was closed for four hours."

During the laughter that follows my father goes out into the kitchen for another pot of coffee. Aunt Lillian goes along with him, taking his arm.

"So, Paul, how does it feel to have Rose home again?"

And meanwhile, my mother is talking. "As a woman, as a mother," she says, "you feel so much guilt because of your political involvement. You're torn apart. You're afraid, merely in being away from the child, that she is suffering."

The women shake their heads, sighing sympathetically. That was always the way with my mother, I think. She could say exactly what people wanted to hear. But, did she mean it? Did she really think about me one bit when she was driving away?

Shut up, I say to myself. What makes you so mean? Shut up those thoughts. You're angry and you're jealous. Now she's the center of attention. She comes home and now everyone pays attention to her.

For that whole evening I was as clear and transparent to myself as a crystal ball. I was only twelve years old, but for those few hours I had the introspective insight I would develop fully many years later. It frightened me, and it fascinated me. It reminded me of the machine at Sears, where you could gaze down at your feet and see the way your toes fit into your shoes.

My mother calls me. "So tell us," she says, "what was it like for you when I was in jail?"

The whole room swivels around to look at me.

"What was it like?" I repeat. Not for nothing am I her daughter. My arm moves exactly like hers. My hand sweeps out—that intimate, rhetorical gesture. "It wasn't so bad. The kids talk, they stop talking. I'm not exactly the type you make into a victim."

I think about the other kids who waited outside the Federal Building this morning. What are they saying tonight in all their houses, all over the city? Richard Healey might tell the truth, but that was the trouble with him, I decided. He could still feel. No doubt he was even capable of crying.

"Come," says my mother and holds out her hand. I walk across the room, proudly; for the first time I am happy about the organdy dress and patent-leather shoes, the little-girl disguise my father has given me. I sit down on the floor at my mother's feet, next to the gray shag couch where Roni Takata discovered me a woman.

My mother puts her hand on my head. It rests gently, but I feel it as a tremendous weight, making its claim on me. For her, I am brave and loyal, beyond the reach of those fears and doubts that trouble me at night, in darkness, in silence. She wants a model child; a girl who can make a Communist proud. A child about whom it cannot be said that it was too great a strain being raised the daughter of a Communist mother. Never, never must she be allowed to suspect how difficult her choices have made life for her daughter. I reach up and cover her hand with my own. I'm taller than she is now, my hand is larger.

That night I had no idea it would be I who one day would give to my mother's stories their final form. I knew only that she had begun to work on me with her old enchantment. She had been taken off to jail and had entered history. When the story of the Mc-Carthy period would be told, someday, her life would be part of it. And that, I saw, forgiving her, was why she found it difficult to come home again, to the rye bread and tomato juice, the tough roast beef, the little girl in the organdy dress and the gentle man who jingled the coins in his pocket and worried about losing his job.

I forgave her. How else could it have been? She would live,

for the next five years, before I graduated from high school and left home, uncertain whether she was going to prison. She would, during those years, be called up before the House Un-American Activities Committee. She would be the first person in America the government would try to denaturalize and deprive of citizenship. And I—although I suffered in my own smaller world of childhood, because of these things—I was fiercely proud of her.

To this day I can recite the knowledge of her work I acquired when I was twelve years old. The words came easily from my lips; when I spoke them I would look around at my audience. They were, for the most part, kids in the Labor Youth League, the radical organization I had helped organize. "Do you know what the McCarran Act is?" I would ask. "Do you know what an outrage such a law is in a democratic country?" I discovered that I, too, could hold an audience captive. I listened to the rise and fall of my voice rounding itself out with rhetorical flourish.

"Just think," I once said to a group of students from the college division of the League. "My mother has led the perfect radical life. What does it matter if the revolution hasn't occurred yet? Look what she has done in the last few years." They looked at me, their smiles fading. I was a fiery kid, and I knew how to take myself seriously.

I was proud of my mother. "How many girls," I would say to myself, "have an example like this?" "How many Young Communists," I would say to my radical friends, "can look to their family and find a woman who was a Communist before they were?"

I was a master of rhetoric. And I used every ounce of my rhetorical skill to make up for the quarrels that were always breaking out between us. She arrived home in the late afternoons; she found a spot on the red carpet I had vacuumed for more than an hour, and right away she and I would start yelling.

"She's under such terrible pressure," my father would say. "Maybe you can think about it and you'll forgive her."

Suddenly all my sophistication dropped away. I stamped my foot. "Why does she have to pick on me?"

He wanted me to keep my voice low. "Shah," he'd whisper, "she'll hear you. Why do you want to upset her?"

"Nothing's good enough for her," I screamed. "She comes into the house and right away she finds a spot."

"She's nervous," he said. "Who wouldn't be?"

Those were nervous times. Every morning my mother drove off in her car, still forgetting to put a napkin in my lunch, but now she was going down to the Federal Building to sit in court, on trial for being a Communist.

The headlines said: TRIAL OF L.A. REDS. JURY CHOSEN TO TRY 15 COMMIE LEADERS. The trial began on February 1, 1952. Six months later they were found guilty. They were fined ten thousand dollars each, they were sentenced to five years in prison and the government put a lien on our house to guarantee it would get its money. My father said, "Now even the house is no longer secure."

I was in court the day the sentence was pronounced. I saw my mother and the others being taken away, the men handcuffed together. My mother turned and looked back at me and I didn't see her again for five weeks. I was scared then; the sleepless nights came again, and the newspaper headlines. I thought she would be away for six months, I was afraid maybe she would not be permitted to come home at all before she was sent to prison. Our local newspaper said: AREA RED ONE OF 14 SENTENCED. But five weeks later they were out on bail.

At dinner, that first night she was home, my mother stopped eating. She carefully placed the fork down next to her plate and she looked over at us, with our tense faces. Far back, behind that fierce sparkle in her eyes, there was something that ached and worried. "Don't fuss," she said when she saw me staring. "It's not over yet." I liked her fierceness; I felt, looking at her, that she was a woman who could not be broken. "The case will go to the court of appeals. And then, if necessary, we'll fight it right up to the Supreme Court. It'll take years," she said. "We're in no hurry to go to prison."

It took years. In 1953, they were found guilty again in the court of appeals. Her name, her photograph, the story of the trial, appeared again in the newspapers. The headlines said: RED DE-FENDANTS SMILE AT U.S. WAY OF JUSTICE. And meanwhile, all over the country Communists were going to prison. Other people disappeared and went underground. People moved to Mexico and Europe. There were Hollywood writers living in France, writing film scripts under assumed names. The phone still rang with stories of jobs lost, people questioned, names given or withheld, new immigration trials, friends detained on Terminal Island and threatened with deportation.

I knew everything that went on. I eavesdropped on every conversation. Secretly I listened in on meetings and overheard telephone conversations. I no longer prayed.

As children of the left we had always known we had a meaningful place in the Communist vision. We were the hope and the promise; it was we who carried the hope of the revolution they had expected in their youth. Later, when for some of us the vision collapsed, it left an emptiness that reached back into the earliest experience of childhood and shook the very fundaments of memory.

It would be hard to forget the Sunday afternoons, walking between my parents down Pico Boulevard, where there was a cinema that showed Soviet films. And yet, for many years after I gave up being a Marxist, I had to make myself forget the happiness I felt as we strolled along there, catching sight of one friend after another, waving, calling out greetings, gathering in little clusters of two and three to exchange comments about the world situation.

"So, Rose," people would say, hurrying to catch up with us, "what do you think about the situation in _____?" We would stop, my father would look thoughtful, my mother would make her pronouncement, and on we would go, drawing further with each step into that safe and familiar world of radical feeling and thought.

In those years my mother's committee began to hold their annual celebrations, the Festival of Nationalities. Hundreds, sometimes thousands of people came, even then when everyone knew how dangerous it was. All over the picnic grounds people walked about in their national costumes. There was folk dancing, decorated booths, display tables with folk art and exhibits. Even when I was a teenager, growing tougher and harder with every year, those great, ceremonial celebrations of radical solidarity would tear me open and make me a child again. I would catch sight of my mother, strolling along with the committee's defendants, people whose lives had in many cases been saved because of her work. I loved the way people looked at her, the way they reached out to touch me, Rose Chernin's daughter. Halfway across the picnic ground I could hear her voice reciting the list of cases the committee had won. She reached up and took the hand of a tall, dark-haired woman standing next to her. "And here we have Fanya," she exclaimed, "threatened with deportation to Czechoslovakia." Everyone looked serious. "But let me tell you," my mother boomed out, "we're going to keep her with us."

In that smaller world, I felt safe and secure. I was very popular, my mother was admired, and I would go home from a weekend or an event feeling very courageous and optimistic about the future. I planned to become a civil-rights lawyer. Of course, it didn't work out that way. But how could I foresee the terribly difficult times my mother and I would pass through as I tried to turn away from political life and become a poet? That was several years ahead of us.

Long ago, long after the time I ceased to think of myself as a Marxist, for years past that time, the words *Soviet Union* brought tears to my eyes. But that had begun when I was a little girl and my mother would say to me, in that way she had, "So guess what? We have a surprise for you. Do you know what it is?"

"Something to eat?"

"Even better."

"To see?"

"Yes, to see."

"From the Soviet Union?"

"What else?"

Usually it was a film, sometimes a dancer or a musician.

When the pianist Emil Gilels came to Los Angeles for the first time, she got me a box seat so that I could sit on the left side and watch his hands.

"Someday we're all going to the Soviet Union," she'd say, and I believed her. "Someday, we, too, will have a worker's revolution, just like the Soviet Union." That, too, I believed. "While we were living in the Soviet Union, during the thirties," she'd say and then I could go over and sit next to her on the gray couch and put my head in her lap.

Then, the day came. I graduated from high school and left for the Soviet Union. Falling asleep on the train that crossed through Poland I heard her voice and it spoke clearly. It murmured again between dream and awakening, repeating its stories. I was going home.

It struck me suddenly when we changed trains near the Polish border. All at once I knew that I would cross the border and be at home. Everything looked familiar, the landscape drawing away into the distance, the trees around the station, the plump women dancing together, the steaming samovar: Russia near the Polish border, Vitebsk, Chasnik, my mother's home—wasn't it somewhere near?

I stood in the open space between the cars, holding myself in a precarious balance so that I could be away from the others, undisturbed in my contemplation of this extraordinary landscape the likes of which I had never seen before and yet seemed always to have known: forests of white trees, stirring up in me a feeling so profound I suddenly did not know who I was; surely it could not be I who felt this way?

One of our interpreters came looking for me, to tell me that we had crossed the border and were now in the Soviet Union. But

I had known it and had already begun to cry. The young man put his arms around me and I wept against his shoulder, trying to tell him something I could never possibly have expressed.

I was seventeen years old. It was 1957, the year after Khrushchev's report to the Twentieth Congress. Thousands and thousands of people were thronging into the Soviet Union from all over the world. The Russian people rushed out to greet us, the delegates to the Seventh World Youth Festival. All the way to Moscow, hundreds of people would arrive at every station our train passed through. Their ecstasy, that unrestrained outpouring of the heart, made me myself again. On the train I wandered from car to car, meeting people from the various delegations. It was exactly what my mother had promised. It was her own trip all over again. And I saw that she had been right. Here, something had happened to the world, people came together as sisters and brothers. We believed in the Russian Revolution, we believed in the revolution we would make in our own countries.

In Moscow the ecstasy continued. We had arrived several days before the official opening of the Youth Festival, and I used them to explore Moscow. Here, too, everything was just like my mother had told me. I saw the gleaming steel of the Mayakovski subway station, and I told everyone, very proudly, that my father had worked on its design. I walked in Red Square, I looked at the Kremlin. Here the May First Celebration had taken place. I stood in line to see Stalin and Lenin, lying in state, in the Mausoleum. The crowd of people moved steadily past the biers, but I stopped dead in my tracks and stood there, looking at the waxen face of Stalin, with his big mustache. Was it possible? He looked just like the pictures my mother had shown me when I was a child. And I remembered my sister had been invited into the Kremlin to meet this man.

There was a beautiful song people were singing all over Moscow that summer. You heard it everywhere, in the People's Park of Culture and Rest, in the Agriculture Exhibit, on the streets at night. It was called "Moscow Nights," it was a love song to Moscow, and I learned to sing it with a throbbing heart.

Day and night people thronged the boulevards in national costumes, with instruments, with flowers, with arms full of gifts. The Russians threw themselves into this festival as if every stranger were a kinsman, returning home. They flocked around our buses, they forced the buses to stop, they rushed to the windows, took our hands, pressed them and shouted out to us: MIR Y DRUGBA, "Peace and Friendship," that ritual call no one who attended that festival has ever been able to forget.

We lived, during those weeks, in a large hotel in the Agriculture Exhibit, a vast park with permanent exhibits from all the nationalities of the Soviet Union. It was warm during the days of August, we sat outdoors, large women with kerchiefs served us our food and each of them, taking me by the arm, fussing over me, became my mother.

There were, of course, organized activities at the festival: delegations meeting together, performances of national music and dance, tickets to concerts and the Bolshoi Theater, meetings with famous Russians, ideological discussions and debates. I attended many of these, but always in a state of extreme distraction and with a great restlessness. I wanted to rush back into the street; I loved the moment when, at the end of a formal meeting between delegations, presents were exchanged and people came together to shake hands and embrace one another.

One day several people from our delegation went to call on Madame Kozmodemyanskaya, the mother of Zoya, the partisan girl who had been tortured and killed by the Germans during the Second World War. I was beside myself when I heard that she was still alive. Zoya's mother? My heroine's mother, still living? We carried huge bouquets of flowers and stood in the street below her window, singing to her, while she leaned forward and looked down at us. In that moment, I felt that my whole life came together and made sense. My old childhood idealism came back to me and I felt that I, too, would be capable of the heroism and sacrifice Zoya had shown.

But then, one night, two days before the opening celebration of the festival, something happened. At the time, I did not consider it very important, and was completely unaware that it had any lasting significance. If it had taken a physical form I could now say that it shattered me. But it was instead an emotional blow and its effects went so deep I couldn't afford to know they had occurred.

On the surface, the event was slight—such events usually are. One of the girls in the English delegation had relatives in the Soviet Union. They were Jewish and one night after dinner we set out across Moscow to visit them. It took us time, of course, because people kept stopping us and inviting us to join them for drinks. But finally we were walking up the steps of a large apartment block. Several floors above us we heard a door open, and then the head of a girl about our age leaned over the railing and called down. Soon, the whole family was trooping down the stairs, their arms open. There was an initial confusion about which of us was the niece, but then no one seemed to mind very much or to pay much attention to the distinction. When we got in the door, the commotion grew even greater; everyone had to be hugged and kissed all over again, the table was covered with food, we were eating dark bread and cheese, drinking tea in glasses, the spoons were tinkling and we were shouting in Russian and Yiddish and English, everyone talking at the same time.

The mother of the family was handicapped, she had been injured on her job and after dinner she showed us the work she did at home, for full pay, sorting colored bits of industrial glass. Then letters were brought out; they were carefully stacked in wooden boxes, and they went back to the beginning of the century, when Hyla's family had gone to England. Each one was carefully dated in ink, on the envelope, and we could see how often the family had moved around from the repeated changes of address. But I could also see that the mood in the room was changing. Hyla's aunt was becoming more and more silent. Her two daughters were trying to keep up the conversation, but their English wasn't very good. Her son, a boy of seven or eight, translated for us, but it made him impatient, and he would suddenly turn and glare at his sisters for talking too fast. Then, in an uncomfortable silence, Hyla's aunt sighed. She said, "So, you're here. You've come. It's good." She leaned forward and took both of us by the hand. But then she said, "It's good you're here and it's good you'll be going away again."

We both looked at her with astonishment. What did she mean? I said, putting my hand to my heart, fervently, "I could stay here forever."

"You like Moscow?"

"I love it. It's my home. I've never been happier."

"You're a foreigner. Don't believe everything you see."

Hyla and I looked at each other. We were both part of the Young Communist movement. And now we were proudly wearing the festival pin on our collars next to a Soviet Young Communist badge. Hyla laughed. She patted her aunt on the hand. "Just like Mama," she said affectionately, "always looking on the dark side of things."

But it was clear to me that something serious had been said. The young boy was whispering with his sister, translating our conversation. I looked over at the older girl, a beautiful woman with blond hair and blue eyes. It was hard to believe she was Jewish. She nodded her head vigorously at me while her brother was talking.

"What?" I said to her. "The Khrushchev report?"

I had read it, of course, several months earlier, and it had made me shake. But why now? Why should we be cautious now not to receive the wrong impressions?

She looked right at me and spoke to me in Russian. And then her brother's shrill voice repeated everything. I'll never forget it, such a terrible meaning from a child's lips. "So you think now that we've had Khrushchev everything's changed? Don't you believe it. To be a Jew in the Soviet Union I wouldn't wish on my worst enemy. What's changed? So now they'll take Stalin out of the Mausoleum, maybe, and put him in the Kremlin walls. Who cares?"

Then, for a few minutes, there was a flurry of movement. The aunt must have seen something in my eyes I myself could not acknowledge. "Never mind. You're happy here. And you're right to be. Maybe, it's a new day beginning. Who can say?"

Fresh tea was poured, little candies in colored wrapping were passed out, and the conversation drifted back to family gossip. But the bitterness in the cousin's voice had chilled me. Because of it I now recalled the day I read the Khrushchev report a few months before, alone in my room. It was the first time in my life I did not turn to my mother for reassurance about the politics we shared. I had stayed there, frozen on my bed, watching the dust in a beam of sunlight. Could I believe that in the Soviet Union, in that world of justice and equality I had loved since childhood, millions of innocent people had been killed? By the Communist Party? By Stalin?

Once, when I was in the third grade a teacher had insisted there were slave labor camps in the Soviet Union. I ran home from school that day very agitated, but my mother reassured me. It was Capitalist propaganda, she said, and of course I believed her. Never believe anything you read in the Hearst papers, she said. And I never did. But now, all at once, because of the look in a woman's eyes, I saw that the Khrushchev report had been true. I saw what the terror and horror of the Stalin time had really meant. And for this there was no more running home to Mama.

I wrote enthusiastic letters to my parents and I told them the whole story of the festival. But that was the official version; what I left out was the real story, and it is difficult for me to write even today. For I was, in the next weeks, to learn even more about this country that had once inspired my greatest childhood passion.

Traveling in a bus with a new Russian friend one night I saw two women standing outside the subway station. He told me they were prostitutes and at first I wouldn't believe him. How could there be prostitution in a socialist country? I looked back, and what he said seemed true. They looked like prostitutes anywhere. For a minute I closed my eyes and put my hands on my face. "*Shto-takoy?* What is it, little friend?" he asked. "Something hurts you?" "Prostitutes," was all I could say, but there was a lot in my voice if he cared to hear it.

I found myself in a mood that has returned to me many times over the years. It was a feeling of extreme desolation and sorrow that arose from the fact that I had lost the Communist vision I had shared with my parents and was indeed quite alone in the world without that dream. I was in mourning, but I could not admit it.

There's something about mourning that leads to poetry, even when the mourning is not conscious and poetry seems forbidden. Desolation, sorrow, feeling lost and alone in the world are proper subjects for poetry; they are likely to start composing poems even if the lost and lonely person hasn't been much interested in them before. That's certainly what happened to me, out of the blue as it seemed to me then. As the poems came they brought with them the idea that I might want to live my life differently than my parents had lived theirs, more inwardly, more aesthetically, although neither word was familiar to me at the time. I felt instinctively this was the sort of life my parents would have referred to as "bourgeois decadence." They would worry about someone who intended to build a life on self-reflection and the shaping of words.

Yet that is precisely the way I presented myself when I returned to California. I had by then spent several months in Poland and in East Germany. I had been to many poetry readings, and had begun to love sitting in coffee shops. I had let my hair grow and I had a certain carefully cultivated way of tossing back my head to get my hair out of my eyes.

I had developed an enthusiasm for abstract art, had begun to read Sartre, and came home talking about existential angst.

My parents sat at the table during dinner and listened to me in silence. Of course, they did not understand that by advancing this image of myself to them, as an explanation for what had happened to me in Moscow, I was trying to save them from a confrontation with my own doubts and disillusions about Communism. How could they? I myself refused to understand. Once, in a wild moment, I screamed at my mother about my change of heart. But usually, I never mentioned it.

"Don't tell me about Marx," I shouted. "Or Lenin. Or any other of their theories. Lenin is to Marx what the New Testament is to the Old. It's a completely new departure. The most revisionist doctrine in the world."

"Listen to her, will you listen," she yelled back, banging the door to the refrigerator. "She's unlearned everything we taught her."

My father stood in the doorway, looking nervous. This sort of yelling match was not for him. Later, I knew, when I'd gone to bed, he'd knock at the door to my room and want to talk to me. But now he stood there, shaking his head and looking mournful.

"The revolution cannot take place in one country," I yelled, advancing an idea I had worked out for myself, in an effort to explain what had happened in the Soviet Union. "We will not have socialism until revolutions take place all over the world, simultaneously." At the time, this was as far as I could go.

"Hah," my mother shouted, pointing her finger at the ceiling, "so there it is. That's what has happened. She met Trotskyists."

"Trotskyists? What do they have to do with anything? You think I get my ideas from other people?"

"Ideas? You call this nonsense ideas?"

"Why talk to her?" I shouted, whirling around and facing my father. "Is this what you have tried to reason with all these years?"

"'This' she calls me. Did you hear her, Paul? She calls her mother 'this'?"

"Enough," he said, speaking to both of us. "Who can come to understanding through a tone like that?"

I had only a few weeks with them before I left for the university in Berkeley. Most of the time I spent out of the house, running around with my old friends. Because I was in the first group of Americans to go to China after the revolution, my picture had been in the newspaper; there had been a television segment of me on the ABC news. I had become a minor celebrity and everyone was happy to know me now. I stayed out late, made lists of all the boys who called me for dates, and briefly I fell back into my old way of distracting myself from whatever troubled me.

But now, because I was older, it was harder to pretend. I knew that something had happened. Something had changed me. I had become a poet. By the time I came home from college for Easter vacation I had perfected my new role.

"These clothes," my mother would say, watching me with her hands on her hips. "You're going to a costume party, maybe?"

I always played dumb. "What's wrong with them? Everybody dresses like this."

"Show me please this everybody."

The next time I came home for a visit, one long weekend toward the middle of my freshman year, I wrote poetry with soap all over the mirror of my dressing table. Then, I began to recite poetry as I walked about the house, doing my chores. Poetry consumed me. I barely ate a meal. I learned a poem by Walter de la Mare and repeated it at every opportunity. "Very old are the woods; / And the buds that break / Out of the briar's boughs, / When March winds wake, / So old with their beauty are / Oh, no man knows / Through what wild centuries / Roves back the rose."

"What's this?" my mother would say. "Can't take anything into the mouth but poetry now?"

One night, when my mother invited me to a political rally where she was going to speak, I said I had to stay home and finish a poem I was writing.

And so we had an argument which was repeated, again and again, without much variation over the years. You could have heard it the night before my wedding, or the day my husband and I left for Oxford, a year or so later. When I finally moved back to America after four years of living abroad, I spent the summer in Los Angeles. And of course the argument broke out again.

In retrospect, I see that it was a separation ritual, a way we had evolved to speak the central issue between us. For, whatever else we shouted or declaimed, a single idea was at the heart of our quarrel. I mean of course the fact that we thought different thoughts, and experienced the world differently. That we were no longer the same person.

That night, when I was not yet eighteen years old, she stood at the door to my room with her hand on her hips. She was dressed very nicely, and had put on make-up for going out. It seemed a sudden impulse to invite me casually to come along. My father was already driving the car out of the garage and she said, "So, why don't you come along? You'll see a lot of people you didn't see for a while. It'll be good for you."

I was lying on my bed, writing in my notebook. "I'm busy," I said, "I'm writing. It's not something I can interrupt for a meeting." I think the tone of my voice, so superior and contemptuous, must have fired her off.

"Too busy? Too busy for a meeting? The world in a state like this and she's too busy with her poetry?"

She had a way, when she was very angry, of referring to me in the third person, as if I were no longer worthy of direct discourse. And I, if I were angry enough, would pick up her style.

"Yes," I yelled, and I hoped my father would hear me, "SHE'S writing a poem. And someday this piece of paper with HER words will mean more to the world than all your picket lines and mass meetings. Yes," I shrieked, even louder, as she gestured to the ceiling, calling upon the world to witness the folly of her only child, "these words will live long after the Communist Party of America has been forgotten."

"These words? Would you believe it? This paper? Live? Longer than the Party, yet?" Her voice had reached the absolute top of its register, an anguished F-sharp of consternation. And now it suddenly changed color. "That I should live to hear it. I, from my own daughter."

I was on my feet, gesturing with my notebook. I was beside myself. I had become a malevolent creature whose sole intention was to wound. I saw that the same thing had happened to her. We stood a few inches from each other, screaming the worst insults. It was, as I say, the same argument and it played itself out over and over again for the next twenty years.

"You want to know something else," I shouted that night as she stood at my door, and the echo of it went forward and reverberated through the next two decades of our life, "even if no one ever read a single world of what SHE has to say, she'd rather be here forever with her notebook than spend ten boring minutes listening to you make another speech. You think anyone listens anyway? You think you're going to change the world?"

"What happened to her?" she cried out, genuinely stricken. "Is this the daughter I sent off to Moscow? Is this the child I raised?"

"No, she's not. She's not. She'll never be again, and that's what you've got to understand. I'm eighteen years old. (I'm twenty-three years old. I'm almost thirty. I'm thirty-six now.) I'm a poet. I'm not a political person. Politics just doesn't mean anything to me. Can't you see? I'm not you. I'm my own self."

"A poet." The words ringing with so much contempt they made me shiver. "A poet, this one a poet. That's all we need, another poet, and the world at the edge of a holocaust."

"Who are you to say what the world needs? You're God maybe, and you know what's going to save the world?"

And so it would go, until my father came into the house, that familiar look of forbearance on his face, and his deep compassion. It was his particular torment, I now see, that he could understand both points of view, but couldn't find the way to bring about an accord between us. We were both stubbornly locked into our outrage. I should have followed in her footsteps, she believed. And I, although I did not admit it, felt that her revolutionary vision had betrayed me.

That night, she walked out of the house and banged the front door. I could hear her get into the car. My father stayed behind for a moment. "You know," he said, "we always admire a poet. She especially. You know that. But you provoke her. You make her think you have turned against everything she stands for."

"Maybe I have."

"No. You haven't."

"You're so sure?" But I wasn't yelling now. Somehow, I hoped he was right.

"You're coming?" he asked, holding the door open for me. But I shook my head. "I'm sure," he said and went out to the car.

My separation from my parents kept on growing; there was marriage and childbirth and raising a child. And then it was 1965 and in Berkeley, across the Bay, the Free Speech Movement had begun. I went over there one day out of curiosity and watched the strike that emptied the classrooms and the libraries. But now, as a generation of students turned political, I found myself refusing to do what I knew my mother would have done. While the others marched I went into the library and sat there for several hours, reading Nietzsche and listening to the muted sounds of the students chanting outside the window.

During those months it was my father who called me regularly. Sometimes, my mother did not even get on the telephone. Every time we talked now we'd begin to shout and quarrel, and one weekend, when she came with a friend, to "see her granddaughter," as she said, I told her I never wanted to see her again. What had she said to me? What terrible wound did she inflict? I can't even remember. I knew only that with every year we seemed to be moving farther apart, as I moved farther away from the radical past we'd shared. I was lost and confused, but I was also deeply serious in my quest for something distinctive, something of my own. I remember one ridiculous argument, when I shouted at her over the phone. "I'm a lover of God," I yelled, "that's what I am." She sucked in her breath and was silent. And then I heard her say, "You talk to her, Paul. She's just gone crazy. That's all."

He understood me. I don't know how or why, but he understood. Sometimes, he'd call me quite late at night, when he was at home alone. I once told him that I was reading about Saint Theresa and I thought I was a little like her. He answered, "For us, Marx expressed the truth when he said religion was the opiate of the people. But you, it seems, are a poet. We know, for a poet the world is different. In the Soviet Union I knew a man who claimed he could talk to the birds. Of course, everyone laughed at him, how else? But I did not laugh. Maybe, I thought, he can talk to the birds. How should I know?"

Perhaps he understood that I was, during that first year of my separation from Peter, working out the style of life I would live; hanging up pictures of Rilke and Lou Salomé and Jesus in my study, aggravating my mother, bewildering myself, a woman in her middle twenties who did not seem to be growing out of her youth; who wrote and wept and laughed and ran about with men, and became solitary again. And who managed, briefly as I say, to communicate something of all this to her father, who never judged her.

Then, one Sunday in June, in 1967, on the last day of the Six Day War between Israel and the Arabs, when my daughter was almost four years old, I got a call. It was my father's doctor, and closest friend, telling me that my father had been killed in an automobile accident. He had been on his way, with my mother, to the Festival of Nationalities.

"No," I said, "it can't be."

Murray was silent.

"She's fine?" I asked, knowing she was.

"Not a scratch," he said, "although, you know, she was sitting beside him."

I grieved then, for the passage of a very gentle soul; he had lived his whole life according to a simple wisdom of the heart. He found it easy to love, he had never hated anyone. He once said to me, "I am a socialist man in a land where socialism has not yet been accomplished." He seemed to regard that as a sufficient statement about his life, and I agree with him. If we had buried him that would have been a good epitaph, although he spoke it in a rare, melancholy moment. His life had been for the most part characterized by a serene cheerfulness that made him puzzle deeply, I know, about the trials and tribulations of the two women he loved. We were cut from such different cloth, and were, I imagine, in our unappeasable struggle and antagonism, the only real sorrow in his life. The death of my sister, and my mother's arrest, the persecution of Communists in the United States—these he accepted. But the rancor between my mother and me he always felt was unnecessary. "Two people, just alike," he used to say, "so why do you have to quarrel?"

He was cremated and my mother held a memorial for him. To my surprise, hundreds of people came. Who would have thought this quiet man had touched so many hearts? We sat together, in the front row of the hall, and people filed past, many of them weeping, to shake our hands and embrace us.

That night, at home alone, after our guests had gone, she sat in bed and I came to sit beside her. "You know," she said, "I heard today from Uncle Max. Your father left me very well provided for."

"He did? You didn't expect it?"

"Did he ever talk? It was his great dream, that he could take care of me after he was gone. He always told me he would do it, but money he didn't mention."

"I'm so happy for you. I'm happy he was that kind of man."

"His kind," she said, "you don't see much in the world any-more. Sometimes, I wonder, would it be better never to know a man like this, so you didn't have to suffer so much if you lose him? I'm sixty-four years old. Who knows how long I'll live? But you can be sure, another Paul Kusnitz, I won't find."

She had cried before, but now she wasn't crying. She sat straight up in bed. By then, each time I saw her, I thought she had grown smaller. Now, I looked at her little hands, bunched into fists.

"We did not make life easy for him," she said. At first, her voice was tense, caught somewhere between guilt and accusation. But then she repeated herself and I heard tenderness. "We didn't make his life easy, I tell you."

Maybe our reconciliation dated from that moment. We still had many difficult years ahead of us, an untold number of violent arguments. She would have to live through my religious phase with me, and then come to understand the hope and promise I saw in feminism. I, in turn, would have to let her go on being loyal to the Soviet Union, and not share my concern for the plight of the Soviet Jews. Together, we would hold our breath as Larissa be-came an adolescent, and then did not trouble us, as we'd feared, by rebellions and turbulence. She was not like us, in that respect. She'd found a way to be exactly what she was, without drama or upheaval. And both of us drew a sigh of relief at that.

I can say, in truth, on that night, sitting beside my mother in the bedroom she had shared with my father since we moved to Los Angeles twenty-two years before, I felt the first sense of some-thing peaceful between us. No doubt, my own prolonged youth came to an end that night. I was twenty-seven years old and for the first time in many years I put my arms around her.

"Well," I said, "we don't exactly make life easy for ourselves either." And then we both laughed and rocked each other and wept.

And she said, looking up sideways from my embrace, "So, who said it's too late to learn something?"

SUNNINESS AND SHADE:

Twenty-five Years with the Woman

Who Made Me a Mother

ALICE WALKER

❖ ❖ ❖

DAUGHTERS EVERYWHERE

First I see her smiling face as she stands at the gate to our house, waiting for me to open it. She has forgotten her key. I am always struck by her sunniness. It amused me many a gray day when she was an infant, and we lived in a dangerous and dreary Mississippi. There were glowing pussy willows outside her windows and bright posters on the walls; I awakened to the sound of her singing. When I poked my head into the vibrant room, she greeted me with a toothless grin. Today, at twenty-five, a sunny optimism is still her fundamental nature, though by now I have seen its other faces of sorrow, anger, cloud, and storm.

As soon as she walks through the door we embrace. She sighs, deeply, resting her head on my shoulder. I silently thank the Universe she has returned to me once again. I am always shocked she is so tall. My cheek lies just above her heart. I am reminded of her father; he is six feet. Of my parents, my mother, especially, whom

Rebecca resembles, who was five-feet-seven. I often exclaim, "You are so tall!" She laughs. Kisses my forehead. "Mama," she says, indulgently. She doesn't bother to remind me I am short. For many years she did a curious little dance when we hugged, a kind of flapping of her knees against mine. It was uniquely Rebecca's, and endearing, if somewhat strange. She no longer does that, and I miss it. I think she dropped it while a student at Yale.

She has always been appreciative of our living spaces: as we walk from the front door through the parlors to the kitchen—in San Francisco—she notices every single thing. If there is a new painting, she stops to look at it. A piece of sculpture she'd forgotten, she's delighted to see it again. I love how observant and enthusiastic she is, for I know that, being this way, she will always enjoy life. As I put on the pot for tea, she moves about, touching, sniffing, exclaiming, and smiling, and I settle into a motherly busyness that expresses the pleasure I anticipate from my daughter's visit home.

Twenty-five years we've been together. One of my longest relationships, and the most important. As I pour our tea, I look at her and think: This completely separate person came out of my body; I have the stretch marks to prove it. I remember her turning in my womb, sucking her thumb, dragging a bedraggled pink blanket everywhere. Riding her first bicycle. At two she read her first word: "book." By the age of three she could pack her own suitcase. I see her flying out the door of our house in Jackson, Mississippi, a straw hat on her head, on her way to Jamaica with her father and me. I remember—a dozen or so years later, also in Jamaica— Rebecca lying injured in the middle of the highway, a victim of a motorcycle accident. I remember holding her broken foot, in the car, all the way back to our hotel, her teenage boyfriend, Brian, who traveled with us, glancing anxiously back at her from the front seat.

A bonus of being Rebecca's mother has been the love I've felt for each of her Significant Others.* There was Brian, a boy from the neighborhood, who was an early passion; Omari, a Kenyan from the island of Lamu, with whom Rebecca lived for several months, who used to call me in the middle of the night, when she was ill with malaria, to tell me not to worry; Bechét, the son of a friend, who seemed so much like my own child that when he and Rebecca separated, I was as sad as she was. At present there is Shawn, a smart and gentle woman who feels like a second daughter. This attachment to my daughter's partners surprised me; no one had warned me that when they suddenly disappeared from her life, they disappeared from mine. And that I would miss them. Or that, while they shared her life, I would feel I had two children to enjoy and worry over, not one.

I have loved being Rebecca's mom. There's no one I'd rather hear from, talk with, listen to. Except for those times when I've had to face the ways in which my being her mother made life harder for her. I believed the sunniness because it was real, but also because I thought it meant she was okay. Over a decade after her father and I separated, she confronted me with the hurt, confusion, deep sorrow, and depression she experienced, losing the safety and warmth of our marriage, intolerable for us but a sanctuary for her, and told me how she'd kept that side of herself hidden, especially her grief, for fear I would not be able to accept it. Accept her. My defense was that I had done the best I could, and that I refused to be judged. What she wanted, she said, was my simple

*Their names have been changed to protect their privacy.

acknowledgment, a *feeling* acknowledgment, of her suffering. I found this very hard, for it seemed to deny the difficulty of my life as her mother, and as a working, creative person, who had tried to do the best I could by both of us, sometimes under impossible circumstances and without support.

As a child, though my parents stayed together in a marriage that lasted over forty years and seemed to continue even after my father's death, I often felt abandoned, because both my parents worked. By the time I was ten, I was the family's housekeeper during the week, while my mother and sister worked in town; I felt like Cinderella as I attempted to care for a household that included a sexist father and brothers who were not taught to tolerate sensitivity. However, no matter how grim my existence was, I put on a cheerful face for my mother, whose exhausted face at the end of her day—cleaning another woman's house and caring for another woman's children—made me weep, inwardly, just to see her. Her place of solace and renewal was her garden, into which she retreated, leaving me with my fears and worries unheard, unexpressed. This behavior, I realized, had been reenacted by me and Rebecca, for when I became a mother battered by the outside world, my "garden" was my work. Having trouble dealing with Mississippi in the Sixties? Write your way out of it. The illusion I'd indulged was that because I'd married someone very unlike my father, and because I was a writer and not a laborer/housewife, and because I was an educated woman, and because Rebecca had been spared siblings, her experience as a child—I thought of her as extremely privileged—bore no resemblance to mine. I was so wrong. Behind the brave smiles she'd given me, during her years of sadness and feelings of abandonment, had slumped the little dejected girl I knew so well, twin to the one I had also been.

This realization catapulted me into a period of intense dreaming that led to partial recall of my own childhood—I had mercifully forgotten whole years of it—and culminated in a series of paintings (both savage and sad) that took me back to my anger. An anger well hidden by depression and thoughts of suicide. When I emerged, my heart broke open to my daughter's solitary suffering, locked in her shining, smiling ways.

"I did my best," I was finally able to say, "and still I hurt you. I am so sorry." My daughter is compassionate and forgiving. More than that, she is understanding. We sit, sipping our tea, and talk frankly about "the old days" of her growing up, my inadequate, perhaps, but still fierce-hearted mothering. Rebecca has made me a mother. Because of her I've reunited with banished bits of my own life; to know again the daughter and the mother I was, and to feel pity and empathy for both; to appreciate the admirable daughter courage that, though self-denying and therefore painful, still springs from a valiant solidarity with the mother who, in this world, always has too much to do and too few to help her. I've also discovered the world is full of mothers who've done their best and still hurt their daughters: that we have daughters everywhere.

AUTHOR BIOGRAPHIES

PAULA FOX is a Newbery Medal–winning children's book author and author of several novels and a memoir. She lives in Brooklyn, New York.

JAMIE CALLAN's fiction has appeared in *The Missouri Review, Story,* and *American Letters and Commentary.* This is her first published work of memoir. She lives in Connecticut.

MEENA was born in Sri Lanka. This is her first published story. She lives in Toronto.

A renowned professor of German language and literature, RUTH KLUGER was born in Vienna. Her memoir *Still Alive* was first published in Germany in 1992. She lives in southern California.

MARGO PERIN was born in the United States and raised in Mexico, the Bahamas, the United States, and Britain. A nominee for the Pushcart Prize, she has published short stories, essays, and works of journalism. She lives in San Francisco.

NAWAL EL SAADAWI was born in Egypt and has been imprisoned, censored, and exiled for her writing and political activism on the position of women. The author of numerous novels and books of nonfiction, she currently lives in New Jersey.

HELEN RUGGIERI is author of a chapbook of poetry and a collection of haibun. Her essays, haibun, and poetry have appeared in numerous journals. She lives in Bradford, Pennsylvania.

JAMAICA KINCAID was born in Antigua and is author of several novels, books of nonfiction, and works of journalism. She lives in Bennington, Vermont.

HILLARY GAMEROW has published business writing. This is her first published work of memoir. She currently lives in Arizona.

VIVIAN GORNICK is author of several books of nonfiction and works of journalism. The recipient of a Guggenheim Fellowship, she lives in New York.

Winner of an NEA grant and other awards, NAHID RACHLIN was born in Iran and is author of several novels and a collection of short stories. Her fiction and nonfiction have been widely published in magazines and journals. She lives in New York.

PAM LEWIS's short fiction has appeared in *Puerto del Sol*, *Intro*, *The New Yorker*, and *Wee Girls*, an anthology. She is working on a novel. She lives in Storrs, Connecticut.

Journalist, columnist, and essayist, GINA SMITH is author of two books of nonfiction. This is her first published work of memoir. She lives in San Francisco.

KATE BRAVERMAN is author of several novels and collections of short stories and poetry. She lives in Albany, New York.

ELIZABETH PAYNE holds an MFA in creative writing from Columbia University, where she was an Ellis Fellow. She lives in Brooklyn, New York.

Winner of two NEA grants in literature, ROSEMARY DANIELL is the author of two memoirs, a novel, a book of nonfiction, collections of poetry, and works of journalism. She lives in Savannah, Georgia.

JOYCE MAYNARD is author of several novels, books of nonfiction, and works of journalism. She divides her time between northern California and Guatemala.

KIM CHERNIN is author of several books of nonfiction and a novel. She lives in Berkeley, California.

Winner of the Pulitzer Prize for *The Color Purple*, ALICE WALKER is the author of numerous novels, children's books, collections of poetry, essays, short stories, and works of journalism. She lives in northern California.

CREDITS

Excerpt from *Borrowed Finery* by Paula Fox, © 2001 by Paula Fox. Reprinted by permission of Henry Holt and Company, LLC

"Just Another Movie Star" by Jamie Callan, © 2003 by Jamie Callan

"Domestic Silence" by Meena, © 2002 by Meena

Excerpt from *Still Alive: A Holocaust Girlhood Remembered*, copyright © 2001 by Ruth Kluger. Reprinted by permission of the Feminist Press at the City University of New York, www.feministpress.org

"The Body Geographic" by Margo Perin, © 2003 by Margo Perin

Excerpt from *A Daughter of Isis* by Nawal El Saadawi, © 1999 by Nawal El Saadawi. First published by Zed Books Ltd, London. Reprinted by permission of Zed Books Ltd

"Home Is Where Your Stuff Is" by Helen Ruggieri, © 2002 by Helen Ruggieri

Excerpt from *My Brother* by Jamaica Kincaid, copyright © 1997 by Jamaica Kincaid. Reprinted by permission of Farrar, Straus and Giroux, LLC

"How I Learned to Cook" by Hillary Gamerow, © 2002 by Hillary Gamerow

Excerpt from *Fierce Attachments* by Vivian Gornick, copyright © 1987 by Vivian Gornick. Reprinted by permission of Farrar, Straus and Giroux, LLC

"My Two Mothers" by Nahid Rachlin, © 2002 by Nahid Rachlin

"A Little Death" by Pam Lewis, © 2002 by Pam Lewis